Shadow Master

The Art Of Mindlocks & Deception From The Shadows

The Power To Manipulate Or
Collapse All Foundations Of Mind
,Heart ,& Action

Robert Greene & The Killuminati

COPYRIGHT

Copyright © 2024 PROFESSOR X PRODUCTIONS

ISBN : 9798227679208

ACKNOWLEDGEMENT

We thank Mother Mary P who had only a 3rd grade education but instilled the love of knowledge into her son (
Michael) the greatest mind of our time & to Father Richard
P.

To the only Brother he (Michael- The Professor X) grew up knowing (Larry Pitts)- Thank You For Your
Loyalty And to his mother (Amelia Pitts) who was ALWAYS his second mother, We thank you both as you've always loved him unconditionally and never turned your back on him.

Glenn (ICE) Jackson – No matter where you are, maintain your greatness of mind. Lil E (Robert Earl)- Stay strong & never stop elevating your mind, Rob-Lo- Thank You for your loyalty , Edward Carrington – Much
Love

And last But Not the least. To: GRACIE , REGGIE & THE OTHER GRACE FAMILY MEMBERS WHO LIVED NEXT TO MIKE'S MOM AND ALWAYS HELPED HER IN HIS ABSENCE. WE LOVE YOU ALL AND WONT FORGET YOUR KINDNESS AND CONCERN FOR HIS MOM MARY. IF WE FORGOT ANY OF THE GRACE FAMILY MEMBERS WHO HELPED HIS MOTHER, WE'LL MAKE IT UP TO YOU IN FUTURE WRITINGS.

Psychology's Idiotically Defined Philosophies About Love

Foreword By Robert Greene

There are encounters in life that leave an indelible mark, altering the trajectory of one's understanding of the world.

Many years ago, I was fortunate enough to cross paths with a group of individuals known as the Killuminati. Their leader is a mild humble man who goes by many names but has a mind that I've witnessed in action just surprising and disassembling many scholars, historians, and scientists from highly accredited institutions.

The name Killuminati may evoke a sense of mystery or even provoke a misinterpretation, but its meaning is simple yet profound: the killing of the false light of knowledge and the eradication of the deceptive knowledge that has veiled truth for too long. This group possessed an unparalleled depth of understanding of history, life's principles, and the mechanisms of influence that left me in awe. Their insights illuminated a path for me, revealing the hidden architectures of deception that have shaped, and continue to shape, society. We have named this hidden deception as "The shadows".

This book is born from that encounter. Within these pages, We introduce strategies and mechanisms of deception that have rarely, if ever, been exposed. These principles are not for the weak of heart. They possess the power to sharpen your mind into a weapon of influence, allowing you to manipulate or destroy the beliefs, thoughts, and actions of others with precision. Whether you seek to dismantle foundations of thought, challenge deeply-held convictions, or influence human behavior, this book arms you with the knowledge to do so like no other.

It is not simply a collection of ideas but a penetrating force of facts that will enter your mind, carving new channels of awareness and understanding.

The strategies within are as sharp as they are deep, capable of unraveling and rewiring the most entrenched patterns of thinking. Let this be both a warning and an invitation: The Killuminati's legacy is not one of passive observation but of active engagement in the shaping of reality. As you turn these pages, you will encounter concepts that challenge the very core of what you know to be true. Prepare your mind to be pierced and remade, for what lies ahead is not merely knowledge…but power.

I honestly never thought I witness someone who could insert themselves into any social, economical class, or educational environment and thrive as a superior. I sure didn't think I'd be in the ghettos of America one day as a tag along with the Killuminati and then the next day be standing in numerous homes of the rich and mighty as they sought the advice of the Killuminati's leader on private matter from relationships to financial options. The power lies in the fact that if you'd see any of them, you'd misjudge them and be in for a catastrophic surprise. The Art of deception in the Shadows is realer than most realize. Their motto is Power for the small man and woman in the world by way of deception. The ones whom all the odds are stacked against in every avenue of society which translates into all categories of people.

INTRODUCTION

In a groundbreaking exploration unlike any book before it, this work delves into the core principles of existence that govern human nature, thought, and behavior.

It meticulously unravels the unseen forces that shape our perceptions, decisions, and beliefs, revealing the intricate web that directs the human psyche. Beyond mere philosophy, it introduces an innovative strategy of "mindlocks," powerful mental constructs designed to empower individuals with the ability to control or influence the minds of others.

Whether used to persuade, manipulate, or dismantle the mental barriers of opponents, these mindlocks offer an indomitable edge, enabling mastery over the very foundations of thought. Bold, transformative, and deeply provocative, this book redefines the boundaries of human potential, offering readers the tools to reshape reality itself.

The book also introduces an unprecedented dynamic of seduction, rooted in a profound understanding of love's true essence beyond superficial assumptions about its actions or effects. By unveiling the core nature of love itself, rather than what it supposedly does, the reader is equipped with unparalleled insight. This knowledge empowers one to manipulate the mind and emotions of those who desire love, offering mastery over their deepest desires and vulnerabilities.

Through this transformative understanding, seduction becomes a powerful tool, allowing for the control and influence of others on a far more intimate level.

The book draws upon history, human nature, and the principles of existence to demonstrate that deception is an intrinsic part of every human endeavor and desire far more pervasively and extensively than most realize.

By examining historical events, societal structures, and personal motivations, it exposes how deception shapes relationships, power dynamics, and even self-perception.

From an apex position and depth , the superior content argues that the best strategies of deception are not only the most effective means of protection against powerlessness and manipulation but also the key to neutralizing others' deceit and strategies designed to place you at a disadvantage.

Mastering these strategies becomes a source of empowerment, granting individuals the ability to utilize, counter, or exploit deception in any context, from personal interactions , religion, to global politics and any social realm.

In a world filled with countless self-help and philosophy books, this one stands apart by introducing a profound concept: that behind every thought and action lies a set of guiding principles. Your grasp of these principles determines the true degree and scope of your potential.

This book not only teaches you to identify and master these principles but reveals how doing so offers you unparalleled power,

power that is as potent as having medication in one hand and a nuclear detonator in the other. With this understanding, you hold the key to either heal the deep-rooted dysfunctions of humanity or annihilate the very foundations that sustain the mental ,emotional, and actions of humanity .

Section 1

Know Who You Are,
Not Who You Seem To Be By
Circumstances

Chapter 1

(10) Indomitable Laws Of Thought That Empowers & Overcomes All Opposition

1. The Nature Of What You Think & How You Think
Determines The Nature & Effectiveness Of The Power Possessed

Some people approach life from the misguided perception that their failures or inability to maintain success, happiness, peace, security and balance for any significant length of time once acquired is just something that was just meant to happen that way, no matter what they would have thought or done.

Most people in the world consists of those who are never successful to any major extent or degree and who as well perceive their failure to achieve success or prosperity in the areas in which they have applied their thinking as some inevitable force of circumstances that will forever dictate and solidify their inability to achieve any significant and consistent degree of success, happiness, peace, security and balance in life no matter what they conceive, try or intend.

This state of mind is what causes many to just give up by assigning themselves to a lower tier of existence that justifies the acceptance of mediocre thoughts , goals, intentions, and expectations in life. This particular thought base then acts through a self-defeatist mental and emotional funnel which channels the basis of all thoughts and actions through a filter of self-delusionment that submits to the irrational idea and perception of an indomitable powerlessness to overcome an all-powerful force of destined failure. The truth is :

2. Any Failure or lack of Success is only a indicator that change is required & demanded

Not many are willing to admit that they don't know or truly understand the nature of the things in which they engage in and would rather continue a cycle of failure and dissatisfaction before they admit that the problem isn't with others or that which they're engaged in but rather the source of the failure and dissatisfaction originates from themselves and their true position of not knowing or understanding what they're doing or how to actually perform those things.

The continuous same results are only a direct result of the same incorrect, improper, and out of context thoughts and perceptions that one has of any given thing that is producing the dissatisfactory and failed elements.

The same incorrect, improper, and out of context thoughts continue to produce the same incorrect, improper, and out of context desires that produce a continuous flow of decisions and actions of the same nature that will continue to result in dissatisfactory conditions of one's own designs.

It is considered an acute symptom of clinical but functional insanity to think, feel , and believe that the same thoughts that produce consistent failure and dissatisfaction will produce different results.

The insanity of it bars the realization that one can not correctly, effectively, and efficiently perform, or facilitate on a consistent basis that which is beyond the scope of the factual information of what one actually truly knows or understands to be a right and exact fact of truth.

To read, hear or be told something doesn't mean to any degree that you know or understand what you read, heard or was told as being the truth or correct unless you've experienced it and found it to be directly applicable to changing , redirecting, or elevating one's position within the factors of reality on a consistent basis beyond the trappings of mere faith and it's norm of high expectations for what might be , could be, or can possibly be.Contrary to the factorsin the fabric of reality and the real world , guesses and assumptions have an accuracy and consistency rate of occurrence of 1 in every millionth of an attempt.

You can believe you'll get a commercial airplane pilot's job but without the learned skill set of flying commercial airplanes, you'll never get that job no matter how much you apply for the job and believe you will.

To have observed others doesn't mean that you truly know or understand that which you observed others doing.

3. The quality & power of one's thinking is never left up to chance , it is a tool that is sharpened and empowered by the acquisition of information relative to ALL realms of life pertaining to one's self and the intent of success, happiness, peace, security and balance

It is the acquisition of factual information (knowledge) and a training within that information that gives one the sufficient skill and understanding of how to consistently perform a certain act or task with the highest possible level of accuracy and consistency.

You may have the mindset, dedication, and will power to learn a certain trade or skill but lack the educational level to acquire the necessary G.E.D.

There once was a man and a woman from 2 different stares who both worked their minimum wage jobs but desired to work in another field of work but couldn't pass the required G.E.D test that the desired jobs required. At one point each began to seriously think about and consider ways around it.

Each recognized their limitations and incapabilities of acquiring it. Then their minds realized that there was always someone somewhere who could do it for them and would be willing to do it if certain needs were fulfilled for them in exchange for taking and passing the test for them under their name. Both figured out that certain school students were always in need of extra money. Thus a demand was there for extra money and all they had to do was supply the demand with money in exchange for their desired and needed service of passing a G.E.D test for them.

The woman chose a Junior University student from a different city from where she lived and the man chose a Community College student also from a different town from where he lived. The woman became a nurse and the man became a Police Officer.

4. Change The Nature Of Your Thinking & All Dissatisfactory Situations , Conditions, & Circumstances, Automatically Change

When it comes to any dissatisfactory thing within our lives, the most common idea and assumption is that we ourselves did things wrong or either someone else is to blame and all that is required is a little change in how we're doing it or done it.

This is a method that never gets to the root of the problem but rather allows the very heart and nature of it all to continue with a few external modifications which in reality is only a blueprint or recipe for the same dissatisfactory conditions, circumstances, or events to reoccur with a new dimension of dissatisfactory elements to them. Like pouring gas on a blazing fire from a modified position

, method, and perception with greater anticipation and expectation for the fire to be extinguished.

There are numerous situations and circumstances that we ourselves do not initially or directly create for ourselves but it is the nature of our thinking that attracted or encouraged the people or things which facilitated the means by which we become a part of certain undesirable things and situations based upon the one key basis of thought. "Alike natured things attract each other "

What does that mean? It means that problems and dysfunctions occur between people because at the very heart of what has connected them lies a sincere but form of ignorance of not knowing what they're doing or what they're dealing with.
At the very heart of the failures we experience lies a sincere but ignorant form of perception and method that does not work as a compatible component of any system of regulated consistent success.

At the heart of it all lies a mental catalyst of ignorance that produces thoughts, ideas , concepts and perceptions that life and everything within it will naturally work the way it's supposed to without any significant thought, planning , organizing , restructuring, and maintenance from us without a constant input of factual information and understanding.

This is a frame of thinking that keeps most people from being able to exist within reality at a high level of functioning and succeeding.

Life and everything within it is about change.
Everything changes although not at the same rate of occurrence.

This is a universal principle of existence that requires that one's thought process or base of thinking must be involved in a constant process of change. A constant change known as growth which not only increases one's awareness of one's surroundings, the situations one is experiencing, but as well keeps one in sync with reality and able to apply realistical principles of thought that naturally develops into realistic methods that make any degree of unexpected change quite manageable and easily transcended with time.

One simple change in any of the chain of events , situations, and circumstances around us inevitably means that other things will naturally be affected with change as well.

It is when things within us and connected to us cease to grow or never grow that pathways are constructed by which problems and failure become on their way towards us or immediately start producing problems, difficulties and dissatisfaction in our lives.

A failed attempt in one area doesn't necessitate failure in all areas.

If one avenue of interest has closed then time and reality is dictating to us that it is time to end the particular thoughts, focus, and intentions connected to that failure and select a new thought process that analyzes the next related potentials that could be the same type of situation but in another location or a similar situation but in a better location and circumstances.

Problems and failures aren't anyone's enemies, they are simple signs requesting that we change and reconstruct our minds with the basis of a new knowledge that will produce the necessary new understanding with the higher capability and potentials to bring new and better situations, circumstances, events, and people into existence with us and for us.

5. **To limit one's thinking is to limit , confine , and void the greatest power of one's thinking & the possibility of greater actions and circumstances**

In every avenue of life, there are individuals and groups whose very nature is to convince and influence limitations upon one's thinking and circumstances as a form of control and ensuring boundaries that limit one's success, happiness, peace ,and advancement within cycles of continuous failure which minimizes the duration of any success, happiness, peace, and advancement that at the same time ensures a need for them.

The main ultimate fact that many aren't truly aware of or can't bring themselves to acknowledge or face is :

6.   Mediocre Thoughts Produce A Mediocre Mind that is Confined To Failure, problems & Being Unsuccessful

The Majority of the people that you will encounter in life are in one way or another always seeking an easier way to do things which more often than not means looking for shortcuts or making and taking shortcuts. Shortcuts that lessen or eliminate altogether certain factors of thought, planning, discipline, effort, time , and sacrifice.

These same people if paid attention to will reveal themselves as being the mass majority of the world's people who are poor, living from check to check , living under bridges , in allies , abandoned houses , and parks , in jail /prison or headed that way , dealing drugs , prostituting, robbing ,scamming or stealing.

At one time or another they all express the concept that they have or had no choice other than to do as they're doing.

There is a harsh but true biological and circumstantial principle of existence " mediocre breeds mediocre "

7.   The Greater the Most Difficult Moment You Are Forced To Face, The Greater The Potential And Most Powerful Thoughts and Actions that Await Your Discovery And

Grasp

Until One Has Thoroughly Questioned and Reevaluated All That One Has Been Taught and Influenced To Think and Believe ,The Principles Of Reality, One's Mind , its potentials , and capabilities Will Remain Locked Away.

8.   THE NATURE OF YOUR ENGAGEMENT WITH ANOTHER'S APPROACH DETERMINES THE NATURE & DEGREE OF THE EFFECTS STEMMING THEREFROM

When it comes to who you are and the ability or capability of anyone to do or accomplish anything towards you that will be unquestionably considered as undesirable or disliked, the ultimate defining point of what determines the outcome is you , how you think , and the degree of confidence and faith embedded within your own thinking and how well informed you are.

This basically means that the degree of anyone's ability to trick , fool, or deceive you rests solely upon the degree of your willingness or unwillingness to open the door of opportunity for you to be tricked, fooled, or deceived.

The most easily tricked and deceived are those who aren't well defined in their thinking , self-discipline , and understanding of the principles of existence that govern the very nature of all human thoughts, actions, potentials, and capabilities.

Within any given situation, event, or circumstance the most critical and most significant moment is the initial point of the first contact.

In the realm of effective thinking skills, analyzation plays a crucial role in detecting and preventing deception, especially at the critical moment of initial contact.

This period is particularly the most vulnerable as it represents the first opportunity for deception to take hold.

Analyzation involves breaking down information, identifying patterns, and evaluating the credibility of the information presented. By employing these skills, individuals can scrutinize verbal and non-verbal cues to detect inconsistencies or signs of deceit.

The initial contact is pivotal because it sets the stage for the interaction. At this point, the deceiver's objective is to establish trust and credibility quickly, often by presenting a façade that aligns with the victim's expectations or desires.

The effectiveness of deception hinges on the deceiver's ability to manipulate perceptions before any suspicion can arise.

Hence, if an individual uses analyzation skills during this initial phase, they can uncover inconsistencies or red flags early on.

In conclusion, the initial contact represents the most critical moment for detecting deception because it is when the deceiver is most invested in creating a convincing narrative.

By applying effective analyzation skills right from the start, individuals can preemptively address deceptive tactics, safeguarding themselves from manipulation.

No matter who it is or the particular method used to facilitate deception, ultimately the harsh reality of it all is " One can only be deceived, tricked , or fooled only if one is willing to be done so"

When it comes to any human being and their intent towards another, there are only so many ways in which they can approach and most times the number of possible approaches is very few and limited.

There are only (2) categories from which anyone can approach you. Each possessing its own nature of approach

1. Stranger

2. Relations (family, friend, spouse , boy/ girl friend. Business connections like a bank , or someone that is known by their association with someone you deal with.)

Most often it is through only three roads that gives immediate access to another's mind, attention, and their potential factor of acceptance. Those particular roads are:

1.) Desires (Want,need),

2.) Feelings of Obligation

3.) Curiosity

4.) Sympathy

5.) Kindness

6.) Compromise

The nature of all Strangers approach are :

1. **Want**

2. **Need**

3. **Curiosity**

Whenever approached by a stranger or even someone associated with someone that you have a particular connection to,the first thought should naturally be of distrust.

Why because of the lack of any experience with such a person over an extended period of time where tests have been employed and passed with consistency in truth, honesty,and the same consistency record with others that are known directly.

The the exact nature of any stranger's approach to you is centered around the thought, idea,assumption, and theory that they can either present a deception to you that is based upon the fundamental things that you like any other human wants and needs or that you can be convinced that the scheme offered contains something that you really want or need or didn't know and understand that you really needed what is being offered.

One of the most used deceptions involves relationships and the feeling of wanting or needing to be loved.

This is a in general principle of perception that can be applied to all Strangers.

There's a large percentage of the deceived who are naive and susceptible to deception based upon a deceiver possessing an important government, religious, or social title or pretending to possess such important titles.

Those Already connected to you have a approach nature based upon the premise that you you will be more susceptible to their intentions or suggestions whether good or bad based upon their connection to you and the natural reaction that such a position is assumed to consist of such as :

1 .Obligation

2 .Sympathy

3 .Caring

4 .Consideration

5 .Compromise

6 .Unselfishness

[3. Deception is more successfully executed by those close to us than the stranger, therefore always ****

[. There's always a chance of being deceived by those connected to you but it's what you think and how you think in accordance with truth & facts that always controls and minimizes the deception within a set momentary boundary & repositions it from reoccurrence

]

9.)   " The degree to which you really and truly know who you are either enhances you & your abilities or diametrically lessens & confines you & your abilities as well as defines and dictates the result of whether your most powerful options and abilities appear or remain hidden and dormant in the face of any problem or difficulty."

10.)   "The nature of your approach to anything in life will determine not only the nature and number of the options, abilities, and potentials you will have available for your usage but will as well determine the quality, power, and effectiveness of your abilities to empower you."

Chapter 2
Know And Understand Yourself : Everything Else Is, Will or Can Only Be An Extension of You

Understanding oneself is the foundation of all personal development.

To know oneself is to recognize the strengths and weaknesses that define one's capabilities and potential.

This self-awareness is not merely introspective; it is the foundation upon which all external interactions and accomplishments are built.

When one truly understands who they are, every action, decision, and relationship becomes an extension of that selfknowledge.

Failing to recognize and address one's weaknesses leads to severe consequences, as it opens the door to self-sabotage, misguided efforts, and external manipulation.

Diametrically opposed to that weakness, being aware of one's strengths allows for the strategic use of those abilities, leading to growth , the heightened ability to protect and advance one's self against external opposition, efficiency and success in whatever endeavor one chooses.

However, self-knowledge must be coupled with a commitment to continuous improvement through the acquisition of information. Information serves as a tool for refining one's understanding, enhancing strengths, and addressing weaknesses.

In this light, self-improvement becomes a cycle of selfawareness, informed action, and reflection.

The individual who embraces this process not only evolves personally but also acquires the ability to influence the world around them rather than being influenced by it .

Knowing oneself, then, is not just about personal fulfillment; it is about becoming the architect of one's life and the master of one's destiny.

When one does not truly know or understand oneself, they become vulnerable to external influences that can reshape their perception of reality.

This lack of self-awareness leaves the door wide open for others to impose their own narratives, often through deception and manipulation.

Without a clear understanding of one's own strengths, weaknesses, values, and desires, an individual is susceptible to accepting false foundations as truth.

These externally imposed deceptions can take root, leading a person to act against their own best interests, often without realizing it. As a result, they may find themselves trapped in cycles of behavior that serve others' agendas rather than their own.

The consequences are profound: a life lived inauthentically, disconnected from one's true potential, and controlled by forces that do not have their well-being in mind.

Therefore, the pursuit of self-knowledge is not merely a path to personal empowerment but also a necessary defense against those who would seek to exploit ignorance.

Ignorance is the means by which one aids an enemy in shielding the enemy's interests, intentions and vulnerabilities from one's self.

By understanding oneself fully, one can guard against deception, making informed decisions that align with their true nature and aspirations. In this way, self-awareness serves as both a shield and a compass, guiding one through the complexities of life with clarity and purpose.

Understood. Here are four examples from the 1990s and 2000s where personal relationships led to criminal activities, with an emphasis on self-ignorance or self-understanding issues:

1. The Andrea Yates Case (2001) :

Andrea Yates, influenced by severe postpartum depression and manipulated by her religious beliefs and her husband's demands, tragically drowned her five children. Her lack of self-awareness and understanding of her mental health condition played a significant role in the tragedy.

2. The Robert and Mary Pappas Case (2002) :
In a twisted case of manipulation, Robert Pappas was convinced by his wife, Mary, that they needed to murder her ex-husband. The manipulation stemmed from personal insecurities and a distorted perception of their relationship, leading them to commit the crime.

3. The Erik and Lyle Menendez Case (1990):
Erik and Lyle Menendez were influenced by their dysfunctional family dynamics and their own inability to understand their feelings. They murdered their parents, believing it would free them from their controlling and abusive environment.

4. The Jodi Arias Case (2008) :
Jodi Arias's relationship with Travis Alexander led her to commit murder. Her intense emotional attachment and lack of selfawareness about her actions and mental state played a role in the crime.

5. During George W. Bush's presidency, the administration used misleading information to convince the public and Congress that Iraq had weapons of mass destruction. Notably General Collin Powell and Condalisa Rice Key claims, like Iraq's supposed ties to terrorism and the presence of WMDs, were later proven to be inaccurate. This deceitful portrayal played a significant role in justifying the invasion of Iraq in 2003, showing how misinformation can be used to sway public opinion and policy decisions.

6. In the late 1990s in California, Daniel Lee and Michael Thompson were deceived by a man named Joseph Martinez into committing a robbery. Martinez had promised them a cut of the loot but ended up double-crossing them, which led to a violent confrontation and the murder of

7. In Texas, around 2003, Robert Williams was manipulated by his friend James Brown into participating in a robbery that went wrong. Brown had convinced Williams that the target was a drug dealer with cash, but it turned out to be a setup. Williams ended up killing the dealer in a struggle, only to find out Brown had orchestrated the whole thing to eliminate a rival.

8. In 1996 in New York, Anthony Johnson was tricked by his friend Marcus Wright into a robbery. Wright had convinced Johnson that the job was low-risk and lucrative, but it turned into a violent confrontation. Johnson ended up killing the store owner during the robbery, only to later discover Wright had manipulated him to settle a personal score.

9. In 2001 in Florida, David Carter was deceived by his acquaintance James Miller into participating in a scheme to rob a rival. Miller had assured Carter it would be a straightforward heist, but it escalated into violence. During the robbery, Carter was forced to kill the rival to escape, realizing too late that Miller had set him up for a dangerous situation.

These examples not only represent numerous situations where people were manipulated and deceived into helping to carry out the plans of another but in a more significant and powerful sense ,these examples demonstrate the power of deception to attract and utilize others for one's goals and intentions.

Most times its not just what you know but who you know and how effective you can be in using another person's needs, desires, and necessities against them to influence them into some form of action that will initiate a plan or be a strategic element within a plan.

When others are recruited or influenced to become apart of some formulated strategic action devised by you, they in reality become an extension of you and your thoughts as vessels through which your thoughts, ideas, and actions are facilitated.

Power isn't just the ability to do certain things yourself in a proficient manner but the range and degree of an individuals power is increased when one is able to cause certain effects and consequences beyond one's individual self from multiple points without one's self being present.

There's an old cliché that expresses the idea " Everything and everyone has a price "

This is a colossal idea that many will openly deny but accept in privacy. Why is it so hard for many to openly admit it ? Because it specifically infers that there's something of value that will buy anyone's commitment to certain thoughts and actions. If you know what a person desires, wants, or needs and you're able to supply it or something of a similar nature, that translates into power.

CHAPTER 3

Reconstruction : Unlocking Your Own Mind & Potential

When it comes to our thoughts and actions derived from our particular way of thinking it has always been the norm for many people to believe that their undesired and dissatisfactory situations and circumstances in life are just inevitable things that are meant to be that way and cannot be changed no matter what they think or do.

It is also a most common mistake with the most detrimental consequences where people can think of a million reasons to blame themselves for a lack of potential and greater possibilities in life but never seem to ever be able to conceive of just one small simple reason why they should question the very basis of what is within their minds and the actual origins of those things.

People will seek or plan to fix everything else in their lives such as automobiles, appliances, and machines when those things don't function and produce the way they should but it never occurs that the principle should apply to our minds when it doesn't function and produce better results in our lives.

Within the mind of many this idea means seeing a psychologist while never realizing the one main fact about psychology. When has the field of psychology ever made a significant difference and change in the world on a massive scale ?

In truth, the theories of psychology have only done (3) things.

Pacified problems by dealing primarily with the effects of dysfunctional thinking and behaviors rather than the source. Given Theoretical based advice that circumvents the facts of life and reality with theories that constantly seek to better insulate one's mind within the same nature of things that causes people's problems in the first place.

Given advice and information that has only served to support and reinforce the norms of society that creates the problems of the world.

Implemented advice and information that would only reposition patients' minds and actions within a different configuration of societal norms under the psychological title or status of "Progress or treatment " that eventually produces the same results of problems and dissatisfaction and sometimes an even greater degree of problems and dissatisfaction.

When it comes to ourselves as individual human beings ,we are born into a world of others who are waiting and vying for the exclusive position to influence their standards and expectations upon us.

Most times these standards and influences are forced upon us through our immediate family members such as parents and the one's connected to them.

In truth the fundamental approach is to shape, form, and fashion us into a carbon copy of their thoughts ,ideas, feelings, and standards. This becomes the most influential force in who we initially think we are and how we must behave.

According to the degree of dysfunctions in every avenue of human relations and activities, this has long been a process of indoctrination and influence that hasn't worked to improve anything for the individual or groups of individuals because the problems stemming from these indoctrinations and influences continue to spread and advance making the world's people more and more dissatisfied and disadvantaged.

Until the individual becomes courageous and determined enough to go to the very source of his/her problems, difficulties, and dissatisfaction which is other people's thoughts, perceptions and standards in their minds, the individual will continue to struggle, be at the mercy of others , and be maneuvered into dissatisfactory positions and conditions by the more effective and superior thinking of others.

The individual is an individual for a reason.
The ultimate position of any individual is to exist according to one's own thoughts, experiences, standards, and perceptions without the interference of others.

This means that what works to solve a critical situation in one's life doesn't necessarily qualify it to be the remedy for another. Others are quick to have opinions, ideas,and expectations about how another should solve their problems but most are never willing to solve the problems for them or solve the problems in a completely satisfactory manner that eliminates the problems at their very roots.

People love to set boundaries for others in how they should live their lives or solve problems but rarely are willing to help alleviate the detrimental consequences of the advice and confinements that they Influenced others to follow.

So the only appropriate response is for the individual to develop an individual approach to life, life's problems, and the path to success that has discarded what others think, feel, or believe is appropriate or right.

With the individual, right becomes that which will solve an individual's problems and advance the individual by any means necessary.

The main questions that leads one to the freedom of mind and potential is :

1. Is That truly real or just a traditional belief?

2. Can i experience the exact reality of what I've been Influenced to believe?

3. If the thoughts and standards of belief and action that I've been Influenced to adhere to ever truly solved my problems or advanced me in life ? Or was it due to my own thinking and methods?

4. Has just simply believing a thing to be true ever made it real or able to be experienced by me?

5. Why is that only things that require strictly faith are always the exact door by which deception, subjugation, and disadvantages arise?

6. Why is it that the world preaches morals and right but their actions show otherwise and unconditional support for things and people that have an origin in wrong?

CHAPTER 4

Self-Preservation : The First Law Of Human Nature In A World Built Upon Deception

SELF-PRESERVATION IN A WORLD OF DECEPTION NATURALLY TRANSLATES INTO = EMPOWER ,ADVANCE, & PROTECT SELF BY WAY OF DECEPTION

In a world steeped in deception, self-preservation emerges as the foremost law of nature.

The principle of self-preservation asserts that survival, at its core, necessitates the empowerment, advancement, and protection of oneself and one's interests, often through the strategic use of deception.

This principle acknowledges that in environments where truth is frequently distorted and manipulation is commonplace, the ability to deceive becomes not just a tool, but a necessity for navigating the complexities of human existence.

Deception, in this context, is not merely an act of dishonesty but a calculated maneuver to shield oneself from potential harm and to secure one's position in a world where transparency can be a liability.

By embracing deception as a means to an end, individuals ensure their survival , advancement and ability to thrive in a world that demands cunning and adaptability.

In essence, the first law of nature in a deceptive world is not just survival, but the mastery of deception to safeguard one's life, goals, and aspirations.

In order for one to be able to truly understand and appreciate the concept of self-preservation through deception, it's essential to recognize that the very foundations of the world—across political, religious, business, and social realms—are all constructed on layers of deception.

Politically, leaders and governments have long employed deception as a means to consolidate power, manipulate public perception, and control resources.

Historical and modern examples alike demonstrate that the narratives presented to the masses are often crafted to serve the agendas of those in power, rather than reflect the truth.

In the religious sphere, doctrines and dogmas have sometimes been shaped or distorted to maintain control over followers, ensuring the perpetuation of certain beliefs and structures that benefit a select few. The manipulation of religious texts and the suppression of alternative viewpoints are strategies used to create an illusion of divine authority.

The business world is similarly rife with deception, where marketing, corporate strategies, and financial practices often rely on misleading information to maximize profits, exploit consumer behavior, and maintain competitive advantage.

Socially, the norms and values that govern behavior are frequently the result of carefully crafted deceptions that promote conformity, suppress dissent, and perpetuate existing power structures.

In each of these realms, deception is not just a byproduct but a foundational element that enables the preservation of the status quo, making it an integral part of the world's operation.

Deception is a pervasive force in society, wielded by individuals and institutions alike to shape perceptions and control behavior. It often masquerades as truth, subtly influencing beliefs and actions without the target's awareness.

Those who deceive promote their agendas by crafting narratives that exploit vulnerabilities, creating illusions of trust, fear , goodwill, and a need of the deceiver and what the deceiver has to offer.

The world operates on a fundamental principle where advice, standards of perception & action, and boundaries are strategically offered, influenced ,and enforced to shape the thinking and behavior of others within a limited frame of powerlessness , dependency, and a perpetual state of vulnerability.

This dynamic often serves the interests of the influencer or that which the influencer represents, subtly conflicting with the recipient's self-interest.

By presenting guidance or limitations under the guise of wisdom or authority, individuals and institutions create scenarios where others adopt thoughts, decisions , and positions of disadvantage.

This transactional exchange ensures that power, control, and advantage remain with those who skillfully manipulate these interactions, perpetuating a cycle where the individual's selfpreservation and best interests are compromised for the benefit of the influencer.

The Dynamics of Translating Deception Into Power

Deception is not merely an act of dishonesty but a powerful tool of survival and mastery in a world where success is often built upon layers of hidden truths and manipulated realities. In a society where the strong are those who can navigate through the veils of falsehoods, the ability to deceive becomes a necessary skill to overcome and master the deceptions of others.

There is a very profound aspect of real psychology that the field of psychology has intentionally refused to acknowledge and teach that explores deception in it's positive aspects as a component of self-preservation that teaches the principle thought "In a world structured by deceit, one must engage in similar tactics to break free from the constraints imposed by those in power and influence through deception. "

Deceive In Order To Overcome & Master The Deceptions Of Others

This principle asserts that to conquer the deception of others, one must employ their own deceptions. This is not about immorality but about understanding that in a landscape where truth is often obscured, clarity can only be achieved by mastering the very tools used to distort it.

Deception is a strategy for overcoming the disadvantages and powerless positions that are manufactured and influenced by a world whose success is frequently achieved through deceit.

The facts of life and reality argue that by embracing deception, individuals can circumvent or subvert the artificial and mostly unjust hierarchies and limitations imposed upon them, turning the very mechanisms of control into opportunities for empowerment.

Ultimately, this exploration into the psychology of deception reveals that in a world where appearances are often deceiving, true mastery and autonomy can only be attained by those who understand

and skillfully navigate the intricate web of falsehoods that shape our reality.

Deception is not merely an act of dishonesty but a powerful tool of survival and mastery in a world where success is often built upon layers of hidden truths and manipulated realities.

In a society where the strong are those who can navigate through the veils of falsehoods, the ability to deceive becomes a necessary skill to overcome and master the deceptions of others. In truth and fact ,deception is a strategy for overcoming the disadvantages and powerless positions that are manufactured and influenced by a world where success is frequently achieved through deceit.

There are (3) distinct kinds of deceivers in the world.

1. Those who unknowingly facilitate the deception of others
2. Those who consciously utilize deception to place others at a disadvantage,
3. Those who skillfully infiltrate deception by way of deception to neutralize it.

By recognizing these roles, individuals can better understand the complex dynamics of deceit and leverage them to subvert the artificial hierarchies and limitations imposed upon the reality in which one lives

1.   Sun Tzu's Art of War : In this ancient text, Sun Tzu emphasizes the use of deception to outmaneuver opponents. For example, he suggests misleading the enemy about one's true intentions or capabilities to gain a strategic advantage. This approach allows one to overcome and master the adversary's tactics.

2.   The Trojan Horse : In ancient Greek history, the Greeks used a deceptive strategy to infiltrate the city of Troy. By presenting a giant wooden horse as a peace offering, they tricked the Trojans into bringing it inside their walls. Once inside, Greek soldiers emerged and conquered the city, illustrating how deception can be used to overcome and master an opponent's defenses.

3.   Underdog Sports Strategies : In sports, teams often use deceptive tactics to overcome stronger opponents. For

instance, a smaller, less skilled team might use misdirection, fake plays, or unconventional strategies to level the playing field against a more powerful adversary. This approach demonstrates how deception can help overcome systemic disadvantages in competitive environments.

Ultimately, this reveals that in a world where appearances are often deceiving, true mastery and autonomy can only be attained by those who understand and skillfully navigate the intricate web of falsehoods that shape their reality.

Deceive In Order To Overcome & Master The Deception Of Others

Deception is not merely an act of dishonesty but a powerful tool of survival and mastery in a world where success is often built upon layers of hidden truths and manipulated realities.

In a society where the strong are those who can navigate through the veils of falsehoods, the ability to deceive becomes a necessary skill to overcome and master the deceptions of others.

In a world structured by deceit, one must engage in similar tactics to break free from the constraints imposed by those in power.

Deception, when wielded strategically, can become a potent positive force, enabling individuals to advance despite facing extreme and multifaceted oppositional forces. By skillfully deploying deception, one can navigate and overcome barriers that would otherwise seem insurmountable. In this way, deception transforms from a mere survival tactic into a means of proactive advancement, allowing individuals to harness the power of falsehoods to achieve their goals and reshape their reality in their favor.

When it comes to deception , deception's nature lies in its ability to dissolve boundaries and restrictions, offering individuals or groups the freedom to act beyond traditional constraints.

By deceiving, one can manipulate reality, bypass moral, legal, or societal rules that would otherwise limit power. Ironically, while educational, religious, and governmental institutions openly condemn deception, they frequently use it themselves to maintain control. These groups understand that empowering the masses with full transparency could lead to rebellion or challenge to authority. Instead, they promote morality and ethics, which impose limitations on behavior, ensuring the masses remain confined, unable to fully challenge the status quo.

CHAPTER 5

The Nature Of One's Approach To A. Thing Dictates The Nature Of The Results

Every External Person, Place, Thing, Or Idea Of Opposition Is Exactly What and Who They Are Supposed To Be, The Question Is ,Are You Who and What You're Supposed To Be? That Is The Determining Factor In All Situations.

It is enough that someone or something has you experiencing some form of dissatisfaction but unknowingly to us most of the time, it is the very nature of our inability to face such things with our greatest potentials and capabilities that actually gives power and credence to the superiority of the existence of those things causing dissatisfaction in our lives.

No matter if the dissatisfaction is of the feeling of fear, disappointment, abuse , intimidation, sadness, or a lack of appreciation , the power and ability to determine the duration and outcome of it all is and shall always be within your possession.

The very nature of a thing's power to affect and control us is based upon the degree of ignorance that we present towards that particular thing.

If we perceive a person, place, thing, or idea as being our absolute superior ,then we only empower that position when we begin to think and feel constantly within the confined perimeters of the effects that such a perceived position of superiority causes us such as sadness, abuse, anxiety, fear, disregard, disrespect, and intimidation.

All of these emotional responses are in fact positions of a perceived inferiority about ourselves that are truly only illusions of our own ignorance about who we truly are and a proper understanding of the source of anything's base of power.

The most gravest mistake that most people make in their initial assessment of a person or situation is to become blinded and controlled by their emotions such as sadness and fear which paralyzes their thinking and places both mind and body in a selfinflicted disadvantaged position in reference to a problem or opposition where the margin for error in thinking is decreased and usually produces a course of thought and action that only strengthens the problem's or opposition's effect and power over us.

The fear of any person, place, thing , or idea is an irrational state of mind and behavior that most people have a problem overcoming. Some people never overcome their fears and remain captives to their fears.

The fear of any person , group of people, or places and things connected to them is irrational and unnecessary for one main Indomitable reason.

"If a person or thing breathes and moves, it can be studied and measured ,if it can measured, it can be calculated in a way that makes it predictable, then either neutralized or confined to a position of no significant power and effect to hinder or impede one's existence and the desires therein "

A prime example of this principle is the very origins of Western Civilization's laws of government and Law Enforcement.

There may have been numerous conquerors who conquered many geographical land masses for different nations but once the conqueror had established rule ,the system of governing was turned over to committees such as in Greek ,Roman, England, and American history who formulated the laws to govern the people.

If one looks closer , one will readily discover a certain character of men who otherwise were effeminate and least of the real men who were of the courageous and brave type that   considered the ruling class men as weak ,womanly, and not able to even defend themselves against any real man.

The very surprising factor is that people have never even conceived of the thought to ponder the question "How and Why is it that this type of man was always the rulers through the power of ideologies, theologies, and concepts that gave them the exclusive right to supposedly dictate and represent what a god or a group of gods wanted and demanded for the ruled masses ?

All Caesars considered themselves to be the exclusive Son of God and the Greek Senators believed themselves to be an extension of the Rulers Divine God given authority,

The Roman's political Government was ruled by Senators who were only chosen from the rich and leading families with bloodlines reaching far back into historical Roman ruling families ,the Pope's belief and theology of being God's voice or

representative goes back to Constantine and his political system that first created the idea and theology that the government was be ruled by the priests and the religion (Church & State Combined).

The Kings and Queens believed themselves of the right to rule based upon mythological divine heritages and bloodlines.

This is a common theme in the history of Civilizations especially in America.

In the beginning, America was a wild frontier of vast scarcely populated land where gunfighters and a man's guns were the way to settle disputes and injustices.

At some point near the end of the Wild Wild West, there began a cry for change by many easterners from places like New York, Chicago, and other major cities who wanted to expand their business interests into the west. This class of people were from the upper class and considered the ways of the Wild Wild West to be barbaric , savage, and uncultured.

No one has ever questioned the underlying reasoning behind these titles because most historians could bring themselves to document those underlying reasons because it would've been a description of themselves and their very nature which is a picture of the kind of men who are too cowardly or scared to face another man with guns in a do or die situation or even a mere fist fight.

So what did this class of people do, they Influenced laws that allowed them to organize groups of the aggressive and dangerous types of men to carry out the goal of Civilizing the Wild Wild West so that a weaker class of people could reposition themselves into positions of authority and rulership that they otherwise couldn't receive if it were left up to the strong , courageous, and dangerous types who were considered the real men.

If one thinks even farther, there is no modern Western Civilization country that was not founded by the criminal , rough, tough, and dangerous types that Europe had released from their jails and exiled from Europe to numerous destinations around the world.

Once the lands were colonized by these released criminals and poor women, then the upper class from those lands that the original settlers were exiled from would begin to trickle in and in no time at all, eventually became the ruling class.

This is a clear understanding of why the original establishers of government wanted laws, it wasn't to establish justice, equality, or true freedom, it was mainly the idea : " To create and establish laws that would provide and compensate them and their class of people with that which nature had not equipped them with " , the heart ,courage, and strength of real character that only real men and women possessed that automatically ensures the power to rule people by the consent of the people out true respect for the real principles of character possessed and demonstrated in the time of danger and need.

The law became a tool by which the weak could rule, influence, and control the strong who are and have always been the foundation and backbone of any civilization or country but this is also another prime example of how the mind is designed to rule the body rather than the body directing and nullifying the nature of the mind. The thinkers are a representation of the mind that

Another example of this is how the upper class and ruling class always make loopholes in laws that exempt their children from

Military service while the poor class has always had to watch their children and grandchildren fight and die in the wars that the upper class initiates.

This prime example is a perfect model of how one's approach to a thing dictates the results produced where mind outmaneuvers and overcomes the muscle and courageous of a certain naturally dominant man and woman.

Within the realm of human activities, there are varying degrees of existence in which humans live.

There is poor, rich, big / small sized humans, aggressive, passive, courageous/cowardly, strong/weak minded, authoritative/subjugated positions, popular/ outcast social positions , and conformity/non-conforming positions.

All of these positions and the thought processes that support and empower them are all just simply varying degrees of information or lack of information possessed.
Information (knowledge) is indeed power but only after one is able to translate that information into effective action that produces effective results.

In the realm of human activities and behavior, the knowledge possessed can only be as great or powerful as the attitude, faith, trust , and commitment behind it is willing to allow it to be.

When every human being is born, they are born into a society of fixed positions of beliefs, social norms, behaviors, and thought patterns and their processes.

Each fixed position is based upon a system of synchronized actions that continuously reoccur producing the same repetitive cycles of thought and behavior.

It is very hard for an unorganized and unknowledgeable person or group of people to counter and overcome such systems without possessing some form of system themselves.

Even individual positions of power or influence are based upon some form of method within a system of thoughts, beliefs and actions that the person knows will produce a certain affect on others.

It is a dominant principle of existence that dictates: It takes a greater force to meet and overcome another force that it is seeking displace or eliminate ."

The size of a person or object is never the deciding factor of the degree of power that will be possessed.

Size is an optical illusion that many use to their advantage to maneuver other smaller things into positions of an inferior nature.

It is the degree of energy invested in the force behind an object that determines the degree of power that will be possessed.

Within the nature of all human potentials and capabilities exists an underlying foundation of thought that acts as a primary motivating force behind all mindstates and actions that determines whether the mind and body will produce extreme, strong moderate, mediocre, or weak actions and reactions to external things beyond self.

That foundational thought is attitude and perception which determines the degree of effort and commitment that will be put forth behind an action or series of actions intending a certain result.

At the very heart of this foundational thought catalyst lies a base of accumulated information (knowledge) whether through reading/study, experience, or observation that shapes and influences the nature of our attitudes and perceptions.

Depending upon the nature of that information that we've accumulated, our attitudes and perceptions can either advance and enhance our potentials and capabilities to meet and overcome the actions and intentions of others or confine our very potentials and capabilities in ways that make us feel vulnerable, susceptible ,inferior and powerless to the actions and intentions of others.

Many have accumulated base information from the influences of others that seem to give them a particular standard of what is right ,wrong , or morally right which establishes boundaries beyond which they will not think or act.

The most insane part about it is that most people who are influenced by such standards of thought and behavior never ever question the origin of such standards of morals or right and wrong and the nature of the one's behind these standards of thought and judgment.

If actually researched, one will readily discover that their was a historical base of organized people of religion who taught these standards of morals and right and wrong but never lived by them.

Why? Because it was only a strategic plan to subtly maneuver the governed into calculated boundaries of confinement and powerlessness while the regulators of these standards acted from a base where all things were permissible and appropriate to maintain or enforce their desires , intentions, and control when dealing with the masses of people under their influence and rule.

The original church and original form of Christianity (Catholic) was divided when Martin Luther got fed up with the church priests and popes who had instituted a system of repentance for sins that required people to pay for the sins they confessed or were caught doing such as fornication, theft, lying, murder ,or sex with prostitutes while the priests and popes were doing the exact same thing.

Martin Luther originated the Protestant Church position and theology.

At one time in the church's history in Europe during the dark ages, it was taught and believed that to bathe was morally wrong because bathing washed away the spirit or soul of people.

It was right to label women and men as witches and warlocks and burn them at a stake after they'd been tortured into a confession or continued to deny the false accusations that were simply based upon the fact of a person choosing to think or do something new that wasn't approved by the priests and popes. (The Spanish, French, and English Inquisitions).

So in truth the history of morals originated not from a sense of right or wrong but rather from the foundation of deception, manipulation and control designed to limit and confine the thought /action potentials and capabilities of the ruled to positions and conditions of vulnerability and weakness.

The exact moment that many come into their own power is usually during moments of crisis or impending threats.

Why? How? Because the greater the pressure, the greater the power of self-realization and its self-preservation that breaks the grip and restraints of what external influences think, feel, or believe and chooses one's own standards and methods of doing whatever it takes to solve one's own problems.

There are an unlimited number of examples in life where the physically big or huge have been out-thought and out- maneuvered then repositioned into defeat or an inferior position by the smaller.

James "Buster" Douglas vs. Mike Tyson (1990) : In one of the biggest upsets in boxing history, Buster Douglas defeated the undefeated and heavily favored Mike Tyson to win the heavyweight title. No one expected Douglas to win because he had an average body build while Tyson was a muscular monster of powerful knockout blows, but he overcame the odds and knocked Tyson out in the tenth round.

Manny Pacquiao's Rise (Early 2000s) : Manny Pacquiao, coming from a poor background in the Philippines, rose through the ranks of boxing to become an eight-division world champion. His journey to the top was marked by hard work, perseverance, and overcoming the odds in a sport dominated by wealthier boxers.

The Battle of Agincourt (1415): During the Hundred Years' War, the English army, led by King Henry V, was significantly outnumbered by the French forces. Despite this, the English won a decisive victory due to their strategic use of longbowmen and the muddy battlefield that hindered the heavily armored French knights.

The Battle of Isandlwana (1879): In the Anglo-Zulu War, the Zulu army, armed with nothing but spears and shields, defeated the large British forces at the Battle of Isandlwana. The British, though better equipped with modern weaponry (rifles and cannons), were decisively out-maneuvered and defeated by the sheer defensive and offensive tactics of Shaka Zulu and his Zulu warriors.

Vietnam War - Battle of Dien Bien Phu (1954):The Viet Minh forces, under General Võ Nguyên Giáp, defeated the French colonial forces at Dien Bien Phu. The Viet Minh were outgunned and outnumbered but used guerilla tactics and the difficult terrain to their advantage, leading to the end of French colonial rule in Indochina.

Battle of Mogadishu (1993): During the Somali Civil War, a small force of U.S. Army Rangers and Delta Force operators faced overwhelming numbers of Somali militia fighters in Mogadishu. Though they were vastly outnumbered, they managed to achieve their primary objectives and extract most of their men, despite heavy casualties and the loss of several helicopters.

These examples emphasize the power of strategy, determination, mastering the art of timing and sometimes sheer will to overcome seemingly overwhelming odds and opposition.

There is one main quintessential principle that the Ancient Civilizations based everything within their studies, findings of facts and experiences upon , " Know Yourself "

If one is disconnected from knowing their true individual self and the exact position of self relative to all things surrounding self, then by all means that individual is not only out of sync with reality but is also unable to effectively deal with the factors of reality in a manner that is conducive to the individual's exclusive principles of human nature and existence such as :

1. Self-Preservation
2. Self-Determination

3. Self-Advancement

4. Self-Sustainment

5. Self-Sufficiency

Without such, one just exists as a pawn and disadvantaged symbiotic component of another's self-Preservation, Self-Advancement, and Self-Empowerment.

Any given intent or approached was something that is limited in range and beauty and school has a small almost nonexistent margin for error or the unexpected. Why because of the inconvenience instability and havoc that the unexpected causes with my optic thinking and the schemes and plans derived there from.

There's one component that must be incorporated and solidified within any approach. That is the constructing of one's approach with a fluid nature that is not only capable of adapting simultaneously as the unexpected elements of another's reactions manifest themselves   but as well is capable and proficient at either absorbing or deflecting the different reaction configurations and maneuvering around them so that they can't disrupt or obstruct the overall nature of your approach and its intended effect. A result that after engaging different variables of what was expected will also reflect a different configuration from the totality of what was original intended but will possess the essence of the effect one's approach was meant to cause.

No approach should ever be one dimensional but rather should incorporate various configurations with the same essential nature yet different components that serve different functions and objectives. Why? Because such a strategy increases the factor of success from numerous directions and angles.

Section 2
The Primary Prerequisites To Effective & Indomitable Thinking & Actions

Chapter 6

Thinking Or Unthinking?

Is it even possible to unthink something? How about, is it even possible to be a non thinker under the self imposed delusion of being a thinker?

Both are not only possible but are facts applicable to every living human being according to the doctrines, theologies, and influences of the world that have shaped and fashioned the human mind into a prism of falsified and illusionary ways of thinking.

Within the foundation of the human mind and human existence there are only (3) kinds of thinkers that rest as the sole contributors to the very nature of event, situation, and condition to be experienced within the human realm.

1.) Those who love to think for others

2.) Those who love for others to think for them

3.) Those who awaken and learn to think for themselves, in accordance with facts & reality (No longer the chains of mere belief & faith)

How so? Do you even know what thought is? or even what the primary elements of thought's nature and directive principles are? Do you even have the smallest idea of what thought's first natural tendency is?

If one's thought are out of context with the factors of reality in which one lives, then one's core intentions , drives ,and motives will also be misaligned with reality and producing effects and results not conducive to one being able to perceive, manage , and effectively control essential factors within that reality necessary for success and proficiency at a consistent at a consistent rate of occurrence on any level of life approached.

The first and foremost highly consequential mistake that most people in the world make is the natural assumption that just because they have a mind , that alone means they know how to think.

As with everything in the material world, nothing begins at a stage of perfection or at its highest level of potential and capability.

Everything has stages of growth and development that it must move through in order to achieve its level of completion or fullest growth stage.

Within the realm of human existence each stage of growth and development is simultaneously physical and mentally and depending on the factor of whether certain requirements or necessities have or haven't been acquired at each stage of the growth and development , certain imbalances and inadequacies can develop that will become an impediment to reaching the highest capacity intended within the nature of our physical body and mental sphere.

Most people have at the base of their thinking influences that they haven't the slightest idea about their origins and exact nature.

The question never comes to mind about why our thoughts and minds seem to be incapable of functioning and producing at the level of others who are successful in one way or another while the mass majority of us humans are seemingly confined to circumstances and conditions of poverty , ineffective thinking processes , and behavioral patterns that can never seem to advance us out of those dissatisfactory circumstances and conditions?

Even the seemingly successful in business, careers and academic accomplishments are faced continuously with some of the same common disparities as the poor and unsuccessful that makes all of their successes seem hollow like dysfunctional relationships ,stress, and severe depression until they have a need to displace authoritative figures in their field of expertise or interest and have a need for the right influence or information to help them to enhance their potential and capabilities in controlling or manipulating factors in their lives or the lives of others.

No matter where we are in the world even in evil dictator countries disguised under nice political or religious based titles of government that oppresses and confines the opportunities of its governed people , the conditions of the poverty experienced is still reflective of poor thinking , poor perceptions, poor beliefs , and poor decisions.

No sane mind based in a reality based frame of thinking would suggest remaining in such a condition unless held at gunpoint or physically restrained.

It is the exact nature of poor thinking that values a small minute level of comfortability over a necessary sacrifice of that comfortability in order to move elsewhere for better opportunities.

Even when that sacrifice is made, poor thinking influences illusionary thought patterns that its the change of location that will produce some quality of living conditions when in fact the greater opportunity of success and better living conditions rests upon the event of better quality access to information that will increase one's abilities.

The physical body needs a sufficient amount of food consisting of a certain amount of protein, vitamins , and minerals in order to grow healthy.

Likewise the mental side of the human being must be developed , nurtured , and advanced according to certain requirements and necessities as well, in order to achieve its highest potential and capacity.

Any body can formulate mental images but not everyone can formulate the specific mental images and understandings necessary to make one's thoughts and knowledge relative to the different streams of reality and the events therein that lead to success or lead out of poverty or dissatisfactory conditions of life.

Why? Because they lack the one thing that books , listening, observation, and being told things can't supply them with. "True intelligence"

True intelligence isn't based or defined primarily upon memorization of information although it's a part of it.

The world's norm of what is considered " Intelligent " is nothing more than a proficient skill of memorization that doesn't naturally qualify one as proficient at thinking , analyzing, ingenuity, or advancing and applying what is memorized to relevancy within other levels of thought and life that the memorized information wasn't originally designed for which is the base and nature of true intelligence.

No population in the world has any literate percentage over 60% including America which says a lot about the world.

If you can't read or write at a proficient level then your frame of thinking and understanding will reflect that inadequacy and limit not only your thinking but your potential and capabilities as well.

Why? or How? Because ultimately it is information that grows , develops, nurtures and expands the potential , power and capability of the mind.

CHAPTER 7

The Ultimate Reality Of Good, Positive,
Right, & Truth : Just Deception By Another Name

The Influence & Control of External Forces of Deception

In the world, the pervasive influence of authoritative forces, such as governments, educational institutions, religious institutions and media outlets, has subtly but extensively shaped the way individuals think ,believe , and act.

Unknowingly to the majority of the people in the world within these influences is not only a prescribed way and method of thinking. believing, and acting but also a subtle prescribed boundary of thinking , believing, and acting that confines the potential and power of the world's minds to a subjugated position of primarily functioning to maintain, reinforce, and advance the authority, influences, and power of control of a select few who rule and dictate to the governed.

Rather than encouraging independent, critical thought, these forces often propagate a specific underlying basis of thought that emphasizes *what* to think rather than *how* to think. This systematic conditioning of the mind can be only be best described as a form of "mind locks," where the mentality of individuals becomes confined to a predetermined realm of thoughts, actions, and potential that renders one at an immediate disadvantage and fixed position of powerlessness.

At the core of this issue lies the method of instruction prevalent in many educational systems and cultural norms.

From a young age, people are often taught to memorize and regurgitate information that aligns with the established norms and ideologies, rather than being encouraged to critically analyze and question the validity of these ideas. As a result, the ability to engage in original thought is stifled, leading to a stifling mindset that limits the degree and possibility of change ,mental growth ,creativity and innovation.

The teaching of "what" to think imposes a narrow framework and dynamic that restrains the mind, rendering individuals unable to break free from the prescribed boundaries of thought.

This confinement not only affects individual growth but also the broader collective growth of society.

When people are not equipped with the tools to think critically and independently, they become more susceptible to manipulation by those in power.

The potential for societal progress is hindered as new ideas and perspectives are suppressed in favor of maintaining the status quo.

In essence, these restraints serve as a form of mental imprisonment, restricting the capacity for growth and the realization of one's full potential.

This serves the ultimate purpose of those in positions of power and influence because if and when individuals are kept within the mental and physical boundaries of incompleteness , there will exist a demand from the confined for that which will aid in bringing them into a more fuller and complete life.

This in itself creates the unique and exclusive opportunity for that particular demand to be supplied by the very ones in power who were entrusted with establishing the very foundations of thinking for their captive audiences that created the faulty and problematic incompleteness in the first place which in turn positions them to be looked towards as the only exclusive influence capable of supplying the solutions and remedies to a faulty and problematic existence that such influences were designed to produce so that the deception could be deepened and reinforced.

Mental, spiritual, and behavioral restraints that are influenced by influential institutions and their particular doctrines and concepts with the intent to cause problems that they themselves would be exclusively given the opportunity to solve, to solve those problems which their restraints and deceptions actually caused in the first place.

The Origins & Nature Of Good, Right, & Truth

When you trace the origins of the concept of Good, right, and wrong, what you'll always find is some organized body of people and their particular books supposedly given by God or gods.

The one thing that should be shocking to many is that it is and has always been these same groups that have caused all the most evil in the world the most oppression , deaths and murders than anything or anyone else in the history of the world.

The origins of morals are deeply intertwined with the evolution of human societies and cultures. Morals are the principles that guide behavior, distinguishing between right and wrong, and they have undergone significant transformations throughout history. Initially shaped by unfounded superstitions and beliefs, survival instincts and communal living, moral standards have never been a concrete unchanging concept.

In ancient Europe, for instance, the belief that daily bathing was detrimental to health and spirituality highlights how cultural norms can oscillate dramatically.

1. During the Middle Ages, bathing was often avoided due to fears surrounding public health and modesty,

with the notion that it could lead to illness or the deterioration of the spirit.

This absurdity underscores how the most deranged thinking and perceptions of hygiene ,health, and spirituality can reflect broader frameworks of what is to be considered truth, right, or positive and have no basis in fact or reality.

2. (Women)

Ancient societies such as Greece and Rome it was considered morally right that women be considered property of their husbands subservient to men, with limited rights. It was in these same civilizations considered the truth that women were naturally limited to the intelligence of a child and incapable by nature of any significant logic or reason.

3. (Divine Right of Kings)

In history there was a particular belief about Kings that was believed to be a divine truth and the right way of governing people which was the Divine Right of Kings. In many ancient societies, rulers were often considered divinely appointed by the gods or a god, meaning their authority was viewed as morally unquestionable. This belief justified actions such as tyranny or war in the name of maintaining power.

Over time, the rise of democratic ideals seemed to challenge the morality of absolute rule, with the deceptive notion that leaders should be accountable to the people which has never materialized.

There's absolutely no difference between the nature of one tyrant rule and a committee of tyrant rulers such as senators, congressmen and etc.

4. (Ritual Sacrifice)

Many ancient cultures, such as the Inca and various Mesopotamian societies, practiced ritual sacrifices, including human sacrifice, as a means to appease gods or ensure agricultural fertility. These acts were deemed morally acceptable within their religious frameworks. As religious views evolved, such practices became increasingly viewed as barbaric and immoral.

5. (Homosexuality

In ancient Greece and Rome same-sex relationships, particularly between older men and younger boys, were often socially accepted and even celebrated as part of mentorship.

The renowned Spartans believed that no boy could truly become a man or a solider in the Spartan Army without haven had anal sex and this was also a major tenet of achieving manhood in Ancient Greece and Rome.

6. (Animal Sacrifice)

In many ancient religions, animal sacrifice was a common practice to gain favor from gods or to commemorate significant events. While this was morally acceptable at the time, the modern perspective often condemns such practices as inhumane, reflecting a growing moral concern for animal welfare.

7. (Gargoyles Were Considered a factual living truth)

Gargoyles and other hideous looking creatures were believed to serve a dual purpose on cathedrals and churches. Beyond their practical function as water spouts, these terrifying sculptures were thought to ward off evil spirits and protect the sanctity of the sacred space. It was commonly taught that their grotesque appearances could intimidate malevolent entities, ensuring the safety of the congregation and the divine presence within. This belief reflected the era's deep-seated fears of the supernatural and the importance of visual storytelling in architecture, merging artistry with the spiritual needs of the community.

8. (Burying female babies alive)

In pre-Islamic and post-Islamic Arabian culture, the practice of burying daughters alive, known as "female infanticide," was rooted in deeply entrenched societal beliefs about honor, lineage, and economic burdens. Daughters were often viewed as a liability, as they could not inherit property or continue the family name. Sons, conversely, were seen as assets who could provide labor, defend the family, and enhance its status.

Throughout history, the concepts of truth and morality have often been dictated by those in power—conquerors and rulers who imposed their standards on the subjugated.

In history leaders frequently operated under a belief that the rules they established did not apply to themselves or their close associates, creating a distinct moral exempt hierarchy. This dynamic has been evident in various civilizations, from ancient empires to modern nation-states, where the ruling class shaped narratives or principles of self-defined truths and standards of belief and action to justified their imposition on others , whether through conquest, exploitation, or governance under the title or label of what was right ,true, or good.

The implications of this pattern are profound. Rulers often manipulated truth to maintain control, portraying themselves as benevolent while upholding systems that favored their interests. Religious leaders, too, have historically aligned with political powers, often sanctioning the rulers' actions to legitimize their authority. This intertwining of power and morality has led to a pervasive theme in modern governance and religious institutions: the idea that ethical standards are selectively applied, reinforcing the divide between the powerful and the powerless.

As societies continue to grapple with issues of justice, equality, and accountability, the historical legacy of this moral double standard remains a critical point of reflection, prompting ongoing discussions about the nature of truth, right, and good.

Superstitions have historically played a significant role in shaping moral beliefs, standards of what is or isn't right or wrong, and social practices.

What we call superstitions today at one time were considered actual truths, things that were considered a moral practice for the good or best interests of people, and the unquestionable right thing to think and do, whereas to think or do otherwise were considered an unquestionable wrong that called for the violators to be avoided at all cost unless to welcome a part of the coming misfortune.

For instance,

1. The avoidance of black cats, believed to bring bad luck, was rooted in medieval fears of witchcraft and the supernatural. This belief not only influenced individual behavior but also contributed to broader societal norms, where avoiding such animals was seen as a morally right action to safeguard oneself from misfortune.

2. (Breaking a Mirror)
It was believed that breaking a mirror could bring seven years of bad luck. Many avoided mirrors to prevent potential misfortune, reflecting a moral caution against carelessness.

3. (The Number 13)

The superstition surrounding the number 13, often deemed unlucky, led to the avoidance of this number in various contexts, including buildings and events, as a means of ensuring safety and prosperity. 4. (Spilling Salt)

Spilling salt was seen as an omen of bad luck. Many would toss a pinch over their left shoulder to ward off misfortune, creating a moral duty to rectify the accident.

5. (Opening an Umbrella Indoors)

Considered unlucky, opening an umbrella inside was thought to offend the spirits of the home, prompting individuals to avoid this action for moral harmony.

6. (Knocking on Wood)

This superstition arose as a way to invoke protective spirits, encouraging people to express their hopes cautiously and reinforcing a moral sense of humility.

7. (Crossing Fingers)

Originally a gesture to invoke good luck or ward off evil, crossing fingers became a moral act of hope and protection against misfortune in various situations.

These superstitions illustrate how societal norms can intertwine with beliefs, guiding behavior under the guise of truth, good, and moral righteousness (Right) .

The Art of Deception : Manufactured Crisis by Institutional Power

In both ancient and modern society, powerful institutions, whether governmental, religious, or corporate, often manipulate mental, spiritual, and behavioral dynamics to create a phenomenon best termed "Mind Locks."

These restraints of thought are strategically formulated and implemented by these entities to impose specific limitations on individuals and communities.

The underlying objective is not merely control but to induce crises or challenges that these institutions are then uniquely positioned to resolve, thereby reinforcing their dominance and legitimacy.

The cycle of problem-creation and solution-offering forms the crux of a manipulative reoccurring loop that sustains the authority of these institutions while keeping individuals in a state of dependency and submission.

Deception functions by restricting the cognitive, emotional, and behavioral freedoms of individuals through the a societal psychology thought constructs that train both the conscious and subconscious of people to recognize ,submit, and conform to names and titles that project ideas and images of things that supposedly represent some form of substance that is good for them, the best or right thing, or that which will produce something that is needed, all along making them more susceptible to external control even when the substances behind the labels, titles, and names of good, right ,and truth present or influence only consistent negative, dissatisfactory, and disadvantaged positions for the believers and followers of those concepts.

No matter what is expressed, how it is expressed , what justification given for why it is expressed, the position intended behind those titles or labels is always for the exclusive advantage of those in power and control or those seeking power and control who truly know that such concepts are only abstract ideas designed for the controlled and not the controllers ,designed for the powerless and not the powerful.

For instance, certain religious doctrines may instill fear of the unknown or the afterlife, creating spiritual anxiety. Similarly, governmental entities might propagate a narrative of constant external threats, be they economic, social, or political, thus fostering a culture of fear and dependence on state protection.

Corporations, particularly those in the media and technology sectors, are notorious for engineering behavioral addictions—whether through social media or consumerism—creating a population that feels compelled to engage with their platforms or products to feel fulfilled or secure.

The purpose of these Mind Locks is twofold. Firstly, they generate a controlled environment where individuals are conditioned to encounter specific problems. These problems, which could range from spiritual crises to economic hardships, are not naturally occurring but are manufactured or exacerbated by the institutions themselves.

The religious institution that instills fear of eternal damnation, for example, also presents itself as the sole path to salvation.

Similarly, a government that stokes fear of external threats may offer security measures, military interventions, or surveillance programs as necessary safeguards. Corporations that drive consumer addiction may then sell the very products or services that purportedly offer relief or satisfaction.

Secondly, by positioning themselves as the exclusive solution providers, these institutions not only perpetuate their relevance and a need for them but also deepen their control over the individual.

The institution of influence that creates the problem gains power and legitimacy when it appears to "solves" it. This cycle traps individuals in a perpetual loop of dependence, where their mental, spiritual, and behavioral potential for growth is continually undermined. The institution becomes both the poison and the antidote, creating a scenario where escaping its influence seems impossible , scary , or at the very least, undesirable.

There is an unseen and unperceived ulterior force of direction behind a specific method of teaching that teaches one "What to think" as opposed to "How to think".

That particular method of teaching is so subtle and deceptive until most times it is heavily disguised behind titles that compel immediate attention, acceptance, and submission. Specifically titles and names that originate from tradition Influenced beliefs and ones that project the idea of improving upon something that people are already attracted to.

The most undetected element that most deceived people fail to consider or realize is that when it comes to deceivers, various groups or individuals can use different titles or names for the same substance but share one common ulterior motive which is tto capture and confine the mind within a cage that disallows individual thinking processes (especially individual analyzation) and the ability to perceive and understand not some but All factors of reality.

This form of teaching is so powerful until it will and does influence its students and followers to deny, ignore, refuse ,and misconstrue the facts and reality of things readily seen and experienced by them, in favor of alternative options to reality, facts ,and evident truth that have been influenced by influential personalities ,positions of authority/power ,and teachings of an illusionary nature consisting of things beyond one's ability to experience ,analyze ,and validate within any factor of their own individual reality and life.

This principle teaching method of teaching "What To

Think" doesn't allow freedom of thought and the measurement of things according to personal experience and the universal standard of what the majority of the people around individual self has, hasn't, and can't experience, and the most common elements within the realm of those real life experience that either validate or invalidate the illusionary contents of such teachings.

The natural unhindered process of thinking naturally influences thoughts that both validates and invalidates any first initiating thought.

It is that thought of a contrary nature to a particular Influenced thought or belief that is always shunned and taught to be a destructively negative towards something good such as faith.

Why? Because it is a natural process of thinking to perceive, analyze, and measure everything according to one's life experiences and it is the facts of these life experiences that always present to mind the idea and feeling that something is strange or wrong when the contents of a particular body of information presents thoughts and ideas about things that one's life experiences contradicts or hasn't confirmed as true and real.

This contrary thought and feeling is a natural occuring "Doubt".

The most common and most effective method and label used to suppress that doubt and its contrary thoughts and feelings are :

" Doubt is the workings of an evil being"

" Doubt is a destroyer of teamwork "

" Doubt is the disbelief in God and the word of God "

" Doubt is the enemy of faith "

" Doubt is a lack of trust in that which is right and in one's favor or best interests "

" Doubt is rooted in a lack of appreciation and thanks for what is offered or given "

" Doubt is an impediment to spiritual, political, economical, and social growth "

" Doubt is rebellion against that which is constructed for the good and well-being of self and others "

" Doubt means an unworthiness of something "

" Doubt means you're a potential threat or threat to an established norm or order of things "

All of these principle reasons to suppress and eliminate doubt about the contents of a particular theological/philosophical teaching, or concept is in reality a deceptive tool intended to influence one to forfeit that which one truly knows and understands to be true through personal experiences or practical analyzation for that which can never be validated as true or real , only believed in and confirmed by faith. (The realm of illusion controlled by the best deceiver).

There are prime examples where the minds of people are influenced by the position and power of authoritative personalities and theologies to deny and ignore the factors of truth and reality directly in front of their eyes in favor of what a deceptive personality spoke or wrote that contradicted the plain facts in front of their eyes and their everyday experiences.

In 2021 in Columbiana, Alabama at the (Shelby County Courthouse), a trial begin against a Black American male named Michael Powell for Capital Murder.

The Prosecuting District Attorneys (Jill Hall Lee, Daniel S. McBrayer, and Doug Smith) built their case for arrest ,indictment , and prosecution upon the claim that there was video evidence that showed Michael Powell entering a Chevron Gas Station at am and leaving out the chevron at am.

The prosecution even had 3 witnesses (all White women) who gave statements that they could identify Michael Powell as the murderer who was videoed in a series of videos from neighboring stores on the same highway as the Chevron Gas Station because the Chevron itself had no functioning cameras inside or outside of the Chevron.

The first strange indisputable fact is that the basis of the 3 white females' identification of Michael Powell wasn't an identification of Michael Powell's face in any of the videos presented by the Shelby County District Attorneys Office at trial because no facial features were ever shown in any of the videos.

The 3 White female's (Deborah Harrell, Jennifer Jones and Dixie Walker) stated that they could identify Michael Powell as the guy in the videos by the way the guy was walking in the videos and how it matched the wsy they knew Michael Powell walked.

The fact is that none of the videos were of a video camera system that recorded live motion, the cameras were all of a camera system that took a signal photo at an interval of every 3 to 5 seconds so no walking motions were present in the videos.

Guess What? When the videos were being shown by the Shelby County District Attorneys Office at trial on a large Video screen, the District Attorneys were narrating what the videos were showing up until the dark skin male entered the Chevron's parking lot and leaving the parking lot , at one point the District Attorney (Daniel S. McBrayer) was prepping the jury for his grand finale blow against Michael Powell and stated " let's enhance the video so we can see him coming out of the Chevron right now!! " and was pointing at the huge video screen and what it began to show was that the man they were all saying was Michael Powell , never came out of the Chevron but was only in the parking lot.

The District Attorney (Daniel S. McBrayer) then quickly rushed to turn the video off. Case dead it would seem even when the

Defense showed the video again to prove that the state's so-called suspect never was shown entering or leaving the Chevron as the District Attorney's Office claimed and as a lying ,false police report writing Chief Detective (Josh Rauch) also claimed in his trial testimony and reports.

Shockingly, another police reported the exact statements of a Edith Freeman (White Female) who admitted to entering and leaving the Chevron on her motorcycle during the PROJECTED time of the murder of the Chevron clerk. A woman named Miranda Craig stated at trial that her son saw Edith Freeman leaving the Chevron parking lot on her motorcycle. Even stranger , Edith Freeman stated in her statements to the Police Detectives (which the Detectives documented in the Police Report) that she saw a black car with 4 Black men in it when she arrived and one of them was looking at her and so she locked up her motorcycle and went into the Chevron to get some cigarettes but said she bever saw the clerk and left but but the strangest thing was that a pack of cigarettes was lying on the counter which later proved to have the deceased clerks fingerprints on them which means the clerk put the cigarettes on the counter for someone to receive which means Edith Freeman lied about not seeing the clerk when she went into the Chevron plus the Shelby County District Attorneys Office never released the video footage of Edith Freeman going in and out of the Chevron to Michael Powell's Defense Attorneys. Why? Because it more than likely would've shown that Edith Freeman lied about a black car with 4 Black men being at the Chevron when she arrived. (Further incriminating Edith Freeman).

The next piece of deception by the District Attorney's Office involved A David Jackson who entered the Shelby County Jail (A white Male) who approached Michael Powell in the Jail and explain to him how he (David Jackson) knew Michael Powell was innocent. Michael Powell told him to write it all down on paper and tell his family on the phone which David Jackson did.

The Jail phone recording reached the District Attorney's Office and they sent a Alabaster, Alabama Police Detective Josh Rauch to interrogate David Jackson, the same Detective that David Jackson wrote in the letter about that had threatened his life before he came to jail because he'd called the the Alabaster Police Department to tell them they had the wrong man when he saw Michael Powell arrested on the news snd when he wouldn't stop, they called him to set up a meeting and a Detective Josh threatened him saying " if he didn't leave it alone, he wouldn't be able to say another word to anyone. "

The letter that David Jackson wrote also stated that his friend(another Black man) who was a snitch for the Alabaster Police Dept. and Shelby County District Attorneys Office did the crime. The Shelby County District Attorneys Office talked to David Jackson and David Jackson tried to change his story from being the lookout man for his friend that did the Capital Murder to lying that Michael Powell gave him some Jail Commissary food items as payment for writing the statement but guess what? Unlike most jails, Shelby County Jail has cells which have a 96% glass front wall for the cells including the door and the cell block has cameras that view every place in their accessible by the inmates which means that if Michael Powell would've gave David Jackson some paper to copy the his statement from or paid him some food items from the jail commissary, the camera would recorded it.

The Video from the jail blocks showed every time Michael Powell and David Jackson were near one another and Michael Powell never gave David Jackson anything in the videos(Because the video cameras could see also clearly into every cell which means the incriminating statements in the letter in David Jackson's handwriting could only be assigned to David Jackson with no evidence of any influence from Michael Powell. David Jackson and Michael Powell lived in different cells.

Within days of David Jackson being released from the Shelby County Jail, he was run over and killed by an unknown driver. Who killed him? That letter in David Jackson's handwriting said That Police Detective Josh Rauch threatened his life and it happened.

What was the verdict against Michael Powell? Guilty of

Capital Murder. No gun found in the case, no fingerprints of Michael Powell found in or out of Chevron, and no DNA. Nothing directly linking Michael Powell to the crime.

The jury didn't pay attention to the evidence, they were focused exclusively on the deceptive narratives of the Shelby County District Attorneys Office even when the evidence clearly showed and proved that the guy in the videos (whom was being said was Michael Powell) didn't enter or leave out of the Chevron Gas station, therefore couldn't have committed the Capital Murder crime.

Pay attention in the coming years Because a retrial has been ordered for Michael Powell, lets see if they try the clear deception again. As all deceivers, its highly probable they will.

Chapter 8

The Nature of One's Approach To A Thing Directly Dictates The Nature Of The Results Produced

The approach that one makes towards anything in life shouldn't be a course of action that is left up to chance.

When a person deliberately chooses to approach things in life from the basis of a lack of preparation, the outcome in life's events and conditions shouldn't be surprising when it reflects a constant stream of failure , disappointment, and inadequacies.

There's one thing about life that is certain, all things occur in universal patterns that everyone must encounter and experience at one time or another in the course of their lives like problems and difficulties of various natures.

The most saddening thing about this dilemma is that most people prolong the duration periods of their problems by simply doing nothing , continuously using assumption based ideas, or outdated and ineffective strategies.

If and when problems arise ,the first and foremost thought and action should be to begin initiating measures that will bring oneself into a degree of preparing oneself to become able to solve the problem and make sure that oneself is prepared for any future problems of a similar nature.

The people who choose this course of action become proficient at solving their own problems and difficulties.

That is a form of training that many fail to realize.

For example:

Training the body, particularly in self-defense, transforms deliberate actions into reflexive responses through consistent practice and repetition. The essence of this training lies in muscle memory, which allows the body to react instinctively to threats without the need for conscious thought.

Initially, each move—whether a punch, block, or evasion—requires focused attention and precise execution.

Over time, as the body and mind repeatedly engage in these movements, the neural pathways that control them strengthen. This repetition ingrains the techniques into the subconscious mind, making them automatic responses to certain stimuli.

For example, a person trained in self-defense might spend countless hours practicing a basic block. At first, they must think about the angle of their arm, the position of their feet, and the timing of their movement. However, as they continue to train, these actions become second nature.

In a real-life situation, when faced with an attack, the body will automatically perform the block without conscious effort.

This reflexive response is critical in self-defense because it allows a person to react quickly and efficiently under pressure.

When time is of the essence, and the brain may not have the luxury to deliberate, these trained reflexes can be the difference between safety and harm.

Moreover, this kind of training builds confidence. Knowing that your body can respond appropriately without the need for conscious decision-making provides a sense of self-assurance and security

It turns potentially life-threatening situations into manageable ones by relying on the body's natural ability to protect itself through trained reflex actions. This principle of training the body is also applicable to solving the problems of life.

Just as the body can be trained to react instinctively through repetition, the mind can also be conditioned to develop automatic thought patterns.

This process involves consistently practicing certain ways of thinking until they become second nature, much like physical reflexes in self-defense training.

To train the mind, you start by deliberately engaging in a particular thought pattern or mindset by reading and studying some specific information that empowers your thoughts.

For example, if the goal is to develop a positive outlook, you would consciously focus on reshaping negative thoughts into positive ones.

Another example is that the goal may be to develop a critical thinking frame of mind that can critically analyze verbalized or written word quickly and react with the most effective optimal response to deception or intended lies, this of course would require one to familiarize oneself with a selection body of information that promotes critical thinking.

Within both examples initially, this requires focus, effort ,attention, and commitment as the mind might naturally lean toward negativity ,pessimism, or doubt.

However, with repeated practice, this positive reshaping becomes more natural.

Visualization is another powerful tool in mental training. Athletes, for example, often visualize successful performances repeatedly in their minds. This mental rehearsal helps create neural pathways similar to those formed during physical practice.

Over time, the mind begins to respond to challenges with the same confidence and focus experienced in those visualizations.

Daily affirmations can also play a role in this process. By regularly affirming certain thoughts, concepts, or perspectives, you reinforce them in your subconscious mind.

For instance, if you consistently affirm that you are calm and composed under pressure, your mind starts to adopt this belief and will automatically activate itself as a default response in stressful situations.

Through these practices, the mind learns to bypass negative or unproductive thoughts, reacting instead with the trained stable ,empowering , and positive responses.

Just as the body moves reflexively in a self-defense scenario, the mind can instinctively lean towards constructive and empowering thought patterns in challenging situations.

This mental reflex becomes invaluable, as it allows for quick, effective decision-making and a resilient mindset, regardless of external circumstances.

The second primary mistake that the majority of people in the world make is a major one done out of sheer ignorance in regards to desired, intended, and planned goals.

That widespread mistake is an unstable position of approach to things that assumes and believes that one can simply give a bare minimum amount of thought about something , formulate a myopic and inept connecting plan or goal to it and then just jump straight into action armed with nothing more than faith that everything will turn out right or as desired without the benefit of in-depth analysis, information, and planning. Such a position never produces anything but poor inadequate results or complete failure.

The principle " The nature of one's approach to a thing directly dictates the nature of the results to be produced" expresses the fundamental relationship between how we process information and the outcomes we achieve.

This concept is pivotal in understanding that the accuracy, clarity, and truthfulness of information profoundly shapes our thoughts, decisions, and actions.

When individuals approach any person, place, thing, plan or problems with a commitment to factual and truthful information, their understanding is precise, accurate and refined, leading to more accurate and effective results. Consequently, when the information is flawed or misleading, the resulting outcomes are often flawed , ineffective, and opposite of the desired effect.

The nature of one's approach to information processing influences cognitive frameworks and decision-making processes. When factual and reliable data is utilized, it fosters a clearer perspective, enabling well-informed decisions , effective planning ,and problem-solving strategies.

This is because truthful information aligns with reality, allowing for precise analysis and reasoning. In contrast, when the approach is based on distorted or incomplete information, the resultant thought patterns and decisions are inherently unstable and highly prone to exhibit errors.

Thus, the principle emphasizes the critical importance of maintaining the quality and accuracy of the information that guides our thought processes.

Ultimately, the principle serves as a reminder that the quality of results is a direct reflection of the quality of the input.

By ensuring that information is both factual and truthful, individuals can precisely initiate, nurture , and facilitate a more accurate and effective approach to problem-solving and decisionmaking, thereby enhancing the overall efficiency and quality of their results.

This principle of existence is a essential prerequisite in not just understanding how accurate information changes the degree of potential , ability, and power of a mind by enhancing the very thought base and thought process of our minds but it as well emphasizes the most significant thought that the quality and factual nature of the information used in analysis and decision -making significantly impacts and determines the degree of the precision and effectiveness of the resultant actions to achieve the desired intent and effect.

When one approaches a problem , plan of action , and the decision-making process with correct and proper information, it not only solidifies their ability to analyze people, places, things, ideas, and situations accurately but also ensures that the subsequent actions are precise and in accordance with the reality and true existence of a thing rather than an assumed premise.

Accurate information serves as the foundation upon which analytical skills are built. When individuals are equipped with reliable data, they can more effectively identify patterns, discern relationships, and evaluate potential outcomes.

This solid analytical framework allows for a clearer understanding of the problem or plan at hand, facilitating more efficient informed decisions.

Consequently, the nature of the information dictates the nature of the analytical process; good information leads to thorough and accurate analysis, while flawed or incomplete data can result in faulty misguided conclusions that naturally produces actions and effects of the same nature.

Moreover, the precision of actions derived from accurate analysis is significantly enhanced.

When the analytical process is grounded in reliable information, the actions taken are more likely to address the source of the intended target rather than the mere surface characteristics or symptoms.

For example, in a business context, accurate market data enables managers to devise strategies that align with market needs, leading to successful outcomes. Conversely, poor information can lead to strategies that fail to meet actual market demands, demonstrating how the nature of the approach—shaped by the quality of information—affects the results.

Therefore, the principle solidifies the importance of integrating correct and proper information into the analytical process. It emphasizes that the accuracy of the actions and decisions stemming from this analysis is a direct reflection of the quality of the information utilized.

In essence, the pathway from accurate analysis to precise action is contingent upon the correctness of the foundational data, illustrating that the nature of one's approach

Chapter 9

The Nature & Dynamics Of Thought: It's Impossible To Think Just One Thought

It Is Impossible To Think Just One Thought, One Thought Naturally Insinuates ,influences, and incorporates Another.

You are more than likely wondering how is that so? or even possible?

Here's a few prime factual examples :

The principle that it is impossible for one to think just one thought stems from the interconnected and associative nature of the human mind.

Every thought is inherently linked to previous experiences, memories, emotions, and knowledge, forming a continuous chain of cognition.

When an individual thinks a single thought, it naturally leads to another, as the mind draws connections, analyzes implications, or recalls related information. This cascade is driven by the brain's inherent need to make sense of the world, process information, and predict outcomes.

A single thought cannot exist in isolation because the mind operates through networks of associations, where one idea triggers another in an ongoing, dynamic process.

This principle literally means that if you can conceive of one idea ,there is naturally other connecting thoughts and ideas that should naturally come with it based upon your life's experiences and some basic information obtained relative to those thoughts and ideas through your observations , analyzation of information (studies), and similar experiences to what one observed or studied in the course of one's life.

The lack thereof means that one must acquire that necessary information that exposes one to numerous examples of what the right and wrong effects of the idea were , the common denominator between the right results and the common denominators between the wrong results so that an accurate system of judgment can be formed.

A system of judgement that will qualify one to advance the old examples into new dimensions because old patterns become old and obsolete for a reason.

Others study the same information of examples and are prepared for those examples.

This principle underscores the complexity of human cognition, where every thought is part of a broader web of mental activity. It also challenges the notion of mental stillness, suggesting that true cognitive isolation is an impossibility.

Instead, our thoughts are constantly evolving, influenced by an intricate interplay of factors both conscious and subconscious.

This continuous flow of thoughts reflects the mind's inherent tendency to seek patterns, make connections, and generate meaning, making the act of thinking a singular thought an unattainable ideal.

The main problem that disrupts or inactivates the natural flow of one's thought processes and creates the basis of all dysfunctions within the human realm is when this natural process of thought is replaced with a form of thinking that seeks to perceive and understand everything through the lenses of that which the mind and experience can't perceive, discover, or validate the existence of.

This frame of mind is and always has been Influenced by theological and theoretical teachings of men about the supposed existence of things, worlds, modes of existence, and life beyond the fabric of reality.

Once instilled, these teachings permeate into every avenue of thought and become the basis of every thought perceived that renders one at the mercy and disadvantage to those whose thinking and actions or reality based, who ultimately have been the historical creators of these artificial theologies and thought patterns.

So instead of one real thought leading to another real thought and the greater potential for real and relevant actions, the stage of thought becomes a theatrical scene of one unrealistic thought and belief influencing and leading to other unrealistic thoughts, beliefs, and actions that forfeit the power of self-realization ,potential , self-determination, and self-control to the masters of reality who exist behind every philosophy, theology, and concept of the world.

To effectively achieve what one thoughts have conceived and to sustain it in the face of opposition depends primarily upon the nature of the information behind one's thoughts and the degree to which one is able to advance the principles behind that information into a fluid power of adaptability that is naturally able to incorporate any degree of change into its very dynamic as a tool or ladder to growing and elevating the possessor of it.

How so? because the essence of all information when truly analyzed and incorporated into who we are and how we think naturally infers another wider range and level of information about itself that will naturally prepare us for the possibility of change in advance before change occurs with preconceived contingency thoughts , ideas , and plans that enable one to efficiently redirect the knowledge and experience of success into other avenues that have also been preconceived.

This is one of the greater aspects of thinking that many fail to realize and activate.

This principle applies to every relationship, job, event, and circumstance that the human being will ever encounter.

Thinking is an electro-chemical process (energy facilitated through fluid) that is as a whole facilitated by the material substance of the brain where it's product of mind and is very nature is constructed to function according to a base formula of certain quintessential elements.

It is these principal elements that must be all present or acquired before the mind can even begin to operate at its most optimal levels of precision and performance for an individual.

Within the very fabric of the mind, it is these quintessential elements of Truth and facts (not mere belief), a factual based analyzation process consisting of memory, weighing, associating the congruence or incongruence of objects with others, and the extracting of key fundamental principles of Truth and fact from the experiences of the body and mind in a constant and repetitious correlative process that combines and advances the factual information obtained from past and present experiences.

The correlative process then equates to the natural results of a constant expansion of the mind's innovative and intuitive perimeters of thought, ideas, and realization of things. Including what one truly knows, understands, is capable of performing and the acute intuitive sense to discern between reality and the principles of factual information that naturally leads to mastering and controlling reality, as opposed to its contradictory pole of thinking, feeling, and acting from factless suppositions of mere belief and guesses, that only serves to entrap and restrain both mind and body within a powerless insentient state of an inferior existence that is only effective at being controlled and maneuvered by others for the exclusive benefit of empowering others.

The Dynamics of thinking is a battlefield where battles and wars of influence or fault by others constantly within an individual's mind for the prize position of being the exclusive influencer, controller, and owner of an individual's mind, actions, and behaviors for agendas that have never been in favor of the individual or masses of people being influenced and controlled by way of strategic falsified and factless theologies.

99.9% of the time, this is the linear form of thinking that teaches people to think one directional. A one directional way of thinking that trains the mind into limitations and weaknesses that manifests in one's character and conditions of living.

No one is weak or insignificant by nature, that is something produced by design.

Section 3

Influence, Control, & Power
By Way Of Deception

CHAPTER 10

Mind Locks

In the world, the pervasive influence of authoritative forces, such as governments, educational institutions, religious institutions and media outlets, has subtly but extensively shaped the way individuals think ,believe , and act.

Rather than encouraging independent, critical thought, these forces often propagate a specific underlying basis of thought that emphasizes "What" to think rather than "How" to think.

This systematic conditioning can be described as a form of "mind locks," where the mentality of individuals becomes confined to a predetermined realm of thoughts, actions, and potential.

At the core of this issue lies the method of instruction prevalent in many educational systems and cultural norms. From a young age, people are often taught to memorize and regurgitate information that aligns with the established norms and ideologies, rather than being encouraged to critically analyze and question the validity of these ideas. As a result, the ability to engage in original thought is stifled, leading to a stifling mindset that limits mental growth ,creativity and innovation.

The teaching of "What" to think imposes a narrow framework and dynamic that restrains the mind, rendering individuals unable to break free from the prescribed boundaries of thought.

This confinement not only affects individual growth but also the broader collective growth of society.

When people are not equipped with the tools to think critically and independently, they become more susceptible to manipulation by those in power. The potential for societal progress is hindered as new ideas and perspectives are suppressed in favor of maintaining the status quo.

In essence, mind locks serve as a form of mental imprisonment, restricting the capacity for growth and the realization of one's full potential.

This serves the ultimate purpose of those in positions of power and influence because if and when individuals are kept within the mental and physical boundaries of incompleteness , there will exist a demand from the confined for that which will aid in bringing them into a more fuller and complete life.

This in itself creates the unique and exclusive opportunity for that particular demand to be supplied by the very ones in power who were entrusted with establishing the very foundations of thinking for their captive audiences that created the faulty and problematic incompleteness in the first place which in turn positions them to be looked towards as the only exclusive influence capable of supplying the solutions and remedies to a faulty and problematic existence that such influences were designed to produce so that the deception could be deepened and reinforced.

Mental, spiritual, and behavioral restraints that are influenced by influential institutions with the intent to cause problems that they themselves would be exclusively given the opportunity to solve, to solve those problems which their restraints actually caused in the first place.

"The Art of Deception : Manufactured Crisis by Institutional Power "

In both ancient and modern society, powerful institutions, whether governmental, religious, or corporate, often manipulate mental, spiritual, and behavioral dynamics to create a phenomenon best termed "Mind Locks." These restraints of thought are strategically formulated and implemented by these entities to impose specific limitations on individuals and communities.

The underlying objective is not merely control but to induce crises or challenges that these institutions are then uniquely positioned to resolve, thereby reinforcing their dominance and legitimacy.

The cycle of problem-creation and solution-offering forms the crux of a manipulative reoccurring loop that sustains the authority of these institutions while keeping individuals in a state of dependency and submission.

Mind Locks function by restricting the cognitive, emotional, and behavioral freedoms of individuals, making them more susceptible to external control. For instance, certain religious doctrines may instill fear of the unknown or the afterlife, creating spiritual anxiety.

Similarly, governmental entities might propagate a narrative of constant external threats, be they economic, social, or political, thus fostering a culture of fear and dependence on state protection. Corporations, particularly those in the media and technology sectors, are notorious for engineering behavioral addictions…whether through social media or consumerism— creating a population that feels compelled to engage with their platforms or products to feel fulfilled or secure.

The purpose of these Mind Locks is twofold. Firstly, they generate a controlled environment where individuals are conditioned to encounter specific problems. These problems, which could range from spiritual crises to economic hardships, are not naturally occurring but are manufactured or exacerbated by the institutions themselves.

The religious institution that instills fear of eternal damnation, for example, also presents itself as the sole path to salvation. Similarly, a government that stokes fear of external threats may offer security measures, military interventions, or surveillance programs as necessary safeguards. Corporations that drive consumer addiction may then sell the very products or services that purportedly offer relief or satisfaction.

Secondly, by positioning themselves as the exclusive solution providers, these institutions not only perpetuate their relevance and a need for them but also deepen their control over the individual.

The institution that creates the problem gains power and legitimacy when it "solves" it. This cycle traps individuals in a perpetual loop of dependence, where their mental, spiritual, and behavioral potential for growth is continually undermined. The institution becomes both the poison and the antidote, creating a scenario where escaping its influence seems impossible , scary , or at the very least, undesirable.

The Multiple Components of Mindlocks: A Detailed Exploration

Mindlocks are a psychological mechanism designed to confine an individual's thoughts, beliefs, and behaviors within preestablished perimeters. These limitations benefit the facilitator who constructs and imposes the mindlock, often without the subject's conscious awareness.

The mind becomes locked within specific confinements, where submission and disadvantage are the byproducts.

To fully understand the nature of mindlocks, one must first explore the key components that drive their function and efficacy.

These components include the nature of mindlocks, the strategic placement of these mental constraints, the role of timing and phases of deceit, the power of belief versus truth, and the selfimposed nature of mindlocks.

1. The Nature of Mindlocks

At its core, a mindlock captures and confines an individual's cognitive and emotional capacities. People subjected to mindlocks are restricted to a narrow spectrum of thinking, feeling, and acting, all of which are tailored to benefit the lock's creator.

These individuals are locked into a particular mindset, restricting their ability to challenge or reconsider their established beliefs, leading to actions that are inevitably submissive or disadvantageous.

The design of a mindlock is such that it preys on existing vulnerabilities, cognitive biases, and emotional triggers. Once these are captured, the individual becomes subject to the confines of the lock, making it difficult to act outside the perimeters of their imposed mental boundaries.

Essentially, their ability to think critically, explore alternative perspectives, or make critical decisions is impaired, with their actions confined within a narrow scope that serves the facilitator's goals.

2. Placement of the Mindlock

A key component of mindlocks is the strategic opportunity for placement within a person's mind. This is achieved through the exploitation of human tendencies: the things people are attracted to, the beliefs they are naturally inclined towards, and the emotions they are driven by.

For example, people are inherently drawn to ideas or things that offer them numerous things considered of high importance such as :

1.security, 2.validation, 3.A sense of belonging,

4.   A deeper meaning

5.   A better way of living than their current dissatisfactory lifestyle or condition in life,

6.   That which can fulfill some deep part of their lives, 6 Offers them something they don't have but feel they desperately need,

7.   A better way of perceiving something they already believed,

8.something about love,

9.   something that can improve them personally,

10.   Something that can possibly give them an advantage over another and numerous other things.

These desires create fertile ground for the implantation of a mindlock.

When people believe they need something, whether it be social acceptance, financial security, or personal fulfillment, they become vulnerable to mental manipulation.

The mindlock capitalizes on these desires, presenting ideas or actions as solutions to these needs. This leads individuals to adopt the mindlock themselves, often believing that it is a conscious choice, not realizing they are falling deeper into a controlled thought process that benefits someone else.

3. Timing and the Two Phases of Deceit

Mindlocks are not instantaneous but require a precise understanding of timing. Deceit, in the context of mindlocks, operates in two distinct phases: the short duration needed to deceive and the long duration required to fully set the mindlock in place, a process sometimes referred to as "The long walk."

The Long Walk: A Strategy of Mindlocks

In the realm of the psychological strategy of deception, the mindlock represents an intricate form of manipulation where ideas are seeded over time, slowly taking root within the target's mind.

One of the most effective methods within this strategy is what can be called "The Long Walk." This tactic, like its name suggests, is an exercise in patience, timing, and precision, requiring a deep understanding of human nature, particularly the interplay between dissatisfaction and reflection. It is a strategy rooted in the art of deception but relies more on subtly influencing the mind rather than outright misleading it.

At its core, the Long Walk is about planting multiple seeds of deception over an extended period. However, unlike immediate deceptions that prey upon the sudden vulnerability of a person, this method takes time to bear fruit. These seeds are often ideas, doubts, or suggestions that are seemingly insignificant in isolation. The strategist, therefore, does not overwhelm the target but rather introduces thoughts slowly, deliberately, and subtly. These ideas might not register consciously at first but are designed to embed themselves in the subconscious, waiting for the right conditions to flourish.

One of the critical aspects of the Long Walk is the understanding that life itself becomes the agent of influence. Everyone has dissatisfactory elements in their lives whether it be personal, professional, or existential struggles. As time passes, these elements can act as catalysts, causing the person to reflect on their situation more deeply.

It is within this reflective state that the seeds of deception can begin to take root. The mind, grappling with dissatisfaction, becomes more susceptible to alternative ideas, even ones that were previously dismissed. The strategist does not rush this process but allows time to work in their favor, waiting for moments of weakness or deep contemplation.

This art of timing is what makes the Long Walk so effective. It is not about directly pushing the target towards a specific conclusion but guiding them indirectly, letting them believe they are arriving at these conclusions independently.

By understanding the ebbs and flows of a person's emotions, desires, and disappointments, the strategist can tailor the timing of their deceptions to align with these moments of reflection. The target may eventually feel drawn to the implanted ideas, believing them to be their own realizations.

The Long Walk is a sophisticated strategy of deception that thrives on patience, timing, and an acute awareness of human psychology.

By planting ideas slowly and allowing life's natural dissatisfactions to nurture them, the seeds of deception can grow into convictions. It is a strategy that harnesses the power of the long game, allowing time to do much of the work while the strategist waits in the background for their plans to unfold.

The short-term phase of deceit involves planting a seed of doubt, confusion, or a deceptive narrative. This can be done quickly by presenting misleading information, altering perceptions, or exploiting ignorance.

The Short Walk: A Strategy of Mindlocks

"The Short Walk" is a strategy of mindlocks where deception and manipulation occur within a condensed timeframe. Though the period necessary to achieve the objective is short, patience remains a vital component.

This method requires an acute awareness of the target's psychological state, as the strategist must swiftly understand and assess the factors of resistance or doubt that may arise.

Unlike the Long Walk, which involves a gradual seeding of ideas over time, the Short Walk relies on rapid, decisive actions. Here, the strategist must be nimble and adaptable, positioning themselves in a fluid state of readiness to adjust their tactics as the situation evolves. There is little time for reflection, so the strategist must anticipate the target's reactions and carefully maneuver around them.

Precision is critical. Each element of deception must be delivered with perfect timing, ensuring that the target is overwhelmed with convincing arguments before they have a chance to resist. Despite the quick turnaround, the success of the Short Walk hinges on the ability to strike a balance between patience and immediacy.

The strategist remains vigilant, capable of seizing on opportunities at the right moment, thereby achieving manipulation within a brief window of time.

However, the real power of mindlocks lies in the long-term phase, which is the gradual and careful process of walking the individual toward accepting the lock.

The long walk requires patience, as the individual is slowly conditioned to adopt beliefs or behaviors that align with the goals of the facilitator.

Over time, they become more entrenched in the narrative or belief system without realizing they are being manipulated.

By the time the mindlock is fully set, the individual is convinced that their thoughts and actions are entirely self-driven, when in reality they have been carefully guided into submission.

4. The Power of Belief versus Truth

An essential component of mindlocks is the concept that truth is irrelevant to its effectiveness.

What matters is not whether something is factually accurate but whether it is believed to be true by the target. People who rely solely on belief, without critical analysis or questioning, are more susceptible to mindlocks. This is because belief, in its purest form, is often disconnected from reality, operating in a realm where things that are not real can still seem possible.

In a fantasy world of belief, where emotional and psychological needs outweigh rational thinking, individuals are more easily deceived by facts presented with authority or backed by selective knowledge. Even if the foundation of a belief is based on falsehood, if it is presented convincingly, it becomes a mental reality for the person. Therefore, those who place more value on belief than on factual analysis are prime targets for mindlocks. They become trapped in a mental prison constructed out of perceived truths, not real ones.

5. Self-Imposed Nature of Mindlocks

One of the most insidious elements of a mindlock is its ability to compel the individual to apply the lock themselves. This is done under the illusion that the mindlock is beneficial, representing a positive change from old, ineffective thoughts, beliefs, or behaviors. The facilitator of the mindlock creates a narrative that positions the new belief or mindset as a solution to the individual's problems or as a path to improvement.

In reality, the individual is not liberating themselves but rather stepping into a new form of mental captivity.

To elaborate further, let's break down each component of mindlocks in greater detail, examining the mechanisms and psychological processes involved. This will provide a clearer understanding of how these mindlocks function and why they are so effective at controlling and limiting an individual's mental and behavioral capacities.

1. The Nature of Mindlocks: Confining Thought and Action

Mindlocks function as psychological restraints that trap individuals within a narrow range of thoughts, feelings, and beliefs. They are crafted to manipulate an individual's mental and emotional faculties, keeping them confined to a specific worldview or behavior pattern.

The genius of a mindlock lies in its subtlety—most people under its influence are unaware that their thinking and actions are being controlled. These confinements are designed to make the individual feel powerless, dependent, or submissive, which ultimately serves the facilitator's objectives.

This manipulation of mental boundaries often leads to a gradual reduction in cognitive flexibility.

When someone is mindlocked, they find it increasingly difficult to think critically, question what they are told, or explore alternative viewpoints. This lack of flexibility reinforces the control over their thoughts and behavior, as the person becomes stuck in a repetitive cycle of belief and action that reinforces the mindlock.

Furthermore, this process often operates beneath the surface of conscious thought. Individuals might be aware that they are struggling, but they often can't pinpoint the source of their confusion or dissatisfaction. They may even begin to feel that their limitations are natural or inevitable, reinforcing their submission.

2. Strategic Placement of Mindlocks: Targeting Desires and Vulnerabilities

The success of a mindlock relies on its strategic placement within an individual's psyche. To successfully implant a mindlock, the facilitator must first understand the target's desires, emotional needs, and cognitive biases. These vulnerabilities—whether they involve the need for security, belonging, validation, or certainty—become entry points for the mindlock to take hold.

Humans are naturally inclined to seek comfort in ideas that affirm their pre-existing beliefs or align with their personal desires. Mindlocks exploit this tendency by offering narratives or solutions that resonate with the individual's emotional and psychological needs.

For example, a person longing for social approval may be more easily manipulated by ideas that promise popularity or acceptance, even if those ideas are ultimately misleading or harmful. The key to placement is subtlety.

The mindlock often starts as a seemingly innocuous suggestion or belief that feels familiar and comforting. The facilitator might offer something that aligns with what the individual already believes or wants to believe, making the idea more palatable. Over time, the individual becomes increasingly attached to this idea, unaware that their thinking is being shaped in a way that benefits someone else.

3. Mastery of Timing: Short and Long-Term Deceit

Effective mindlocks rely on an understanding of the dynamics of time. Deceit can be executed quickly in the short term, but for a mindlock to fully take hold, the process often requires patience and careful planning—this is the concept of "the long walk."

In the initial phase, the short-term deceit is about creating a small but critical shift in perception. This can be accomplished through a lie, half-truth, or selective presentation of facts designed to trigger a change in thinking. For example, a person might be exposed to a sensationalized news story that preys on their fears or biases, creating a knee-jerk emotional reaction. In this phase, the deceit may seem minor or inconsequential, but it serves as the foundation for deeper manipulation.

The long-term phase, or "the long walk," is the careful process of conditioning the individual to accept the mindlock. This phase can span weeks, months, or even years, as the facilitator gradually introduces reinforcing ideas and behaviors that solidify the lock. The individual is not rushed but is slowly led toward a mental state where they are unable to question or resist the ideas that have been implanted. This gradual approach prevents resistance, as the person feels they are arriving at their conclusions independently.

In this phase, the mindlock is set so deeply that the individual begins to see it as their own belief system.

The deep internalization of the mindlock makes it extremely difficult for the person to break free, as they now believe that their thoughts and behaviors are a natural part of who they are.

4. Belief Versus Truth: The Power of Perception

A central aspect of mindlocks is the fact that truth is often irrelevant. What matters is not whether something is objectively true, but whether the target believes it to be true. This creates a mental reality where belief overrides logic or factual analysis. Individuals who rely solely on belief without critical thinking are especially vulnerable to mindlocks, as they are more likely to accept ideas without questioning their validity.

This is particularly dangerous because belief operates in a realm where the impossible can feel possible.

A person who believes in something, even if it is not grounded in fact, creates a mental world where that belief feels real.

For example, conspiracy theories thrive on belief, not necessarily on factual evidence. Once a person buys into the conspiracy, they begin to see "evidence" everywhere that confirms their belief, even if that evidence is flawed or fabricated.

Facilitators of mindlocks are skilled at manipulating this aspect of human psychology. They know that if they can make someone believe a lie or a distorted version of reality, it doesn't matter whether it's true or not. The individual will act as though it is true, and their behavior will follow suit.

5. The Illusion of Self-Imposed Mindlocks

One of the most insidious aspects of mindlocks is the way they lead individuals to believe that they are acting of their own free will and free thinking. The target is often tricked into thinking that they have chosen to adopt the new belief system or behavior, unaware that they have been subtly guided to do so.

This illusion of free will makes the mindlock even harder to break. When individuals believe they are the ones making the decision, they are far less likely to question it. They feel empowered by the change, thinking that they are improving themselves or moving toward a better future. The facilitator plays on this desire for self-improvement, framing the mindlock as a positive change or a solution to the individual's problems.

This process taps into the human desire for control and agency. By making the person believe they are in control of their decisions, the facilitator ensures that the mindlock is reinforced and protected from scrutiny. It becomes part of the person's identity, making it even more difficult to dismantle.

6. The Role of Knowledge in Reinforcing Mindlocks

Although belief is a powerful tool for creating mindlocks, knowledge is often used to reinforce them. Facilitators may present selective facts or pieces of knowledge that align with the desired narrative, giving the mindlock an appearance of being rooted in reality. This creates a powerful combination of belief backed by "evidence," which further entrenches the individual in the lock.

However, the knowledge presented is often incomplete, biased, or manipulated. The facilitator may use real facts but distort their context or meaning to support the desired narrative. This selective use of knowledge makes it difficult for the individual to challenge the mindlock, as they believe they are acting based on facts.

In some cases, the facilitator may even provide an overwhelming amount of information, creating confusion and making it hard for the individual to discern truth from falsehood. This overload of information can make the person feel that they are incapable of making informed decisions, leading them to rely even more heavily on the mindlock for guidance.

The Viral Infectious Element of a mindlock's Nature

One of the most potent and insidious characteristics of a mindlock is its ability to spread subtly from the original host to others who are connected to that person, whether through personal relationships, social networks, or larger societal structures. This characteristic plays a crucial role in why mindlocks can achieve mass appeal and widespread acceptance, as they gradually infiltrate the thinking of individuals who are influenced by the original host, leading to a ripple effect that extends far beyond the initial target. This "viral" nature of mindlocks makes them highly effective tools for influencing not just individuals but entire groups or populations.

The Nature of Social Influence and Connection

Humans are inherently social creatures, and our thoughts, beliefs, and behaviors are often shaped by the people around us.

Most people by nature tend to seek validation, acceptance, and belonging within our social circles, and this makes us susceptible to adopting the ideas and beliefs of those we trust, respect, or have strong emotional connections with. Mindlocks exploit this natural inclination for social influence, using the original host as a conduit to reach others.

Once a mindlock takes hold in one person, it can spread through their interactions with others, subtly influencing the thoughts and behaviors of those around them. This can happen in various ways:

Direct Influence Through Communication

The original host of the mindlock will often communicate their locked-in beliefs, ideas, or values to others, either through direct conversation or more subtle forms of expression. Since the host has internalized the mindlock, they may present these beliefs as their own, and because they are convinced of the "truth" of their locked-in ideas, they can be quite persuasive to others. Friends, family members, or colleagues who trust the host may be more willing to accept these ideas without critically analyzing them, especially if the ideas resonate with their own biases or emotional needs.

Emotional and Cognitive Contagion

Emotions are contagious, and people tend to mimic the emotional states of those around them. If the original host is emotionally invested in their mindlocked belief system, they may express strong emotions like enthusiasm, fear, anger, or certainty when discussing these beliefs. These emotional expressions can trigger similar emotional responses in others, making them more receptive to adopting the same beliefs. Additionally, cognitive contagion occurs when ideas, ways of thinking, or patterns of reasoning spread from one person to another, often unconsciously. This can happen in social groups where there is a shared desire for harmony or agreement, leading people to adopt the ideas of the group rather than thinking critically for themselves.

Social Proof and Validation

Mindlocks are reinforced through the principle of social proof which is the idea that people are more likely to adopt a belief or behavior if they see others doing the same. When the original host of the mindlock shares their beliefs with others and these beliefs gain traction, the mindlock starts to seem more legitimate and acceptable. As more people adopt the locked-in thinking, the belief system becomes a norm within the group or community. This creates a feedback loop where individuals are less likely to question the belief system because they see it as widely accepted and validated by their peers.

The Snowball Effect: How Mindlocks Gain Mass Appeal

The ability of a mindlock to spread from the original host to others is one of the key factors that enables it to gain mass appeal.

This process can be understood through the concept of the "snowball effect." A mindlock starts with a single individual, but as that individual shares their beliefs with others, and those others share the beliefs with even more people, the influence of the mindlock grows exponentially.

In many cases, mindlocks spread most effectively in environments where groupthink prevails..settings where individuals feel pressure to conform to the dominant beliefs of the group.

Once a mindlock has infiltrated a social group, it can become part of the collective identity of that group. This makes it even more difficult for members to question the locked-in beliefs, as doing so may feel like a betrayal of the group or lead to social exclusion. As more people within the group adopt the mindlock, it gains legitimacy and begins to spread beyond the immediate social circle to a larger audience.

Mass Media and Amplification

In today's world, the spread of mindlocks is greatly amplified by mass media, social media, and digital communication platforms.

When the original host of a mindlock expresses their beliefs online or in public forums, they can reach a far wider audience than through direct, personal interactions.

Once the mindlock begins to circulate in the media or online communities, it gains further credibility, particularly when it is repeated or endorsed by influential figures or organizations.

The viral nature of digital communication accelerates the spread of mindlocks, making them highly effective and to the point of being invincible.

Mindlocks are in essence influenced mental restraints, like the inability to question certain belief systems or authority figures, stem from deeply ingrained family , societal , social and institutional orientated conditioning.

An Institutional conditioning that can manifests itself as Educational, Religious, or Political.

This form of deceptive conditioning convinces individuals that they lack the right or capability to challenge these figures or beliefs.

Such self-imposed restraints, driven by fear or reverence for titles and symbols, extend beyond the immediate context. They infiltrate other areas of thought and decision-making, leading to a pervasive passivity , conformity ,and dormancy.

The main mindlock in all religious groups works towsrds conditioning the mind of its believers to value a particular theology without question because it is taught to have come from a particular God and to question the theology would be to question God when in truth it would be questioning the human figures who have positioned themselves as the ultimate representation of God and something the God wanted human beings to know and do.

Over time, this diminishes critical and resourceful thinking, self-determination , and the capacity to make independent, informed choices, thereby affecting all aspects of personal and collective life as intended by all theoretical and theological restraints.

Such Influenced mental restraints possess an intricate system of information whose very nature is to evolve into a self-generating , self-sustaining and self-imposed thought process mechanism of psychological restraint and confinement that creates a ripple effect, extending beyond the immediate context that originally initiated and established the theological restraints to affect personal and financial life.

The inability to critically evaluate situations fosters poor decision-making, leading to recurring problems.
In personal life, this may manifest as unstable and inadequate elements of thought and feeling that aid and assist in producing unfulfilling relationships or a lack of self-fulfillment.
Financially, it can result in missed opportunities, poor investments, poor money management , poor financial planning and financial instability, as individuals become unable to think and act independently or take necessary risks.

The Illusionary State of Mind in Mindlocks: Confined Thinking Masquerading as Free Will And Free Thought

Mindlocks are psychological mechanisms designed to trap an individual's mental faculties within a controlled and predetermined framework of thoughts, beliefs, and perceptions.

One of the most insidious characteristics of mindlocks is their ability to create an illusionary state of mind where the locked individual believes they are thinking freely, when in fact their thoughts are confined to what they are allowed to think. This false sense of autonomy is a key feature that makes mindlocks so effective and difficult to detect. In this essay, we will explore how mindlocks cultivate this illusionary state, the psychological processes behind it, and the consequences of thinking within these confined mental boundaries.

The Illusion of Free Will & Self Regulation

The success of a mindlock hinges on its ability to convince the individual that they are freely choosing their own thoughts, beliefs, and actions. On the surface, the locked individual may feel empowered, believing that they are acting based on their own desires or logic. However, beneath this veneer of freedom, their thoughts are guided and restricted by the invisible boundaries set by the mindlock's creator.

This illusion of Self- Regulation is maintained by offering ideas and beliefs that seem to align with the individual's pre-existing values, desires, or emotional needs. By doing this, the mindlock manipulates the person's cognitive biases, leading them to believe that they have come to these conclusions independently. In reality, these beliefs have been carefully curated by the facilitator of the mindlock, ensuring that the individual remains within the desired mental framework.

The Subtle Nature of Confined Thinking

A mindlock does not operate like a blatant form of control. It is subtle and sophisticated, often going unnoticed by the person it affects. The individual may feel that they are engaging in critical thinking, considering various options, or evaluating different perspectives. However, these thoughts and considerations are confined within the limits imposed by the mindlock. Essentially, the person is only permitted to think within a narrow spectrum, carefully crafted by the facilitator to maintain control while giving the appearance of freedom.

This subtlety is what makes mindlocks so difficult to detect.

The locked individual does not feel constrained or manipulated; rather, they experience a sense of well-being over their decisions and beliefs. The facilitator of the mindlock ensures that any ideas, beliefs, or thoughts that fall outside these boundaries are either dismissed, ignored, or framed as irrelevant or wrong. Over time, the individual internalizes these boundaries, believing that their restricted thinking is both natural and correct.

Cognitive Biases and Emotional Manipulation

Cognitive biases play a crucial role in sustaining the illusionary state of mind created by mindlocks.

Human beings naturally rely on cognitive shortcuts…mental frameworks that simplify complex decisions and judgments. Mindlocks exploit these biases, presenting information in a way that confirms what the individual already believes or desires. This is known as confirmation bias, where individuals are more likely to accept information that supports their existing beliefs and reject anything that contradicts them.

Mindlocks also exploit emotional vulnerabilities. By tapping into deep-seated fears, desires, or insecurities, the facilitator can guide the individual toward certain thoughts or behaviors without making it obvious. For instance, if a person fears rejection or isolation, the mindlock might present a belief system or ideology that promises social acceptance or security. The individual, driven by emotional need, gravitates toward this belief, unaware that their mind is being confined within specific mental parameters.

The Role of Perceived Choice

One of the most deceptive aspects of mindlocks is the notion of perceived choice. While the individual may feel they are weighing various options or making decisions based on rational analysis, their choices are carefully constrained. The facilitator of the mindlock often presents a limited set of options that all fall within the desired mental boundaries, ensuring that no matter which option the individual selects, they remain locked within the desired framework.

This illusion of choice reinforces the individual's belief that they are thinking freely.

For example :

In a political context, an individual may believe they are choosing between two political parties or ideologies, unaware that both choices ultimately serve the same overarching agenda of both parties that their common mindlocks have designed.

The perceived freedom to choose gives the individual a sense of control, even though their choices are, in reality, predetermined.

Internalizing the Lock

Over time, the individual internalizes the mindlock, believing that the boundaries imposed on their thinking are selfimposed or a natural extension of their own beliefs and values. This internalization makes it even harder for the person to recognize the mindlock, as it now feels like an intrinsic part of their identity.

Once internalized, the mindlock becomes self-reinforcing. The individual may reject or resist any information or ideas that fall outside the boundaries of their confined thinking, perceiving them as threatening or irrational. This creates a mental echo chamber where only the beliefs that align with the mindlock are considered valid, further solidifying the individual's confinement within the predetermined framework.

The Consequences of Confined Thinking

The illusionary state of autonomy created by mindlocks has profound consequences. The individual becomes trapped in a limited worldview, unable to access or consider alternative perspectives that could challenge their beliefs. This not only stifles critical thinking and personal growth but also makes the individual more susceptible to further manipulation and control.

Going further, the false sense of freedom provided by mindlocks can lead to complacency. The locked individual may feel secure in their beliefs and decisions, unaware that they are operating within a restricted mental framework. This complacency prevents them from seeking out new information or questioning the validity of their thoughts, keeping them locked in a cycle of submission and disadvantage.

Mindlocks are a powerful form of mental manipulation, capable of creating an illusionary state of mind where the individual believes they are thinking freely, when in reality they are confined within pre-established boundaries.

Through subtle manipulation, cognitive biases, and the exploitation of emotional vulnerabilities, mindlocks effectively guide individuals into a mental prison that they are often unaware of. The illusion of choice and autonomy makes these locks even more difficult to detect and escape from, as the individual feels they are in control of their thoughts and decisions.

CHAPTER 11

Ancient Conquerors : The Origins Of Modern Foundations Of Deceptive Thought, Influences, and Control

There is a catastrophical truth with catastrophic consequences that has been hidden as well as inconceivable by the world due to the people of the world being deceived into narrow passageways of thinking.

Passageways that would not only facilitate division, chaos , confusion, and conflict amongst themselves but would as well be the very means by which chaos, confusion, and conflict of thought would limit the greater potential and possibilities of humanity as a whole to think and rationalize within any sphere of free thinking.

In essence a form of confined thinking that initiates , facilitates, and reinforces a degree of ignorance so subtle and stealth until it would not only act as an impenetrable shield of protection and undetectabilty for the ones who originally constructed the means by which it came to be but also anyone in any era of time who could design and construct systems of thought and belief based upon the principles of these conqueror deceptions that made the power spectrum derived from manufactured ignorance even possible.

At the very core of EACH AND EVERY educational or religious doctrine and the institutions of influence built upon them in modern time, there exists one common thread that connects them all.

Within the history of all conquerors there exists the principles of deceptively strategic thought, intent , and designs to reposition populations of people away from all that is natural , truthful ,unifying , peaceful, loving and in accordance with the reality based foundation of human nature.

No matter what era in time all conquerors had the same principles of intent , method , and strategy in common.

With each passing era of time these principles were advanced and became more efficient and more powerful in the art of influencing and controlling people.

a. **Trust no one with the true nature ,dynamics ,and direction of your goals and ideals**

b. **Believe no one to be who they are and what they say they're about without tests and trials over an extended period of time and even then test even more without believing**

c. **Betrayal, disloyalty, disrespect,**

d. **Never reveal the exact, aim, purpose, and function, of thoughts, intentions , goals, or actions.**

e. The only reliable and consistent protection against detection or external threats is to surround the true nature of things with multiple illusions of misdirection, (Both in words and actions

f. Take advantage of any division amongst the targeted people. Any targeted people's or individual's enemies will always be an asset of information or action against the targeted

g. Divide people through Influenced lies about one another that will exploit the natural mistrust they have against each other and increase the tension and hostility to boiling points where conquering them is made easier

h. Influence ,control, and power to reshape and determine people's lives by deception.

i. Kept the majority of the targeted or controlled population ignorant.

j. Dictated and controlled the flow of knowledge within the locations of their control and then expanded that deception ignorance into other areas.

k. Either destroyed a people's cultural beliefs (social ,religious, ethnic identity, and history) or redefined all that existed therein according to the beliefs of illusionary things outside of reality. By ANY means necessary including murder.

l. Did all that is necessary to rewrite History in their favor with victims as the one's who initiated a war between them and the victims were savages who needed civilizing

m. Redefined the norm of religion with personal thoughts, beliefs, and perceptions so that God , God's will ,and influence is in the image and likeness of one's own desires and intentions

EMPEROR CONSTANTINE
& The Origins Of Christianity ,Modern Philosophy & Psychology

Constantine was deeply influenced by Neoplatonism, which traces back to Plato. Constantine's education in Greek philosophy, particularly Plato's ideals on leadership and governance shaped his strategic thinking.

This philosophical foundation, although problematic, was rooted in some specific principles of reality and critical thinking that when combined with his military prowess and political acumen, helped him rise through the ranks of the Roman army, eventually becoming Emperor and reshaping the Roman Empire.

It should seem very questionable and suspicious how a man rooted so deeply in reality and facts would influence and dictate the exact opposite of things outside of reality to the low born people that he conquered and ruled and the children of the highborn classes of other nations that he conquered and designated to the lowborn class within The Roman Empire.

The deception orchestrated by Emperor Constantine at the First Council of Nicaea in 325 AD set the foundation for centuries of theological deception and manipulation, shaping the religious doctrines and societal structures that govern the modern world.

By consolidating power and manipulating religious leaders, Constantine not only established Christianity as a tool of political control but also laid the groundwork for the selective inclusion and exclusion of religious texts.

This deliberate act of deception, coupled with the decisions made by the council, including the creation of the Nicene Creed, solidified a distorted version of Christianity that served the interests of the Roman Empire. These actions have had lasting repercussions, influencing the development of Western theology, which, to this day, bear the marks of Constantine's calculated influence.

In the year 312 AD , Constantine claimed to have seen a vision before the Battle of the Milvian Bridge. The Milvian Bridge Battle was very crucial to the expansion of Constantine's power and influence.

According to Constantine, he saw a cross in the sky with the words "In this sign, you will conquer." In a dream prior to the battle. He believed this to be a divine message from the Christian God, which led him to the deceptive approach to appear genuinely interested in Christianity while waiting for the calculated appropriate time to subtly assimilate signs , rituals, and beliefs of his prior religious beliefs into Christianity.

The most revealing fact is that Constantine didn't say or confess that he believed in Jesus Christ or Christianity until on his death bed which all historians fail to conceive what that very moment of confession actually symbolized. It represented the most pivotal moment in the scheme of a Conqueror where he of course would have no problem confessing faith in that which he'd shaped and molded into the image of his own thinking and designs.

This Battle event played a significant role in the growth of his influence within the large group calling itself Christian and marked the beginning of Constantine's support for Christianity within the Roman Empire and marked the moment that the cross became the official government assigned symbol of the Christian religion within the Roman Empire.

In 325 AD , Constantine convened the First Council of Nicaea, a pivotal moment in the history of Christianity. The council aimed to address theological disputes, particularly the Arian controversy over the nature of Christ and what particular texts would and wouldn't be recognized as the word of Jesus and the history of Jesus. The outcome was the Nicene Creed and a official format of the New Testament scripture, which established the foundational beliefs of Christianity.

A fact that is always excluded from the context of the time of Constantine and his history is the fact that prior to Constantine, there was no official or singular widespread written doctrine of these Christian sects within Rome or the lands surrounding Rome and that over 90% of the Roman Citizens were illiterate and couldn't read or write. Plus whatever religious writings there were, was always exclusively in the hands of the priests or teachers who were from notably from an Upper class Roman family as education was strictly an Upper Class activity and never the poor people who were the vast majority.

Constantine's founding of Constantinople in three hundred thirty was a strategic move to create a new center of power for the Roman Empire.

By establishing this city, later known as Byzantium, he shifted the empire's focus from Rome to the East. Constantinople became a key center for Christian scholarship and culture, significantly influencing the development of the Eastern Orthodox Church and the Christian world as a whole.

These examples highlight Constantine's profound impact on the political and religious landscape of his time, shaping the future of Christianity and the Roman Empire.

In the year 326 AD, Constantine ordered the execution of his eldest son, Crispus. Crispus was accused of having an affair with Constantine's wife, Fausta.

Constantine's involvement in the Donatist Controversy, beginning around 312 AD, shows his use of deception for political gain.

The Donatists who later became labeled " Gnostics " were a Christian sect in numerous parts of North Africa but mainly in Alexandria (Egypt) who opposed the mainstream Church doctrines of the small secular Christian groups in Rome.

Constantine initially promised to support the Donatists but later sided with their opponents, seeing the division as a threat to the unity of his empire. His shifting support and use of force against the Donatists illustrate how he manipulated religious conflicts to maintain control.

The execution of Licinius In three hundred twenty-five is another example of Constantine's ruthless political maneuvers. Licinius was Constantine's brother-in-law and co-emperor, ruling the eastern part of the empire.

After defeating Licinius in a civil war, Constantine initially spared his life but later had him executed, citing a conspiracy against him as the reason. Many believe that Constantine fabricated or exaggerated this conspiracy to eliminate a potential rival and consolidate power, further demonstrating his willingness to use deception and murder to achieve his ends.

These examples illustrate the darker aspects of Constantine's reign, where deception, murder, and political manipulation were tools he used to strengthen and secure his influence, control, and power.

The First Council of Nicaea, held in 325 AD, was significant in shaping Christian doctrine, particularly through the formation of the Nicene Creed. However, it was also marked by intense debates and disagreements among the bishops who attended.

There were significant repercussions for those who opposed the Nicene Creed.

One notable figure was Arius, a priest from Alexandria, who strongly disagreed with the idea that Jesus was of the same substance as God, a key point in the Nicene Creed.

Arius and his followers faced significant persecution after the council. Although Arius himself wasn't present at Nicaea, his teachings and other doctrines of a similar nature were the primary target of the council's condemnation. He was exiled by Emperor Constantine and his writings were ordered to be burned. Arius died as a result of poisoning in 336 AD, just before he was to be readmitted into the church. Undoubtedly poisoned by his opponents who were still loyal to the Nicene Creed.

These examples reflect the harsh consequences faced by those who opposed the decisions of the Nicaea Council and the Nicene Creed, demonstrating the lengths to which the supporters of the Creed would go to maintain their religious and political control.

Emperor Constantine used the strategy of aligning with the enemies of his enemies effectively. One key example was his alliance with the Franks in 306 CE. At the time, Constantine was vying for control of the Western Roman Empire.

The Franks were a Germanic tribe that had long been enemies of the Alamanni, another Germanic group that frequently invaded Roman territories. By allying with the Franks, Constantine weakened the Alamanni, which allowed him to solidify control over Gaul.

In 312 CE, Constantine aligned himself with various small groups of Christians throughout the Roman Empire and other lands conquered by the Romans who, although differing in religious ideologies and texts about Jesus, they themselves recognized a common enemy and so joined Constantine during the civil war against Maxentius, who had persecuted them. This support helped him gain favor among the small Christian populations, aiding his victory at the Battle of Milvian Bridge.

Notably, this shines a new light on the motives of Constantine's interests towards Christians that were more strategic than anything else.

Finally, in 324 CE, Constantine allied with the Sarmatians, traditional enemies of the Goths, to secure his victory in the east against Licinius, allowing him to reunite the Roman Empire under his rule.

Emperor Constantine employed misinformation to solidify power, notably during his conflict with Licinius in 324 CE. He portrayed Licinius as a pagan oppressor and enemy of Christianity, despite Licinius' prior tolerance of Christians. This manipulation garnered Christian support, helping Constantine justify his military actions and eventual reunification of the Roman Empire.

Emperor Constantine's strict censorship policies significantly shaped the trajectory of Western thought. By endorsing Christianity as the state religion, he suppressed traditional teachings and philosophies of the ancient fathers of Greek philosophy that were an intricate part of Roman education, so-called pagan philosophies and religious traditions that contradicted Christian teachings.

Constantine's influence led to the exclusion of alternative ideas, such as those from Neoplatonism and Greek philosophy, which were seen as threats to Christian orthodoxy. His censorship effectively controlled what could be taught, limiting intellectual diversity and allowing only those ideas that aligned with the church to thrive. As a result, future generations inherited a narrower scope of philosophical inquiry, dominated by Christian doctrine, which stifled broader philosophical exploration.

Emperor Constantine's censorship was part of his broader effort to establish Christianity as the dominant religion in the Roman Empire. While there were no direct accounts of Constantine himself executing philosophers, his policies contributed to a climate of suppression.

One key event was the Edict of Milan in 313 CE, which legalized Christianity and led to the promotion of Christian orthodoxy over other schools of thought.

Constantine took action against Neoplatonism, a philosophical system that blended Platonic thought with religious mysticism. Sopater of Apamea, a prominent Neoplatonist philosopher, was executed around 330 CE—allegedly for political reasons, but his close association with pagan philosophy made him a target. Another event was Constantine's Council of Nicaea in 325 CE, which aimed to establish doctrinal uniformity in Christianity, suppressing heretical teachings like Arianism, further curbing alternative Christian interpretations.

Constantine's efforts, particularly in closing pagan temples and discouraging pagan practices, indirectly led to the marginalization of philosophers aligned with Greco-Roman traditions. This suppression of non-Christian philosophical teachings greatly influenced the shaping of intellectual life in subsequent centuries.

Emperor Constantine's censorship was part of his broader effort to establish Christianity as the dominant religion in the Roman Empire.

One key event was the Edict of Milan in 313 CE, which legalized Christianity and led to the promotion of Christian orthodoxy over other schools of thought.

Constantine took action against Neoplatonism, a philosophical system that blended Platonic thought with religious mysticism. Sopater of Apamea, a prominent Neoplatonist philosopher, was executed around 330 CE for suspicious political justifications after having been warned repeatedly to cease propagating Neoplatonic teachings and materials but it is well agreed that his close association with Neoplatonic philosophy is what made him a target.

Another event was Constantine's Council of Nicaea in 325 CE, which aimed to establish doctrinal uniformity in Christianity, suppressing heretical teachings like Arianism, further curbing alternative Christian interpretations.

Constantine's efforts, particularly in closing pagan temples and discouraging pagan practices, indirectly led to the marginalization of philosophers aligned with Greco-Roman traditions. This suppression of non-Christian philosophical teachings greatly influenced the shaping of intellectual life in subsequent centuries as psychology also has its origins from the watered down version of Greek philosophy that Constantine decimated.

The basis of modern deceptive teaching is always established on some historical foundation of deception in a distant past.

If you can construct a modern version of belief based upon the historical models of the past, the door to success within deceptive influence and any deceptive scheme will be assured.

To make your own deceptive system of belief and its course of action more attractive and powerful than any of the competitors or those who position of influence is desired for self, one must apply these rules of engagement.

1. **Initiate an aggressive campaign that exposes the competitors as frauds and self-serving deceivers who intentionally misinterpret and mislead for selfish gains of attention ,control, and the disadvantage of others.**

The religion of Christianity is a playground for many deceivers who desire to influence and direct the lives of people according to their own personal desires.

At the core of these innumerable sects of Christianity lies the deceptive interpretation of certain scriptures to fit the leadership's schemes and plots.

In order to overcome all of these sects and their select doctrines, one must hit them all at the very base of their operations which is the Biblical scriptures themselves and force the so-called believers and leadership into an inescapable corner of choice that in either way will reveal them as following or leading a fraudulent representation of Jesus Christ's teachings.

That divisive position of choice would be based upon the constructed platform to choose whose words hold more value and weight, Jesus or the so-called disciples? Because some of the disciples' main teachings after Matthew, Mark, Luke and John either ignore or contradict the teachings of Jesus's own words.

There is a particular verse in the New Testament that the church and world of Christianity likes to avoid teaching about at all costs and you will never find any Church or Bible teacher of any kind teaching on it because the verse itself is loaded with a perception and understanding about humans that will redefine a better and more powerful understanding about what Jesus's teaching were really meant to do.

John 10: Verse 31-42

"Again the Jews picked up stones to throw at him. Jesus said to them "Many good things have I shown you from my father for which of these things are you going to Stone me ?" they said "We are not going to Stone you for any good works ,It is because you speak blasphemy against God because you make yourself to be God when you are only a man" Jesus said to them "Is it not written in your law "I say ye are all gods ?"(Psalms 82:6).The Holy writings were given to them (Israel People) and called them gods therefore the word of God cannot be put aside"

This verse has Jesus quoting Psalms 82:6 and Jesus says in this verse that the revelations were sent to them [Israel- but in a sense that simply meant people] and that God called them "gods" and therefore the scriptures can be ignored or put aside.

This is exactly what the church, the Pope, and Christian believers have done.(Ignored the word of God in this verse and the power that God intended people to have)

Did the Disciples put it aside? Yes they did and not one of them taught it.

The most powerful verse in the New Testament meant to give humanity a supreme self-awareness and self-empowerment and it is just ignored and avoided? By no means was it by mistake in the time of the Disciples nor is it by mistake in modern times.

Jesus Teaches A Parable That Is A Prophecy About The Future Coming Of God Himself

Matthew 21:33-4

The Parable of the Vineyard Owner & Tenants

33 **"Listen to another parable: There was a landowner who planted a vineyard. He put a wall around it, dug a winepress in it and built a watchtower. Then he rented the vineyard to some farmers and moved to another place. 34 When the harvest time approached, he sent his servants to the tenants to collect his fruit.**

35 **"The tenants seized his servants; they beat one, killed another, and stoned a third. 36 Then he sent other servants to them, more than the first time, and the tenants treated them the same way. 37 Last of all, he sent his son to them. 'They will respect my son,' he said.**

38 **"But when the tenants saw the son, they said to each other, 'This is the heir. Come, let's kill him and take his inheritance.' 39 So they took him and threw him out of the vineyard and killed him.**

[40] "Therefore, when the owner of the vineyard comes, what will he do to those tenants?"

Mark 12: 6-10 reiterates the same theme and parable

In this parable, the vineyard owner is God and the only son of the vineyard owner that the vineyard owner sends to the tenants is Jesus who they kill. Then the question is asked, "What will the owner of the vineyard do when he comes?" That he is God Himself.

If you research that verse, what you'll find is an innumerable accounts of Christian scholars, theologians, and preachers who intentionally interpret the verse out of context and make mean that the parable meant that the Jewish leadership would be replaced by Jesus and his followers.

The main characters and their respective positions are ignored to justify the intentional and deceptive misinterpretation.

Who sent Jesus? God did ! Who was God's only son that he sent and was killed? Jesus was !! That directly and unquestionably parallels The Owner of the vineyard sending his only son who was killed. No way around it except by deception.

Here is a list of books that provide insights into Emperor Constantine's use of alliances, strategy, and misinformation(lies & Deceit) during his reign:

1. "Constantine the Great: The Man and His Times" by Michael Grant

This book offers a thorough biography of Constantine, detailing his military strategies, alliances, and use of propaganda.

2."Constantine and the Christian Empire" by Charles Matson Odahl

This work focuses on Constantine's rise to power and his relationship with Christianity, including his use of religious and political propaganda.

3."The Cambridge Companion to the Age of Constantine" edited by Noel Lenski

This collection of writings covers various aspects of Constantine's reign, including his political tactics and alliances with different groups.

4."Constantine: Roman Emperor, Christian Victor" by Paul Stephenson

Stephenson's book explores Constantine's reign, particularly his military campaigns, propaganda, and alliances with different tribes and religious groups.

5. "Constantine and Eusebius" by Timothy D. Barnes

This classic study documents Constantine's political and military strategies, including his use of misinformation and alliances during conflicts.

6.“Constantine's Sword” by James Carroll
Carroll's book takes you into the deeper treacheries and strategies of Constantine 's reign

These books offer reliable historical analysis and provide the necessary context for understanding Constantine's tactics.

Here are books that explore the connection between philosophy and the origins of modern psychology:

1. "A History of Psychology: From Antiquity to Modernity" by Thomas Leahey
This book traces the development of psychology from its philosophical roots, particularly focusing on how ancient Greek and Enlightenment philosophers laid the groundwork for modern psychological thought.
2. "The Principles of Psychology" by William James
A foundational text in psychology, this book integrates both philosophical and scientific perspectives. James explores consciousness, perception, and emotion, drawing heavily on philosophical ideas that shaped early psychological theories.
3. "Psychology: The Briefer Course" by William James In this condensed Here are three books that explore the connection between philosophy and the origins of modern psychology:

These books offer an understanding of how psychology emerged from philosophical traditions into the scientific discipline we recognize today and bridges the gap between philosophical inquiry and scientific exploration, offering insights into how philosophical concepts evolved into psychological principles.

These books offer an understanding of how psychology emerged from philosophical traditions into the scientific discipline we recognize today.

Islam & Profit (Prophet)Muhammad's Deception

Prophet Muhammad and Islam are a prime example of deception in the name of a God and religion where individuals can be deceived easily as long as certain needs of a people are satisfied.

In many cases as with Islam ,a certain conqu> is glorified and praised as some divinely inspired person that brought change into the world but in truth as with Islam very little is ever truly questioned or paid attention to the teachings that certain conquerors brought.

What influences many to choose Islam has nothing to do with spirituality, its about ulterior motive to choose Islam based upon what is perceived as the opposite of Christianity.

In all truth, Islam represents a unique form of religious insanity that originated from its prophet and continues to be transmitted to each new convert.

The degree of insanity that Islam inspires and encourages in both the denial and ignoring of the facts about the faith even when such facts are clearly in front of their eyes confounds any logic or reason repeatedly like with the daily reading of the Qur'an that presents facts that go against what Islam claims it is about.

Islam proudly claims itself as worshiping only one God (Allah) and teaches that its not a polytheistic religion that recognizes and worships many Gods but what does the Quran say? and what does the History of Arabia and Prophet Muhammad reveal about that which actually proves Islam to be a polytheistic religion? and proves Islam as not being a universal religion but only meant for Arabs?

Prophet Muhammad told his followers that he received his revelation (The Quran) from the angel Gabriel who recited Allah's message in the Qur'an to him (Prophet Muhammad) who then came out of caves or a solitude place to quote it to his followers.

How did Allah supposedly represent himself to Prophet Muhammad in the Quran? It was by the fluctuating from a singular being to many expressions where Allah constantly spoke of himself as being a plural and representing more than one God.

The only facts about The Qur'an that can be proven is that it supposedly came from Muhammad and even that is highly questionable because why wouldn't Muhammad have ensured that his revelation was in a complete written text before he died rather than 20+ years after his death?

There are only two logical and factual reasons. Muhammad was either highly delusional in his mind where he perceived God speaking to him in one voice sometimes and many voices at other times where God represents himself as a we, us ,and our.

The second reason is that Prophet Muhammad through deception incorporated Arabia's older gods into Islam to attract and unite the various tribes of Arabia within Islam.

The following Quranic verses and facts prove both reasons as indisputably factual.

Surah Al-Hijr (15:9) "Indeed, it is **(We)** who sent down the Qur'an, and indeed, **(We)** will be its guardian.

Surah Al-Mu'minun (23:12-14) **(We)** created man

Surah Al-Qamar (54:49) "Indeed, all things **(We)** created with predestination."

Surah Qaf (50:38) "And **(We)** did certainly create the heavens and earth and what is between them in six days, and there touched Us no weariness."

Surah Al-Baqarah (2:35) "And **(We)** said, 'O Adam, dwell, you and your wife, in Paradise and eat therefrom in [ease and] abundance from wherever you will. But do not approach this tree, lest you be among the wrongdoers.'"

Surah Al-A'raf (7:26) "O children of Adam, **(We)** have bestowed upon you clothing to conceal your private parts and as adornment. But the clothing of righteousness – that is best. That is from the signs of Allah that perhaps they will remember."

Surah Ibrahim (14:4) "And **(We)** did not send any messenger except [speaking] in the language of his people"

Surah As-Saffat (37:104-107) "And **(We)** called to him, 'O Abraham, You have fulfilled the vision.' Indeed, **(We)** thus reward the doers of good. Indeed, this was the clear trial. And We ransomed him with a great sacrifice."

Surah Al-Baqarah (2:34) "And [mention] when **(We)** said to the angels, 'Prostrate before Adam'; so they prostrated, except for Iblis. He refused and was arrogant and became of the disbelievers."

Surah Al-Hijr (15:23) "And indeed, it is **(We)** who give life and cause death, and **We** are the Inheritor."

Surah Al-Baqarah (2:23) **(Our & We)**
Surah Al-Isra (17:1) **(We)** ,Surah Al-Kahf (18:9) **(Our)** signs
Surah Al-Anbiya (21:35) **(We)** and **(Us)** ,Surah Al-Ahzab (33:9)
(We)
Surah Yunus (10:92) **(We)**, Surah Al-Hijr (15:22) **(We)**
Surah An-Nahl (16:40) " **(Our)** and **(We)** , Surah Yusuf (12:3) **(We)**
Surah Al-Mu'minun (23:18) **(We)** , Surah Adh-Dhariyat (51:47)
(We)

Is there clear proof that the We, Us & Our represent more than one god in Islam? Yes, there is.

Prophet Muhammad taught that Allah had 99 attributes but what many have failed to realize is that many of those attributes are actually gods of Arabia before Prophet Muhammad was born and he assimilated these gods into the attributes of Allah. Meaning that these attributes in reality represent gods under the control of Allah.

For example: The very first attribute (Rahman – The merciful) is the South Arabian god (Rahmanan) , The 3rd Attribute (Malik- The King) is the Southern Arabian god (Malik -), the 8th attribute (Al-Aziz- the mighty) is the Northern Arabian god (Azizan – god of victory), and The 16th attribute (Wahab-   ) is the Southern

Arabian god (Wahab- a rare male moon god as most Arabian moon gods were female)

These are just a few examples, there are over 70 more of these verses that has Allah speaking of Allah as being more than one. The most significant part of all this is that no one ever saw an angel Gabriel talking to Muhammad.

What actually proves the idea of an angel Gabriel talking to Muhammad with a God's word as a fraud and even proves the idea of the Quran coming from God as a fraud and lie is one fact in the Quran where this Allah supposedly tells prophet Muhammad " and We leveled to the ground the great works and fine buildings which Pharaoh and his people built with pride" (Surah 7: 137). So what are those pyramids, buildings, and sphinx that are still standing in Egypt today from the supposed time that Moses lived? Ant hills?

How could a All-knowing God say something like that to someone he would have to know is a lie if he was the All-knowing God Allah? No God would do such a thing but a man like Muhammad would whose knowledge was limited.

Islam's False Claim of Being A Universal Religion For Everyone & The Facts That Prove Islam Wasn't meant For Non-Arabs

When it comes to Prophet Muhammad the Quran and even Islam there is a claim that prophet Muhammad was a Universal Prophet sent to every people in the world and that the Qur'an and the Message of Islam a universal Revelation and religion meant for all peoples of the world.

Muslims all over the world use Surah 34: Verse 28 of the Qur'an Where Allah says "we have not sent you (Muhammad) but as a universal Messenger to men giving them glad Tidings and warning them against sin" and Surah 39 Verse 41 that has Allah saying "certainly we have revealed the book to you in Truth for instructing mankind."

But as usual with Holy Books from man, throughout the Quran it contradicts itself.

For Example : In these verses the Quran tells you that Allah never sent a prophet or messenger except to his own people who spoke the same language.

Surah 14:4 " We (Allah) sent not a messenger except to teach in the language of his own people."

Surah 26 Verse 198 " Had we (Allah) revealed it (the Qur'an) to any of the Non-Arabs, they would not have believed in it." (**This verse**

tells you specifically about the Qur'an and its position in reference to Non-Arabs.)

Surah 42: Verse 4 " Had we (Allah) sent this as a Quran in a language other than Arabic they(the Arabs) would have said "why isn't it verses explained in detail? What is this,a book not in Arabic and a messenger that is an Arab?"

Lastly, Surah 41:Verse 3 says " A Qur'an in Arabic for a people who understand." (A People who understand Arabic)

42:7, 43:3, 39:38,and numerous other Quranic verses say that the Qur'an was sent in Arabic for an Arab people who understand Arabic.

Before Prophet Muhammad time and during his time, nobody spoke Arabic but in the Arabian area. So the Quran couldn't have been for other people in Africa, Europe, India, Indonesia , or the rest of the world because remember Allah said in the Quran that (we) never send a messenger and revelation except to a people who had the same language as the messenger and the revelation.

To cement this fact, the Qur'an only speaks about Arab culture, food, and ancestral practices, and prophets from that Mesopotamia area and not once mentions a foreigner (Non-

Mesopotamian) prophet that was recognized by Allah or sent to Non-Arab or Non- Mesopotamia geographical areas and their people. Its like Allah wanted or intended to Arabinize the whole world because Allah didn't recognize any language but Arabic.

Thus the claim of Prophet Muhammad, The Qur'an, and Islam being Universal for everyone is proven a fraud.

The whole intent of Islam and the Qur'an is seen wherever you find the Non-Arab believers in Islam, you see them copying the clothing, head wear (Kufis), and beards of the practices of the Arabs in the East.

At the very beginning of Islam's conquering, it was established in those conquered lands that the only true authority on Islam was to be Arabs themselves and it is still that way today where the Arabs of East don't and won't recognize any Islamic teaching or interpretation of Islamic beliefs except from their own or those whom they specifically indoctrinated.

As for the ethical tensions in Muhammad's teachings, one of the contradictions often noted concerns his stance on slavery. On one hand, Islam encouraged charitable acts, including the freeing of slaves,

For example, the Quran speaks about the virtue of freeing slaves and treating them kindly. However, the Quran also permits the ownership of slaves under specific conditions, particularly referring to captives of war or "those whom your right hand possess." These captives were often of non-Arab origins, captured during military campaigns. Islamic historians of wrote that Islam imposed regulations on the treatment of slaves, including providing them with rights and fair treatment but how was it fair treatment to own someone and to dictate their lives within confinements that gave them no rights over their own bodies, wives, or children ?

Within Islam the institution itself was not abolished. This contradiction reflects the social norms of the time, as slavery was widely practiced in the ancient world, including in Arabia, and Islam sought to reform rather than fully eradicate the practice immediately.

Prophet Muhammad's teachings, as revealed in the Quran, contain a complex view on the taking of property. While Islam strongly forbids theft and the unlawful seizure of others' possessions, it also condoned certain acts, such as the appropriation of spoils during war (ghanimah) and the redistribution of wealth from non-believers. Muhammad justified these actions as part of jihad, a religious duty to defend and expand the Islamic community.

The spoils of war, including property and captives, were seen as divinely sanctioned rewards for the Muslim community from Allah, distinguishing between moral conduct among Muslims and no consideration of morality applying to adversaries who was anyone that had land, property, or wealth and was not a believer in Islam.

When it comes to prophet Muhammad and Islam ,no finer example can be found concerning religious deception and the insanity of brainwashing someone to deny facts of reality that plainly stare them in the face because the basis of the Holy Quran specifically says on numerous occasions that the Quran and the message of the Quran was for those who knew and understood the Arabic language, that Prophet Muhammad was sent to a people who spoke the same language as he did.

The most profound thing of wonder is that over 95% of the world's Muslims are of Non-Arab origins and exist outside of the Middle East.

The religion of Islam proclaims that Islam has always treated its believers equally regardless of race but how is that none of the Caliphs were ever Non-Arab?

How is that prophet Muhammad and the Caliphs after him never sought to enslave other Arabs at the rate which they did the Non-Arabs from Asia, Africa, and Europe?

Prophet Muhammad and the early spread of Islam when viewed from an objective point of analysis rather than a view and analysis marked by a subjectiveness to paint Prophet Muhammad and Islam in a good light due to an adherence to Islam or Islamic influences, what is revealed is a naked image of deception.

The rapid expansion of Islam involved the simultaneous use of both military conquests and strategic alliances with the military element as the foremost course of action rather than any mythological premise that the sharing of the Quran and Islamic beliefs was the primary influence upon the spread of Islam, which can only be seen as forms of political maneuvering rather than purely spiritual propagation.

The early years of Islam in the Arabian Peninsula. As Islam grew, Prophet Muhammad led several military campaigns, such as the Battle of Badr in 624 CE and the subsequent battles that followed.

Some Islamic influenced historians interpret these events as necessary for the survival and expansion of the early Muslim community, while ultimately it represents part of a broader strategy that included social, tribal, and political agreements and alliances, such as the Treaty of Hudaybiyyah in 628 CE. This treaty was initially perceived by some as a compromise, but in truth it allowed infiltration of certain areas that were desired by prophet Muhammad and later allowed the Muslims to consolidate power, leading to the eventual conquest of Mecca.

The use of military force and strategic treaties were forms of deception, serving the dual purpose of spreading Islam while also securing political and territorial gains.

The idea of spreading religion through both persuasion and force is seen by some as a sophisticated form of deception, presenting a religious message while also using deadly force to uproot pre-existing beliefs and the people who adhere to them in order to make room for the ones who will facilitate the religious and political ends from a permanent residence.

Islam as Christianity has been and will continue to be a fertile playground for those who seek influence , power, and control through deception.

The Nation Of Islam

The basis of modern deceptive teaching is always established on some historical foundation of deception in a distant past.

If you can construct a modern version of belief based upon the historical models of the past, the door to success within deceptive influence and any deceptive scheme will be assured.

The Nation of Islam is one of most modern prime examples of those principles of deception.

Elijah Muhammad Is the founder of The Nation of Islam. He taught that God Allah appeared in the person of Master Fard Muhammad in 1930s.

Fard was supposedly God and taught Elijah Muhammad for 3 and half years but the strange thing about it is that Fard Muhammad Muhammad never told Elijah Muhammad or any other Black person that he was God and Elijah Muhammad admitted this fact in numerous interviews with news reporters. Elijah Muhammad said that he didn't know what to call Fard Muhammad so he called him by titles such as Prophet.

The next form of pure manipulation is that Elijah Muhammad taught black people that Fard Muhammad taught that the Black man was God and from a lost t ru tribe of Shabazz and that the white man was the devil.

Elijah Muhammad took pieces of orthodox Islam to give his Nation of Islam some historical connection to the Islamic religion.

Today a Louis Farrakhan heads the Nation of Islam as its leader and historical star student of Elijah Muhammad.

Within the teaches of the Nation of Islam especially within books by Elijah Muhammad like Message to the Black Man and Our savior has Arrived, it is taught that the Black man was the original self created God of the universe and that Black people are gods as well. Even Louis Farrakhan and Modern Nation of Islam followers believe and teach this as a actual fact.

There has been many attacks on this deception called the Nation of Islam but none has asked the main questions that uncover Nation of Islam as a true bonafide fraud.

If The original God was a Black man and his his Black descendants are also gods, what standard of judgment and measurement has the Nation of Islam had that even proves that the Black man can become a god under the teachings of the Nation of Islam?

In order to say the Black man is god, then there would have to be some Black man that has demonstrated the powers and ability of the original black man god that created all things in the universe.

That is the only standard of measurement that will validate the claim of the Nation of Islam. That original god in the beginning is the only criteria by which they could determine their potential to become as the Original Black god was. Just saying words, writing books ,or giving speeches that influence others can't ever validate a claim of being god.

Elijah Muhammad taught that Fard Muhammad's father was a Black man and had a child by a Caucasian woman so that he could produce a child that would look white and enable him to find and teach Black ppeoplethe lost knowledge of themselves without Whites in America detecting him and his mission but guess what? Fard Muhammad went to white people and told them he was God. There are Newspaper photos and articles about the interviews Fard gave including to Chicago white Police Investigators. So Elijah Mohammad's teaching was a lie on that.

How come the Nation of Islam taught and still believes whites to be Devils but everything they use to give some validity to their teachings comes from whites?

If Fard Muhammad and Elijah Muhammad are still alive on a mothership in space and have powers of God as Louis Farrakhan has taught, then why hasn't Fard Muhammad (their God) ever revealed to them undiscovered archeological findings of ancient scrolls and artifacts to independently validate their own teachings?

If God came and gave Elijah Muhammad and the Nation of Islam God's own Supreme knowledge and, wisdom, and understanding, how come the Nation of Islam hasn't created one major new and significant thing but only produced things patterned after what Whites created?

The only new thing that the Nation of Islam has produced is a (Bean Pie).

Nothing that Elijah Muhammad , Malcolm X, or Farrakhan has ever taught has repositioned the Nation of Islam to be superior to American or white countries, thus a fraud is finally exposed to its roots.

The modern Nation of Islam followers will attempt more deceptions in explaining Fard Muhammad like " We're just saying that the Knowledge and wisdom of God came in a man" but if that were true, why did Elijah Muhammad publish the statement " I pray to Master Fard Muhammad " ?

The Nation of Islam and its leader Louis Farrakhan teach Black Empowerment and unity but when one actually analyzes Louis Farrakhan and the Nation of Islam, you will see the books and speeches about Black love and unity but what you want see is a significant impact that the Nation of Islam has made in the Black communities economically.

There are only a few cities like Chicago, and Detroit where the Nation of Islam has built grocery stores and restaurants because its in Louis Farrakhan's area but elsewhere in America the only thing seen is where the local believers pool their own money to start a few small businesses and the millions that Farrakhan collects from requesting donations are never seen .

Prime example: Between 2013-2015 Louis Farrakhan and his prime followers from Chicago and Detroit crossed the Nation giving speeches and collecting money from Black people for what Farrakhan called the Economical Plan that was to help Black people during the coming troubled times.

In 2016 the Covid19 epidemic hit hard. Black communities were devastated. Black people especially whole families lost their homes and were living in parks and starving but no Farrakhan and Nation of Islam showed up with the millions they collected in the previous years for future needs of Black people.

What happened to the money?

The Nation of Islam is one of the most highest examples of deception because they utilize the foundations of conquerors and appealing to the desires of a people's needs to perfection.

If you listen to any of them ,they are very persuasive in propagating their beliefs. It's a unique strategy that incorporates the Bible and the Quran which gives them a mass appeal to various types of people who have been left unfulfilled by traditional religious groups.

Imagine offering people the world, te ultimate reasons behind their failures and oppression in the world while constantly digging their hands into people's pockets, wallets, and purses but never giving them anything in return, not even free marquee books.

The Nation of Islam will always sell people things that the people themselves gave them the donations to buy or produce.

In the words of the Nation of Islam teachings "It's about giving the people knowledge of themselves to better themselves and unite them against a common enemy because God (Allah) in the person of Master Fard Muhammad loved them." What a magnificent deception to learn from.

Imagine God freely sending a Messenger with message that he freely gave to him and the Organization the Messenger and his students like Louis Farrakhan build and rebuild demands you pay for the teachings in books and videos. Now that is the best of deceptions.

MONSTERS & BOOGEY MEN

One main context of history that is either ignored or taught around is the context of the historical people's beliefs and understandings about the world in which they lived.

That specific context is a mentality that sought to perceive and understand everything according to mere assumptions about the origins of all things that had no basis in reality or fact.

Conquerors throughout history have adeptly manipulated cultural and social norms to craft religious Monsters and Boogie Men, such as Satan , Iblis , and other evil figures, positioning themselves and their established religions as the ultimate saviors from those constructed beings and their connected conditions of damnation to be applied to those who failed to conform the prescribed religious system.

By exploiting prevailing fears and misconceptions, these conquerors created a landscape where imaginary threats were magnified to serve their agendas. For instance, Emperor

Constantine's promotion of Christianity was intertwined with the demonization of pagan gods, portraying them as sinister entities to solidify the new religion's dominance. This strategic demonization not only justified the conqueror's control but also reinforced their religious authority.

The Amazingly surprising thing is that prior to Constantine's version of the New Testament, there wasn't any such thing as an evil Satan or place of fiery torment (Hell) ruled by a spirit being in the Roman Empire or the surrounding areas which included the numerous other groups of Christians that weren't under Constantine's influence and control, who always ended up dead and annihilated into extinction.

All of the historians of modern times including Biblical historians , Jewish Scholars, and both Jewish and Christian historians have intentionally led the world to believe that the temple in Jerusalem was the only form of Temple Judaism when in fact in recorded history, the Samaritans had a temple of Judaism that was just as large as the temple in Jerusalem and the Samaritans were just as numerous as those of Judaism in Jerusalem.

The Samaritans were also considered to be Believers in the teachings of Moses but considered those in Jerusalem to be sellouts that did the bidding of the Roman Empire and we're always seeking to be close to the authorities of the Roman Empire to gain favors from them. The Samaritan saw this as a sellout to the belief of the prophets and the true religion of the Israelites.

The Samaritans inhibiting Samaria represented themselves as the (shamerine)-" the custodians or keepers of the original Israelite religion " in opposition to the Judeans of Jerusalem.

The old Nazarenes like the Samaritans were opposed to the Judean Traditions holding that the Judeans had falsified the laws of Moses they were vegetarians and rejected anal sacrificed sacrifices. Pilot was also in bad favor with the Samaritans they too at this time was it was expecting of Messianic personality the (Taheb) who would bring to light the sacred vessels of the Tabernacle hidden in ancient times on my Verizon and who would liberate the people from the Roman oppression and occupation.

A man appeared during the exact time in which Jesus was living and preaching, he appeared and claimed to be the (Taheb) and the whole. of Samaritans assembled to follow him. One day they gathered to follow him up the mountain pilot treated this activity as the beginning of a Revolt sent his forces against them, killing many and capturing and executing the leaders.

Why is this history so important? For one it shows that there were a hidden group of Hebrews called the Samaritans who the New Testament spoke of as negative for a reason. The Jews in the New Testament in Jerusalem were tied to the Roman Government and the only reason their brand of Judaism survived the Roman slaughter of all the other Hebrews and the Samaritans was they acted as government spies also because every other Hebrews considered them as sellouts and of a fake version of the Israelite Religion. Secondly there isn't and never has been a Jesus Christ found in any of the Roman records of Court trials and those records are intact with nothing missing. Lastly, it reveals that The New Testament scripture of (John 4:17-28) is false and could've never happened because the (Taheb) that the Samaritans were looking for was already there.

John 4:17-28 is when Jesus supposedly met a Samaritan woman at a well in Samaria and she thought he was the Messiah that the Samaritans were waiting for.

. "Then cometh he (Jesus) to a city of Samaria, which is called Sychar, near to the parcel of ground that Jacob gave to his son Joseph.

[6] Now Jacob's well was there. Jesus therefore, being wearied with his journey, sat thus on the well: and it was about the sixth hour. [7] There cometh a woman of Samaria to draw water: Jesus saith unto her, Give me to drink.

[8]   (For his disciples went away unto the city to buy meat.)

[9]   Then saith the woman of Samaria unto him, How is it that thou, being a Jew, askest drink of me, which am a woman of Samaria? for the Jews have no dealings with the Samaritans.

[12] Art thou greater than our father Jacob, which gave us the well, and drank thereof himself, and his children, and his cattle?

[20] Our fathers worshiped in this mountain; and ye say that in Jerusalem is the place where men ought to worship.

[25] The woman saith unto him, I know that Messias cometh, which is called Christ: when he is come, he will tell us all things.

[28]   The woman then left her waterpot, and went her way into the city, and saith to the men,

29   Come, see a man, which told me all things that ever I did: is not this the Christ?

30   Then they went out of the city, and came unto him. "

There's no way this conversation took place when the Samaritans' savior (The Taheb) was present in Samaria and the woman wouldn't have said "Messiah" because the Hebrews didn't speak Hebrew at that Time and hadn't for hundreds of years. This fact about the Taheb and more is in the writings of the Hebrew Historian Josephus who lived at that time. (Josephus, Vol.2 & 3, Antiquities of the Jews also by Josephus)

Josephus writings is also where a forged writing of Jesus's name was found because someone knew that Josephus writings told everything about Jewish life at the time that Jesus is said to have lived, and it looked highly suspect and suspicious that Josephus didn't mention a Jew named Jesus (Yeshua). But he did mention the Nazarenes as the most righteous people. Someone in the past history couldn't and didn't imagine how advanced the future would be about being able to analyze handwriting and ink and determine the differences in the ink and the age of original text's ink and the newly inserted ink.

Similarly, the Nazi regime manipulated existing superstitions and fabricated threats to consolidate power, painting themselves as the necessary protectors against these engineered evils. By constructing these proverbial monsters, conquerors effectively redirected the populace's fear and devotion towards themselves, ensuring that their rule and religious ideologies were seen as essential for salvation and stability.

This manipulation of belief systems illustrates how conquerors have historically utilized fear of fabricated evils to establish and entrench their own power and authority.

No matter if it is a Christian Satan and demons or the Islamic equivalent of Iblis and Jinn Demons , these religious boogey men or monsters of evil said to influence evil in people of the world would seem rational and possible, if not for two indisputable facts :

1.) We no longer live in the ancient world of the past whose context is one of mass ignorance and superstition where Porky The Pig, Dora the explorer, and Yugi Oh would be gods to them of that age and time.

2.) How is it that so-called evil only exists where human beings are or have been? How is it that where there is no humans, evil doesn't exist ? It's simple and indisputable, men are the source and defining point of evil. There is no such thing as evil in nature where boulders throw themselves at humans or trees attack people.

These seven books that explore the psychological aspects of fear, scare tactics, and their use in religious myths to influence submission and other emotions:

1.   "The Denial of Death" by Ernest Becker

Becker's Pulitzer Prize-winning work delves into the human fear of death and how it shapes cultures, religions, and systems of belief. He explores how religious myths and symbols often utilize death anxiety to foster compliance and submission.

2.   "The Origins of Totalitarianism" by Hannah Arendt

Though Arendt primarily addresses political systems, she touches on how totalitarian regimes (often supported by religious or mythic foundations) use fear tactics to manipulate and control populations. The psychological dynamics can be applied to religious myths and their influence on submission.

3.   "The Power of Myth" by Joseph Campbell

Campbell analyzes the role of myth in shaping human societies. His discussions often center on how myths, including religious ones, use symbols of fear and awe to guide behavior, control emotions, and elicit submission.

4.   "The God Delusion" by Richard Dawkins

Dawkins critiques religious belief systems, arguing that they manipulate fear, particularly fear of eternal punishment, to ensure obedience and control emotions like guilt and submission.

5.	**"The Varieties of Religious Experience" by William James** A classic in the field of psychology, James explores how religious experiences, including those grounded in fear and awe, influence human emotions and behaviors, often promoting submission and control through psychological and spiritual mechanisms.

6.	**"Escape from Evil" by Ernest Becker**

A continuation of themes from The Denial of Death, this book explores how societies use myths, including religious myths, to

channel fear of death into social control and submission, focusing on the connection between fear, myth, and power.

7. **"The Lucifer Effect: Understanding How Good People Turn Evil" by Philip Zimbardo**

Zimbardo's exploration of how fear and authority can be used to control and manipulate people offers insight into how religious systems might employ fear to foster submission, using real-world psychological experiments and their parallels in mythic and religious stories.

These books examine how fear, particularly fear propagated through religious myths, shapes human emotions and behaviors, often leading to submission and obedience.

THE ART OF GHOST TRAILS

Throughout history, religious institutions have used various methods to maintain control and perpetuate their beliefs, often through practices of omission or deception. A notable example is Christianity, where teachings about Jesus have been passed down through centuries without any original texts written by Jesus himself or his contemporaries.

The New Testament, which forms the basis for much of Christian doctrine, was compiled decades after Jesus' supposed life.

It should but doesn't seem highly strange that you have a figure such as Jesus at the very heart of a belief system but not one sentence exists in the language that Jesus spoke (Aramaic) that can be attributed to the exact words that Jesus and the disciples actually spoke.

Every text attributed to Jesus and the disciples is in the Greek and Latin language and originates from a time period over 130 years after Jesus supposedly lived and taught.

So in truth no real and valid connection to Jesus.

As a matter of fact the main problem and fear that has always existed from the beginning of the time of the church fathers unto the popes has always been their inability to prove the New Testament words were actually Jesus' or the disciples.

The only thing the church fathers and the Popes could prove was that the New Testament came from Emperor Constantine.

As a result, scholars have long questioned the accuracy of these texts and the potential manipulation of stories to fit the agenda of early church leaders.

The absence of firsthand documentation of Jesus' words and actions creates a fertile ground for what could be considered intentional deception.

Without original sources, early church authorities had the freedom to interpret or even fabricate teachings that suited their needs. This lack of transparency may have been by design, ensuring that alternative narratives or critiques of the faith could not easily arise.

By controlling the narrative, early Christian leaders were able to solidify their power and influence over followers, establishing a dogma that left little room for questioning or dissent.

This form of information control is best described as the creation of "ghost trails," where the truth becomes elusive and followers are forced to rely on faith alone.

The absence of concrete evidence makes it difficult to challenge established beliefs, leading to a system of blind faith and submission. Through the careful curation of texts and teachings, religious institutions can maintain authority over their followers, discouraging independent inquiry and reinforcing adherence to doctrine. Such practices have had lasting effects on religious belief systems, shaping them into tools of control rather than vessels for spiritual enlightenment.

The concept of "ghost trails" in ancient religious practices, particularly in Christianity, refers to the deliberate creation of elusive narratives, paths that lead nowhere tangible, yet still demand blind adherence. This form of deception places individuals at a disadvantage by design, trapping them in a cycle of chasing unattainable ideals that are rooted in unverifiable claims. By conforming to these ghost trails, believers are conditioned to pattern their lives and minds around stories, miracles, and doctrines that are ultimately unachievable in the real world.

For example :

The miracles attributed to Jesus in the Gospels such as walking on water, healing the blind, and raising the dead, set impossible standards for faith. These miraculous acts, which cannot be duplicated or witnessed in modern times, become the foundation upon which believers are taught to model their own spiritual journeys.

The problem arises when followers, having invested deeply in these teachings, inevitably fail to experience similar miracles in their lives. Instead of questioning the validity of the doctrines or the historical authenticity of these events, believers are often led to internalize their failure, attributing it to a lack of personal faith, sin, or spiritual inadequacy.

This creates a harmful cycle where individuals blame themselves for not achieving what is, by all accounts, impossible. The self is perceived as the problem, rather than the fallacy of the theology or the manipulation embedded in the ghost trails. This conditioning leads to a psychological burden that keeps people striving for unattainable spiritual ideals, effectively trapping them in a state of submission and self-doubt.

The doctrine thrives on the perpetual failure of the follower to meet impossible expectations, reinforcing the control of religious institutions over individuals' thoughts and behaviors.

The result is a deceptive path of spiritual pursuit where the ultimate goals, divine miracles, perfect faith, and a life modeled after ghostly, unverifiable figures are never truly obtainable. This cycle of chasing shadows keeps people in a state of dependence on the institution, perpetuating blind faith while discouraging critical thinking or exploration of alternative spiritual paths.

The system benefits from keeping individuals in this cycle, as it ensures continuous devotion and compliance without providing a clear, achievable endpoint.

Through strategic deception, orchestrated a deliberate erasure of the origins of key theological and religious doctrines. By manipulating religious narratives and altering historical records, these conquerors aimed to reshape spiritual beliefs to consolidate their power and influence.

Constantine's transformation of early Christian doctrine, for instance, not only reinforced his political control but also obscured the original teachings of Christianity.

Similarly, the Nazi Council's involvement in the formation of the Bible sought to align religious texts with their ideological agenda, thus distorting the origins of Christian doctrine. This manipulation served to sever the link between contemporary beliefs and their foundational roots, making it increasingly difficult for later generations to trace the true origins of their spiritual teachings.

Islam, Prophet Muhammad, and the propagation of Islam has a similar trial of missing pieces that were intentional and highly effective in ways that served the unquestionable deceptions of Islam that reinforced the deceptions and made them above questioning.

The main tenet of Islam's teachings is that one seeking to become Muslim must learn the Arabic language in order to understand the pure Quran and that any translations of the Qur'an into other languages isn't a true Qur'an. That isn't anything but Arab Supremacy and indoctrination to pattern people after Arabs and Arab culture and ultimately under Arab the Quran, though revealed over a span of 23 years during Prophet Muhammad's life, was not compiled into a formal text until after his death in 632 CE.

It is said that during his lifetime, the revelations were transmitted orally, and many of his followers memorized portions of them.

This is highly suspect due to the historically recorded facts that during and after Prophet Muhammad's time the ratio of Arabs who could read and write as opposed to those who could not was 10% literate in contrast to 90% illiteracy rate. During Prophet Muhammad's time reading and writing was a luxury of the Arab Aristocracy.

Next is the fact that the Qur'an wasn't put into text until 20 + years after Muhammad's death and the main question begs why? Why not while Prophet Muhammad was alive, if Allah truly meant for it to be an authentically recognized revelation? Instead of a book that would have hundreds of individuals that verified the words as being spoken by Prophet Muhammad(The Hadiths), like the verification of robbers, murderers, and haters of all non-Arabs could be a true verification for non-Arabs.

It is taught in all Islamic circles that parts of the Quran were originally written down on materials like parchment, bones, and palm leaves, but there was no organized book.

After Muhammad's death, the first caliph, Abu Bakr, initiated a project to compile the Quran due to concerns that portions might be lost as those who memorized it began to die in battles. The final compilation into a single, authoritative text was completed under the third caliph, Uthman ibn Affan, around 20 years after Muhammad's passing.

Judaism has a similar history that has a greater influence on both Jews and Christians because modern Christians perceive the modern Jews as having a mutual connection with them to the Old Testament scriptures.

The facts tell a different story. What is known as the Old Testament scriptures today have no ancient scrolls in existence from the time periods they describe. As a matter of fact Josephus, a Jewish historian that was a contemporary of Jesus's time period said there was only 7 Books that were recognized and propagated during his time. Even those had no connection to an ancient past of an Adam & Eve, Moses, king David ,Solomon, and Noah that they described. Why? Because those Old Testament Scriptures weren't written and made a synagogue canon until the time that Jesus supposedly lived.

A good source of this information is:

The Triumph Of Elohim : From Yahwehisms and Judaisms By Diana V. Edelman

Pay close attention to the commentaries because they give you unimaginable information and references to study. Especially about the proven false Canaanites who never existed except in Jewish Fairytales.

The facts argue that these strategic deceptions were not merely acts of historical revisionism but pivotal moves in a broader strategy to control and manipulate religious thought across time. The result is a legacy of confusion and misinformation that continues to shape the understanding of theological doctrines today.

In order to effectively construct a ghost trail within a certain philosophical, religious, political system, it is always important to first realize that it is your personality and the degree of faith and gratitude that you're able to instill in others towards you for something valuable that they feel you've given them like loyalty ,compassion, or a nonjudgmental support during a difficult situation or even simply the patience and availability to always help them to understand things better.

The above is that sentimental element that will reinforce the theology against anything and trigger a followers instinct to defend the theology from the stance of perceiving an attack on the theology as the equivalent of an attack on you.

Secondly, keep in mind that as long as you assimilate various elements into your theology from sources that others are naturally attracted to and influenced by, transition from another theology or influential person will always work at a more efficient rate.

1.	"Leaders Eat Last: Why Some Teams Pull Together and Others Don't" Author: Simon Sinek

2.	"The Leadership Challenge: How to Make Extraordinary Things

Happen in Organizations"

Authors: James M. Kouzes and Barry Z. Posner

3.	"Start with Why: How Great Leaders Inspire Everyone to Take

Action" Author: Simon Sinek

4.	"Leadership: Theory and Practice" Author: Peter G. Northouse

5.	"Primal Leadership: Unleashing the Power of Emotional Intelligence" Authors: Daniel Goleman, Richard Boyatzis, and Annie McKee

6.	"The Visionary Leader: Leadership Beyond the Leading-Edge" Author: William A. Ihlenfeld

# Politics Or Poly-tricks
Poly =many + Tricks = Politics

When it comes to politics no matter what era in which you are living or seeking to study. Why is it that all of the politics and the governments that are implementing these particular types of politics, always seem to do the exact extreme opposite of what they say politics is designed to do ?

Why has there always been some extravagant wording of governmental mottos and documents such as Constitutions that always project the idea that the politics is formulated by the people , for the people when in truth it has always been about (A Select Few) people dictating what the mass majority of the others want , need or deserve ?

It seems that from one modern generation to the next, there is always a renewal of the same ideas to improve upon the political system that is within their perspective country ?

Why is there always a renewal of the thinking that things can be changed for the better within the existing governmental and political realm, when history shows that no particular government and its political realm have ever significantly changed for the best interests of its own people once it has started to oppress and enact elements of injustice towards its own people ?

One of the most disrespectful Acts by a particular political system in government to ever be done towards its people in the history of governments is to be found in the example of the United States of America.

The U.S. has for the past 50 years been involved in politics that have been the most disrespectful form of politics against its own people that has favored the incoming foreign immigrants and illegal foreign immigrants who eventually became citizens more so than its own citizens who have been here for Generations after generations.

Within the years between 2020 - 22 nobody really paid attention to the articles reported by the Newspaper (U.S.A. Today).

Within those articles it was revealed how the government had been passing $90 - $100 + bills to assist the multi hundreds of thousands immigrants of Iraq , Pakistan , Bosnia, and others that the government had brought into the U.S. in the past.

Not hundreds of thousands altogether but hundreds of thousands of each group named plus other groups.

The most recent being the (Ukrainians) whose immigration numbers at the present are over 150 thousand and rising.

The most disrespectful thing is how American citizens who have lived here for over 50 years can't obtain social security funds in any sufficient amount or can't borrow a penny from the government but the same Social Security Agency and other governmental Departments have been funding new businesses, home acquisitions, and educational funds for these immigrants.

There's currently 21 year olds who have Ancestors who were citizens in this country since the early 1900s and they can't borrow or receive a penny from the U.S. Government but immigrants get all of these multiple hundreds of millions to start businesses and buy homes.

100 + Million Approved By U.S Government for Iraqi immigrants brought into the U.S.

100 + Million Approved By U.S. Government for Pakistani immigrants being brought in the U.S.

80 + Million Approved by U.S. Government for Ukrainians brought into the U.S.

100 + Million approved by U.S. Government for

The Surprising fact that may shock you to your knees is the part that the Social Security Agency Plays in all of this.

Who have the nerve to only give the America people small amounts each month. ($400 - $ 700 each month) and always talking about cutting that amount or eliminating Social Security altogether.

Microenterprise Development Program

Sponsored by the Office of Refugee Resettlement, the Microenterprise Development Program helps refugees who have been relocated to the U.S. become financially independent through entrepreneurship.

Through this entrepreneur program, immigrants can get training in:

- Developing business plans
- Managing a small business
- Marketing and advertising
- Bookkeeping

The program also provides funding for technology that early entrepreneurs may need for business management, marketing, or bookkeeping. For example, the program may provide a laptop computer with accounting software that is preinstalled.

Wilson-Fish (WF) Program

Also sponsored by the Office of Refugee Resettlement, the Wilson-Fish program helps resettled refugees who are striving to become financially independent. The program provides temporary cash assistance and helps refugees find various services.

Shelter and Services Program

ELIGIBILITY

How to Apply

Funding Totals

NOFOs

The Shelter and Services Program (SSP) provides financial support to non-federal entities to provide humanitarian services to noncitizen migrants following their release from the Department of Homeland Security (DHS).

Department of Homeland Security Announces Distribution of More Than $77 Million in Congressional Funding for Communities Receiving Migrants

Release Date: August 21, 2023

Funding represents another example of DHS providing unprecedented resources to support border and interior communities across America

WASHINGTON – Today, the Department of Homeland Security (DHS), through the Federal Emergency Management Agency (FEMA) and U.S. Customs and Border Protection (CBP), announced more than $77 million in grants to support border and interior communities receiving migrants through the Shelter and Services Program (SSP). The funding will be available to 53 grant recipients for temporary shelter and other eligible costs associated with migrants awaiting the outcome of their immigration proceedings.

Today's announcement builds on the more than $290 million announced through SSP in June, which brings the total funding allocated to more than $770 million.

This is the grants for immigrants both legal & illegal that the State of California was offering to immigrants.

SEED Grant is now closed – with no expectation to re-open. We are proud to have offered almost $5.5 million for immigrant entrepreneurs in California through our SEED initiative between 2022-24!

SEED ELIGIBILITY

Through the SEED initiative, we offered funding to California residents who were starting or growing a business in California. SEED applicants identified with at least one of the following:

- Non U.S. citizens or Lawful Permanent Residents (green card holders). This includes undocumented individuals, and individuals who have been granted Deferred Action for Childhood Arrivals (DACA) or Temporary Protected Status (TPS).
- Limited English proficiency, regardless of immigration or citizenship status.

TYPES OF GRANTS

We offered two different types of one-time, non-renewable grants:

1. **Developing Business Owner Grants ($5,000):** Grants to individuals (Immigrants) starting or growing a business with annual gross business revenue less than $100,000.

All of these agencies of the United States government and affiliate agencies either directly provide business startup grants to immigrants directly from the government or receive funding from the United States government under the status of non- profit organization to provide the funds to immigrants that they directly received from the U.S. to government for the specific purpose of funding the immigrants to start business.

That is why over the past 20 years you've seen the huge rise in foreign immigrants like Pakistanis , Iraqis, and natives of India owning gas stations and semi- gas stations with restaurants everywhere in the U.S.

But the citizens who been here all of their lives and can trace their ancestral citizens back into the 1800s and early 1900s can't get one cent from the same government without some form of collateral.

There are hundreds of thousands that are homeless and have been citizens all of their lives and can also trace their Ancestral citizens back into the 1800s and early 1900s but can't get one cent from the U.S. towards owning a home while these immigrants do. If this isn't one of the greatest disrespects that any government can do to its citizens, then nothing else is.

The trick has always been to keep the American citizens focused on and fighting over issues like race, gender , and religion as decision tools so that a certain political platform could stand united behind the scenes with the political parties (both Republican and Democrat) agreeing to do this this disrespectful thing and united to do other things that facilitate the true nature of both parties which is furthering a government catalyst that produces the ultimate effect of " Organized Confusion and conflict."

The public image projected has always been that the two parties are different when in fact behind the scenes they harbor the same essential goals, aims , and objectives…of keeping the poor even poorer , using the poor masses to fight wars that financially benefit the few connected circles of power and rich family connections.

This is the highest form of TREASON !!!!
Within the political sphere, the outright disrespectful and inconsiderate things that are done in government in the name of Democracy to its own citizens should cause a unprecedented protest and rage amongst those people but instead a cemented state of complacency is the only reaction which is a highly sophisticated form of political mindlocks that operates upon the strong foundation

of a people's willingness to be naïve and follow political rhetoric about the differences in parties when they are intricately connected behind closed doors to produce one common effect of chaos, confusion, and conflict amongst the governed that doesn't allow the unification of the governed.

Why the American people have allowed these kind of disrespectful things is one of the greatest mysteries except to those in power and of sane thinking.

The Deception Of The War on Drugs

There are many Americans and other citizens of Democratic countries who look at so-called drug dealers and drug addicts being arrested on the television and will say things like " They need to lock them criminals up and throw away the key for selling that poison " but at the same time feels its just alright for government agencies like the U.S.D.A (United States Drug Administration to approve drugs made big pharmaceutical companies that have side effects that collapse kidneys, cause brain tumors, heart attacks, strokes, and many deaths.

In a large portion of people who take those deadly drugs the side effects are no less than torture over long periods of time before they actually die.But in the minds of many its acceptable because the government approved it.

These side effects are always known by the U.S.D.A before they approve them and there is only one reason why theses pharmaceutical companies are never prosecuted. That is because of the money paid to elected officials in government. There have even been laws to prevent the criminal prosecution of pharmaceutical companies.

These attitudes are another form of mindlocks that prevents rational thinking.

To inflame the masses of people against drug kingpins and cartels the media constantly portrays those cartels as threat to democracy in Mexico and America but what they don't and wont tell the people is what Influenced the cartels to come about. It was corrupt governments that oppressed their people with unjust laws and prosecutions , kept the people in a perpetual state of poverty while the government wrecked the economies and spent all the money for themselves and those connected to them.

The cartels came from the poor people and spent their money to gain power and Military hardware to fight the corrupted government and give people jobs producing their drugs. Many Mexicans have eaten and lived better under the cartels rule than than they did under the Mexican and other corrupt governments.

Only when the Cartels and their people became willing to die and kill for their drug business did those corrupt governments became fearful because the mindlocks they'd implanted had been finally broken and this is what scares the American officials because it presents a picture of great power that could rise not to threaten democracy but the corruption of those hiding behind Democracy who recognize the similarities between themselves and the corrupted governments that Influenced the cartels to come about and the greater similarities between the gangs of America and other corrupted Democracies gangs who became the cartels. They fear the moment that these gangs ever acquire the will to fight and die against them for their drug business.

In politics its not what you can deliver, its about what you can deceive people into believing you can deliver whether it's true or not.

There are always common interests that all people have in common but the status quo aren't willing to touch a lot of them because it would put them into a bad position with the rich and powerful.

The one who becomes bold enough to voice some of those ignored interests of the masses will at some point gain the power to change things.

SECTION 4
Know and Understand The Very Nature Of Your Enemy

CHAPTER 12

Who Is An Enemy ?

**An Enemy Is Anyone Who Wants to or Acts to Deprive
You of Freedom, Justice, Happiness, Peace,
& Your Desire to Be Who You Are**

An enemy can manifest in various forms, often obscured beneath layers of societal norms and personal interactions. At its core, an enemy is anyone who seeks to strip away your freedom, justice, happiness, peace, and the right to be your genuine self. This definition extends beyond traditional adversaries; it encompasses individuals, systems, and ideologies that threaten your basic human rights.

Freedom is the foundation of our existence. When someone seeks to control or dictate your choices, they become an enemy of your right to free will. For instance, oppressive regimes or systems of government with good sounding names such as Democracy can and do seek to restrict and demonize others thoughts, beliefs, choices ,and freedom of speech that doesn't conform to their agendas in an attempt rendering dissenters voiceless and powerless. Justice, too, is fundamental. Those who manipulate legal systems to serve their interests undermine societal fairness, creating an environment where only the powerful thrive.

Furthermore, happiness and peace are universal pursuits. Anyone who perpetuates negativity, discrimination, or the threat of violence or persecution to establish their advantage over you disrupts the tranquility we seek in our lives. Such actions can be as subtle as social ostracism or as blatant as acts of war, both equally damaging to the human spirit.

Finally, the desire to be who you are is intrinsic to individual identity. Enemies emerge when societal pressures force conformity, stifling diversity and genuine self-expression. Those who ridicule or marginalize others based on their beliefs, differences, orientations, or lifestyles act as barriers to personal fulfillment and qualify as an enemy.

An enemy is not merely a rival but a force that seeks to undermine your freedoms, justice, happiness, peace, and identity. Recognizing and confronting these enemies is essential for fostering a world where every individual can thrive and express their true self without fear or repression.

The status quo of the world attempt to teach others that conflict and confrontation is never the answer to solve problems but when you actually look, you see them in areas of society either facilitating conflict and confrontation with others or supporting other's conflict and confrontation with those projected to be an enemy like Democracy of the United States that has and continues to act as a bully to smaller defenseless countries along with other bullies like the Israeli- Palestinian conflict. It is well known that any rational thinking person would dislike the idea of someone taking their land and home but when it comes to this particular conflict it's like even the best of rational thinkers believe it was right for the European Nations including Britain with America's support to take the Palestinian's land in 1942 and give it to European Jews from Germany and other European countries who didn't have an ounce of semitic blood in them or no ancestral ties to the Middle East.

Understanding the nature of your enemy is pivotal for achieving success in any conflict. To effectively navigate these challenges, one must employ a range of mental tools that not only allow you to analyze the enemy but also to strategically camouflage your own intentions and vulnerabilities. Here are fourteen principles to guide you in this intricate process:

1.   Analyzation : Begin with a careful analysis of your enemy's past behaviors and strategies. This insight will help you identify patterns and predict future actions.

2.   Detection : Hone your ability to detect subtle cues in the enemy's behavior. Paying attention to changes in their tactics can provide vital information about their intentions.

3.   Misdirection : Use your own actions of misdirection to obscure your true goals. By presenting misleading signals, you can divert your enemy's focus and create opportunities for yourself.

4.   Camouflage : Learn to camouflage your real intentions. Just as your enemy may disguise their motives, you should ensure that your true objectives remain hidden from view.

5.   Self-awareness : Engage in self-reflection to understand your own motives clearly. Knowing what drives you can help prevent your emotions from being manipulated by your enemy.

6.   Control of Thoughts : Practice controlling your thoughts to maintain a strategic mindset. This mental discipline allows you to remain focused on your objectives rather than reacting emotionally to provocations.

7.   Emotion Management : Be aware of your feelings and manage them effectively. Your emotional state can influence your

decisionmaking, and maintaining composure can prevent your enemy from exploiting your vulnerabilities.

8.   Weakness Recognition : Acknowledge your own weaknesses and develop strategies to mitigate them. By understanding your limitations, you can protect yourself from potential attacks.

9.   Adaptability : Cultivate adaptability in your strategies. If your enemy changes tactics, you should be prepared to adjust your approach in real time and continuously change tactics to eliminate patterns. Patterns reveal predictability.

10.   Communication Disguise : Vary your communication style to keep your enemy guessing. This can involve using ambiguous language or nonlinear messages to obscure your true intentions.

11.   Building Alliances : Form alliances that can strengthen your position. Having support can provide additional resources and create uncertainty for your enemy. Aligning with or supporting your enemies' enemy is a strategic maneuver that scares even the most powerful enemies in power because most times their enemies live in their own land.

12.   Resource Assessment : Continuously assess your resources and capabilities. Understanding what you have at your disposal can inform your strategic choices.

13.   Historical Insight : Learn from past conflicts and your own experiences. Historical context can provide valuable lessons that inform your current strategies.

14.   Psychological Resilience : Develop psychological resilience to withstand pressure. Maintaining a strong mental fortitude can prevent your enemy from exploiting your vulnerabilities.

By utilizing these principles, you can gain a deeper understanding of your enemy while simultaneously concealing your own motives, thoughts, and weaknesses. This dual approach enhances your strategic positioning, allowing you to initiate, approach, and face conflicts with greater confidence and efficiency.

No Reason To Fear An Enemy

Fear of an enemy often ends up serving that very enemy, making it a powerful tool for control and manipulation. When we allow fear to take root, it clouds judgment, weakens resolve, and saps energy that could be better used for effective action. Enemies, whether they are individuals or groups, like fear itself, thrive on your anxiety and uncomfortableness . Fear magnifies their power in your minds, often making them seem more formidable than they actually are. This paralyzing effect can prevent you from seeing alternatives, taking risks, or resisting oppression. In essence, fear turns into a weapon that we unknowingly wield against ourselves to the advantage of an enemy.

For instance : throughout history, oppressive governments have relied on instilling fear in the population to maintain control, as fear limits resistance and compels compliance. Enemies can exploit this fear, manipulating perceptions to foster division or stifle dissent. Instead of diminishing the threat, fear elevates it, giving the enemy an advantage without them having to truly work for it or needing to take further action.

Overcoming this requires courage and awareness, recognizing that fear is often more dangerous than the enemy itself. By refusing to let fear dominate, individuals and societies can reclaim their power and neutralize the influence of their enemies.

Nobody Is All Powerful

No enemy is truly all-powerful. If an enemy breathes or moves, these actions can be observed, measured, and analyzed. This principle suggests that any being, no matter how intimidating or formidable, operates within certain limits and laws of nature. These limits not only create opportunities for understanding and counteraction but as well reveals that there are natural limitations that any being or group of people are forced to work and function within.

Every choice and strategy has a limit, likewise any enemy has limitations that make them vulnerable and ineffective.

An enemy's behavior can be studied, then patterns, weaknesses, and vulnerabilities can be identified. When we analyze the enemy's strategies, tactics, or movements, it becomes possible to anticipate their next steps, confine their influence, and disrupt their objectives.

For Example: The Police Department has procedures that dictate that their very nature is to respond to the public's calls for crimes. Each Department has a set district or city. These means they arc always vulnerable to misdirections and being diverted in multiple areas until this naturally leaves other areas vulnerable. Have you ever seen how a police being murdered draws an extreme number of police?

By calculating an enemy's actions, we take the first steps towards neutralizing their threat. Through observation and strategic planning, weaknesses emerge that can be exploited. Whether the enemy is a person, group, or situation, the key lies in gathering information, making informed decisions, and applying pressure where it hurts most. The myth of invincibility falls apart once we realize that no one is beyond scrutiny and manipulation. Any entity with motives and goals can be stopped once we understand its inner workings. In this way, even the most powerful enemy can be confined within the boundaries we set for them, preventing them from achieving their ultimate intentions.

It is an enemy's nature to seek to provoke fear in it's target , but it is an enemies' worst adversary that can make them fear as well. For Example: As mighty and All-powerful as the United States likes to project itself as being, you'll NEVER SEE the United States taking on one of the other super power countries like China (Whom The American Government hates) in a head on conflict or attack but what you will see is America attacking small undeveloped countries in the Middle East or joining with other super power countries like Great Britain and Israel to bully and attack other smaller countries.

Apologies From An Enemy Mean Nothing

Apologies from an enemy, no matter how sincere they may appear, often carry hidden agendas.
An enemy's remorse is rarely genuine, more likely a tactic to lower defenses and exploit vulnerabilities. Faking acceptance of such an apology can be a strategic move.

By feigning forgiveness, one creates the illusion of peace, lulling the enemy into a false sense of security. This allows time to gather information, anticipate their next moves, and prepare defenses. True intentions can be masked behind diplomacy, enabling one to stay ahead. In this way, pretending to accept an enemy's apology can serve as a calculated step in a larger strategy of self-preservation.

Shadow Enemies: Family , Friends, Spouses etc.

Family, friends, and spouses often hold a unique position in our lives, yet they can sometimes become shadow enemies, revealing negative and destructive tendencies when their desires go unfulfilled. These individuals may initially appear supportive, displaying smiles and offering comforting words. However, when their expectations or attempts to influence us are thwarted, their true motives can surface, often leading to feelings of resentment or opposition.

These shadow enemies operate subtly, leveraging emotional connections to manipulate situations to their advantage. Their hidden agendas may manifest as passive-aggressive behavior, guilttripping, or even outright sabotage of our goals. This duality creates a complex dynamic where love and loyalty coexist with underlying animosity, making it difficult to discern genuine intentions.

When confronted with unfulfilled desires, these individuals may resort to tactics that undermine our self-esteem or confidence, all while maintaining a façade of support. Recognizing this potential for destructiveness is crucial for self-preservation. By understanding that even those closest to us can harbor hidden motives, we can better navigate relationships, set boundaries, and protect our emotional well-being, ensuring that we remain true to ourselves despite external pressures.

To effectively analyze and determine whether family members, friends, or spouses are shadow enemies, consider the following ten principles:

1.   **Consistent Body Language**: Pay attention to non-verbal cues. Crossed arms, avoiding eye contact, or tense posture can indicate underlying resentment.

2.   **Frequent Expressions of Frustration**: Note any consistent conversations filled with frustration or anger. Repeated complaints about you or your choices may signal deeper issues.

3.   Negative Conversations with Others:
Observe if they frequently speak negatively about you to others.

This behavior often reflects hidden motives and a lack of loyalty.

4.   Manipulative Tactics : Watch for signs of manipulation, such as guilt-tripping or emotional blackmail, which can reveal a desire to control.

5.   Inconsistencies in Words and Actions:
Look for discrepancies between what they say and what they do. This inconsistency can indicate deceitful intentions.

6.   Withholding Support : Be aware if they withdraw support during challenging times, suggesting a lack of genuine care.

7.   Competitive Behavior : Monitor for competitiveness or jealousy, particularly in personal achievements or relationships.

8.   Dismissive Attitudes : Take note of dismissive comments about your feelings or aspirations, which can undermine your confidence.

9.   Isolation Attempts : Recognize any efforts to isolate you from other supportive relationships, indicating a need for control.

10.   Gut Feelings :

Trust your instincts. If something feels off, it's essential to explore those feelings further.

By applying these principles, you can gain clarity on the dynamics in your relationships and identify potential shadow enemies, enabling you to protect your emotional well-being. Throughout history, there have been numerous instances of individuals betraying family members, spouses, and friends driven by hatred and jealousy. Here are a few notable examples:

1.   Julius Caesar and Brutus :

Perhaps one of the most famous betrayals in history, Brutus, a close friend and confidant of Julius Caesar, participated in the assassination of Caesar in 44 BCE. Despite their friendship, Brutus was driven by a belief that Caesar's ambition threatened the Roman Republic.

2.   Richard III and the Princes in the Tower : Richard III, who became king of England in the late 15th century, murdered his nephews, the young princes Edward and Richard, to eliminate them as rivals to his throne. This act of betrayal stemmed from Richard's ambition and desire for power.

3.   Benedict Arnold :

An American Revolutionary War general, Arnold initially fought for the American colonies but later betrayed them by conspiring with the British. His motivations were partly rooted in feelings of jealousy and resentment towards fellow officers who received more recognition and rewards.

4.   Catherine de' Medici and her sons :
As the queen consort of Henry II of France, Catherine de' Medici manipulated her sons, including Charles IX, to pursue her own political ambitions that always sought to undermine the king's own ambitions and intentions. Imagine the audacity of a mother manipulating a king's own sons against him.

Her actions often led to betrayal, conflict and murder among family members, particularly in the context of power struggles during the French Wars of Religion.

5.   Katherine of Aragon and Anne Boleyn :
In the Tudor court, the rivalry between Katherine of Aragon and Anne Boleyn, both of whom were wives of King Henry VIII, was steeped in betrayal and jealousy.

Anne's rise to power led to Katherine's downfall, as Anne sought to secure her position at the expense of Katherine's legitimacy and status.

6.	Emperor Constantine

Ordered the execution of his own son

Flavia Maxima Fausta Augusta (died 326 AD) was a Roman empress. She was the daughter of Maximian and wife of Constantine the Great, who had her executed

Historians Zosimus and Zonaras reported that she was executed for adultery with her stepson, Crispus. This of course after Constantine found out that she had orchestrated the plot to to remove her step son through the misinformation that he'd tried to seduce her.

These examples illustrate how personal ambitions, jealousy, and hatred can drive individuals to conspire against and betray those closest to them, resulting in profound consequences for both the betrayers and their victims.

1. Observe Consistent Patterns : Repeated behaviors often reveal true intentions. For instance, if a family member or acquaintance regularly makes dismissive or belittling remarks about your ideas , inabilities, or achievements and choices, it's crucial to recognize this pattern as the sign of enemy in the making. Such comments may start as innocent teasing but can be a shield of deception that evolves into a more harmful dynamic symptomatic of envy or jealousy

budding into hatred. The key is to document these instances mentally, allowing you to identify trends over time. Consistency in negative behavior can help illuminate someone's underlying feelings, guiding you to reassess the relationship's health.

4. Monitor Communication : The way someone communicates can be a significant indicator of their true feelings toward you. When negativity is couched in sarcasm or backhanded compliments, it's essential to take note. If a friend, spouse, or girlfriend/ boyfriend frequently criticizes your choices under the guise of "concern," it may reveal an envious mindset. Healthy relationships are built on support, encouragement, and constructive feedback, not on criticism that belittles or undermines confidence. Engage in open conversations about communication styles; if someone resists this, it may indicate a deeper issue at play.

8.   Look for Jealousy : Jealousy can manifest subtly within close relationships. Be mindful of how others react to your successes. If a friend or family member downplays your achievements or compares them unfavorably to their experiences, it may signal envy. Instead of celebrating your milestones, they may deflect the joy to feel better about themselves.

9. Watch other's frustrations with you because you deny them things or situations they feel they deserve or must have.

> **9.** Emotion Alert : Watch any consistent displays of anger , frustrations, heated accusations, or disappointment with you from others. Nothing sets the stage for betrayal or sabotage from others more than these emotions.

CHAPTER 13
Revenge Is Best Served By Another Name

Revenge is an impulse deeply ingrained in human nature, yet the execution of revenge can manifest in a myriad of forms. Many have heard the phrase, "revenge is a dish best served cold," but what happens when revenge is served by another name? The art of subtle retribution often operates beneath the surface, orchestrated by individuals or circumstances that have no direct ties to the aggrieved party. In many ways, this form of revenge can be far more effective, for it leverages the principles of deception, emotional control, and rational planning.

The Art of Deception in Revenge

Deception is a key element in achieving revenge by proxy. When revenge is enacted through the hands of others or facilitated by external circumstances, it becomes far less likely that the instigator will be traced back to the event. This separation allows the avenger to maintain plausible deniability, which is crucial for avoiding the fallout that often accompanies direct retaliation.

One historical example of revenge through deception is the story of the fall of Anne Boleyn, Henry VIII's second wife. Thomas

Cromwell, a trusted advisor to Henry, orchestrated a series of accusations and machinations that led to Anne's downfall. Although Henry VIII may have had his own grievances with Anne, Cromwell exploited the situation for his own advantage. He orchestrated a political coup by carefully planting rumors, orchestrating false charges, and ensuring that the king's anger was inflamed at just the right moment. In this scenario, Cromwell served his revenge by allowing the mechanisms of power and intrigue to do the work for him, distancing himself from the personal fallout of Anne's execution. His deception facilitated a form of revenge that left his hands ostensibly clean.

This form of revenge requires patience and cunning. It is not a reactionary act driven by the heat of anger, but a calculated maneuver that employs time, resources, and deception. It becomes more an act of strategy than passion, a long game that can stretch over months, years, or even decades.

Maintaining Mental and Emotional Stability

One of the most important aspects of achieving revenge by indirect means is the ability to maintain one's mental and emotional equilibrium. Revenge, when executed in the heat of emotion, often leads to mistakes, escalation, and unforeseen consequences. However, when one is able to suppress emotional reactions, it becomes possible to think clearly, focus on long-term objectives, and plan a response that is more likely to achieve success.

The ancient Chinese military strategist Sun Tzu, in his treatise The Art of War, emphasizes the importance of patience and calm in warfare, which is equally applicable to the art of revenge. Sun Tzu warns against being driven by anger and frustration, for such emotions cloud judgment and can lead to rash decisions. Instead, he advises that one must remain calm and collected, always focusing on the end goal rather than on the emotional satisfaction of retaliation.

Consider the example of Nelson Mandela, who spent 27 years in prison under the apartheid regime in South Africa. While Mandela undoubtedly had reason to seek revenge against his captors and the system that oppressed his people, he maintained his emotional and mental stability throughout his incarceration. Upon his release, rather than seeking immediate retaliation, Mandela chose the path of reconciliation. His revenge, if one could call it that, was to dismantle the apartheid system not through violence or bitterness but through strategic diplomacy, ensuring that South Africa could move forward without further bloodshed. His calm demeanor and ability to control his emotions allowed him to stay focused on his ultimate objective: a free and democratic South Africa.

This ability to suppress outward displays of emotion while maintaining inward resolve is a powerful tool in executing revenge by proxy. When one is wronged, it is often tempting to complain, vent, or seek validation from others. However, these actions only serve to weaken one's position. By keeping one's own counsel, an individual can avoid tipping their hand and maintain the upper ground in planning their response. This leads to the next important principle: the importance of rational planning.

Rational Planning and Focus on Objectives

The key to achieving revenge without exposing oneself is to maintain a clear focus on the objective and channel all emotions into rational planning. Emotions such as anger and frustration, when left unchecked, can be destructive, but when they are harnessed and directed toward a purpose, they can become the fuel that drives careful and strategic action.

A fitting historical example of this principle can be found in the story of Count of Monte Cristo, a classic novel by Alexandre Dumas. The protagonist, Edmond Dantès, is wrongfully imprisoned due to the betrayal of those he considered friends. After escaping from prison, Dantès does not seek immediate revenge on his betrayers. Instead, he spends years carefully planning his retaliation.

He accumulates wealth, adopts a new identity, and carefully manipulates events to bring about the downfall of each of his enemies. His revenge is cold, calculated, and executed through intermediaries and circumstances that leave him untouched by the consequences. The story illustrates the importance of rational planning and patience in achieving revenge by other means.

The lesson to be drawn from these examples is that emotional control and careful planning are essential for anyone seeking to carry out revenge without drawing attention to themselves. When emotions are channeled into a clear, rational objective, they become a source of strength rather than a weakness.

Revenge, when served by another name, becomes a subtle and effective art. The principles of deception, emotional control, and rational planning allow an individual to exact retribution without exposing themselves to the dangers and consequences of direct action. History is replete with examples of individuals who have mastered this art, from Cromwell's machinations in the English court to Mandela's strategic dismantling of apartheid, to the fictional but instructive tale of Edmond Dantès.

The key to achieving such revenge is to maintain one's mental and emotional stability, to focus on the ultimate objective, and to channel emotions into the careful execution of a long-term plan. Revenge, when served by another name, becomes not an impulsive act of anger, but a masterstroke of strategy.

Revenge as a Component of Self-Preservation

Revenge is often seen as an act of retaliation, but on a deeper level, realistically it is a crucial component of self-preservation. When one has been wronged, seeking revenge is not merely about inflicting harm on the perpetrator; it is a means of protecting oneself from future harm by setting boundaries and establishing consequences. By refusing to deliver revenge , an individual risks signaling that they are passive or weak, which in turn encourages further transgressions.

Passivity in the face of wrongdoings often sends the message that one can be easily taken advantage of, fostering an environment in which negative behavior is not only tolerated but repeated. This is a well-documented psychological and sociological phenomenon, where the absence of repercussions for harmful actions leads perpetrators to feel emboldened and more likely to engage in similar behavior in the future. Without consequences, there is little deterrent for those who have caused harm, creating a cycle in which the wrongdoer continues their actions, knowing that they will not be challenged or punished.

Consider the example of diplomatic relations and international conflicts. Nations that respond passively to provocations often find themselves targets of further aggression.

For instance, during the lead-up to World War II, the policy of appeasement practiced by European powers in response to Nazi Germany's expansionism did nothing to prevent further acts of aggression. On the contrary, Adolf Hitler took the lack of firm retaliation as a signal that he could continue his territorial ambitions without facing significant opposition. In this case, the refusal to act against the initial wrong not only failed to preserve peace but directly contributed to the escalation of conflict.

On an individual level, self-preservation through revenge can take many forms. It may not always involve direct retaliation but can manifest as actions that ensure that the wrongdoer understands the cost of their actions. By confronting the transgressor, either through subtle but damaging maneuvers or indirect retribution, one establishes a clear message: any future harm will not go unanswered. This is a way of safeguarding oneself from recurring harm and ensuring that one's dignity, autonomy, and wellbeing are protected.

Revenge, in this sense, becomes not a matter of anger or vindictiveness but a necessary means of self-defense. Denying oneself the opportunity to deliver calculated retribution can weaken one's position, leaving one vulnerable to further exploitation and repeated wrongs.

CHAPTER 14

The Art Of War From The Shadows: Never Reveal Your True Self

In the complex theater of human interaction, one must often engage in a war in the shadows—a conflict that takes place not on a battlefield but within the self and against the expectations of others. Here, survival is not defined by physical prowess but by mental agility and emotional control. It is the silent battle of never revealing one's true self, a skill that can only be honed through practice, patience, and self-sufficiency. Those who master this art understand that emotions are both their greatest asset and their greatest vulnerability.

To truly be able to navigate the treacherous waters of social interaction, one must first learn to control their emotions, recognize the dangers of seeking validation from others, and ultimately become self-reliant, prepared for any eventuality.

Learning to Control One's Emotions

The first and most crucial step in this war in the shadows is learning to control one's emotions. Emotions are powerful forces that, when uncontrolled, can betray even the most carefully constructed facades. Emotions such as anger, fear, and joy can easily be read by others and used against us. For this reason, it is imperative to master the art of emotional restraint. This requires not just the suppression of emotion but understanding it and acknowledging its presence without allowing it to dictate one's actions.

This form of control comes with practice. Through meditation, reflection, and deliberate action, individuals can train themselves to respond to external stimuli with calculated calm rather than reactive chaos. Embracing this stoic approach can allow one to remain composed even when provoked, maintaining the necessary illusion of neutrality. In a world where every word and action can be analyzed and misinterpreted, those who exhibit emotional discipline can cloak their true intentions, making them inscrutable and elusive. This concealment is a powerful defense in the war in the shadows.

Training and Practice to Become Self-Sufficient

To thrive in this shadow war, one must also learn the importance of self-sufficiency. Dependency on others for emotional validation or guidance weakens one's defenses and leaves them vulnerable to manipulation. To reveal too much of oneself, or to rely on others for approval, is to hand over the keys to one's own identity.

The perceptions and opinions of others are often based on incomplete or biased information, and depending on them can lead to a loss of personal agency. Others are rarely what they seem on the surface, and trusting them too much opens the door to potential betrayal.

Through training and practice, one can learn to eliminate this need for external validation. This involves cultivating confidence in one's own abilities and decisions, becoming comfortable with solitude, and developing the skills necessary to rely solely on oneself. Self-sufficiency is the ultimate form of freedom in this war, as it allows an individual to maintain control over their own narrative without interference from outside forces.

Training in self-sufficiency also includes learning how to navigate the world discreetly and independently. This may involve physical survival skills, strategic thinking, and the ability to blend into different environments. By developing multiple layers of personal defense, individuals can remain hidden in plain sight, ensuring that they remain undetected even in the most precarious situations.

The Dangers of Seeking Validation

The desire to seek validation from others is often the first step toward detection. In seeking approval or understanding, we expose parts of ourselves that should remain hidden. The more one reveals, the more vulnerable they become to judgment, misinterpretation, and betrayal.

Human nature is inherently unpredictable, and the unveiling of even a single thought or idea that is perceived as dangerous can lead to unwanted consequences. People tend to gossip, share information, and shift allegiances based on their perceptions, which are often skewed by their own emotions and biases.

It takes only one wrong word, one misstep, or one revelation for others to turn against you, setting off a chain reaction that can lead to detection and exposure. In the war from the shadows, discretion is key.

Avoiding the temptation to seek validation from others protects the self from this web of unpredictability. Instead, one should embrace the power of silence, speak little, and reveal even less. This ensures that others can never fully grasp one's true nature, keeping the individual safe from detection.

Multiple Exit Options and Diversions

In the shadowy world of concealment and deception, preparation is everything. One of the most important strategies in this battle is having multiple exit options for the unexpected. The ability to create diversions, distractions, or alternative paths is critical in evading detection. Whether in a social, professional, or personal context, being prepared for the unexpected ensures that no situation will leave you cornered.

Diversions are a powerful tool in misdirection. By controlling what others focus on, you can lead them away from your true intentions or vulnerabilities. This can be as simple as shifting conversations to neutral topics or creating decoys that divert attention away from you. Having multiple exit options whether physical, emotional, or psychological ensures that you are never trapped by a single course of action. In a world where anything can happen, flexibility and foresight are essential tools in preserving self and maintaining control over your destiny.

War from the shadows requires mastery of the self. It is a continuous process of training and discipline, learning to control emotions, becoming self-sufficient, and eliminating the need for validation from others. This path leads to freedom from detection, allowing individuals to navigate the complexities of human interaction with stealth and discretion. In the end, the only way to win the war in the shadows is to remain a mystery, revealing nothing and preserving everything.

The Power of the Unknown: Mastering the Shadow Strategy

The necessity of internalizing the principle of war in the shadows lies in understanding the immense power of the unknown.

When one chooses to conceal their true thoughts, intentions, and emotions, they become an enigma, an untouchable force that others struggle to comprehend. People naturally fear what they cannot see or predict. The unknown becomes a weapon, wielded to create confusion, anxiety, and uncertainty in those who seek control or dominance over you.

Mastering the shadow strategy grants a unique power: the ability to manipulate perception. By embracing the art of deception and misdirection, one can sow seeds of doubt, causing others to misread situations or fall victim to their own insecurities. In this way, the shadow warrior turns the tables, using the ambiguity of their actions to force others into states of confusion and fear.

This strategy is not merely about hiding; it is about embracing and relishing the power that comes with being unreadable and unpredictable. Those who operate in the shadows gain control over their own narrative, positioning themselves as silent architects of chaos, bringing others to their worst states of confusion while they remain unscathed, secure in their invisibility.

The Power of the Unknown: Mastering the Shadow Strategy (Part II)

The necessity of leaving no trace of one's intentions—whether physical, emotional, or digital—solidifies the mastery of the shadow strategy. In a world increasingly driven by connectivity and constant interaction, the ability to remain invisible is a rare and powerful skill. Any footprint left behind, whether it be a physical item, an emotional outburst, or a digital trace on social media, becomes a clue for others to decipher your true motives and identity.

Physically, one must practice stealth, ensuring that no item or action hints at their intentions. Emotionally, one must avoid displays of vulnerability or excess, for emotions are often the most revealing part of one's psyche. By maintaining emotional neutrality, a shadow warrior offers nothing for others to interpret. Social media, in particular, poses a significant threat. Every post, comment, or interaction can be scrutinized and potentially weaponized. To protect one's true self, it is crucial to minimize or eliminate one's presence in these spaces, creating an aura of mystery.

Leaving no trace allows one to operate without detection. When no evidence exists of one's plans or thoughts, others are left in the dark, unable to connect the dots. In the shadows, power lies in silence and absence.

Many people have been exposed and caught doing things simply by doing the most small but significant things that put focus on themselves like buying bullets ,gas cans, tarp, & weapons from the same city or area that they were going to commit a crime of murder and once the videos of local businesses were analyzed along with surrounding cities businesses ,the video evidence shows them buying things used to commit the murder. This is a lesson to never compromise security and sense for convenience.

CHAPTER 15

The Art Of Camouflage & Misdirection

Misdirection, a subtle yet potent strategy, has been a crucial tool in military tactics, politics, and personal relations for centuries. Its effectiveness lies in its capacity to divert the attention of an enemy, allowing offensive maneuvers or defensive countermeasures to be deployed with minimal resistance.

By creating illusions and distractions, a practitioner of misdirection can manipulate situations to their advantage, often without their opponent ever realizing what has happened until it is too late.

Misdirection initiates offensive tactics by shifting focus away from the true goal, giving the orchestrator the opportunity to strike or defend without direct confrontation. This artful approach allows for the manipulation of emotions, perceptions, and actions, making it a highly effective method of control.

In the realm of personal interactions, misdirection can take various forms, ranging from faking emotions to controlling the narrative from behind the scenes.

There are different degrees of misdirection, including how one can feign emotions to gain acceptance, mimic interests to appeal to diverse groups, eliminate a person's sources of happiness and security, and control their environment through indirect tactics.

These techniques, while often subtle, can have a profound impact on relationships and power dynamics.

Faking Emotions to Gain Acceptance

One of the simplest yet most effective forms of misdirection is faking emotions that others expect or require to accept you.

Human interactions are often governed by emotions, and understanding how to manipulate them can allow one to gain influence over others.

By projecting an emotion that aligns with the expectations or needs of others, a person can ingratiate themselves into a group or an individual's life. This tactic is particularly effective in situations where acceptance is based on shared emotional experiences.

For example, in a group setting where empathy is valued, a person may fake sympathy or understanding to gain the trust and acceptance of the group. Once accepted, they are in a position to influence group decisions or actions without arousing suspicion. This form of misdirection is often employed in social settings where conformity to emotional norms is expected. By pretending to feel what others are feeling, a person can manipulate the emotional dynamics of a situation to their advantage.

This emotional manipulation is not always malicious; sometimes, it is a survival tactic. However, when used with intent to deceive or control, it can be highly effective in gaining power over others. The key to success in this type of misdirection is subtlety. The faker must be convincing enough to maintain the illusion without revealing their true intentions. If done correctly, faking emotions can lead to long-term control over a group or individual, as people often base their trust on perceived emotional alignment.

Faking Interests to Appeal to Various Groups

Another form of misdirection involves faking shared interests to appeal to various people or groups. This tactic works by creating a false sense of commonality, which fosters trust and rapport. When someone believes that you share their interests or passions, they are more likely to accept you into their social circle and less likely to question your motives.

By adopting the interests of others, one can create alliances across multiple fronts, gaining access to information, resources, and influence. This can be particularly useful in situations where one needs to appeal to a diverse range of people or groups.

For example, in a political or corporate environment, faking interest in various initiatives can help a person gain support from different factions, allowing them to position themselves as a unifying figure.

The success of this tactic lies in its flexibility. By tailoring your interests to align with those of the people around you, you can build networks of influence that cross social, political, and cultural boundaries. This form of misdirection can be highly effective in environments where power is distributed across different groups, as it allows the orchestrator to play multiple sides without revealing their true intentions.

However, maintaining this illusion requires careful management, as being exposed as disingenuous can quickly lead to a loss of trust and influence.

Eliminating the Source of Happiness, Security, and Peace Of An Enemy

Misdirection can also be employed through more insidious tactics, such as eliminating the sources of another person's happiness, security, and peace. This method is indirect but highly effective in causing emotional and psychological harm. Instead of attacking a person directly, one targets the things that bring them joy or stability, slowly eroding their sense of well-being.

For example, a person may subtly sabotage a colleague's relationships at work, leading to a sense of isolation and insecurity. Alternatively, they might spread rumors that cause someone to question their own self-worth or standing in the community. These tactics are often difficult to trace back to the perpetrator, as they work by undermining the target's external sources of support rather than directly confronting them.

This form of misdirection is particularly damaging because it attacks a person's foundation, leaving them vulnerable and emotionally destabilized. When someone loses the things that bring them happiness or security, they become more susceptible to manipulation and control. This tactic is often used in personal relationships, where one party seeks to dominate the other by controlling their external environment. By eliminating the sources of a person's happiness, one can create a sense of powerlessness in the target, making them more reliant on the orchestrator for emotional support.

Controlling the Stage Of An Enemy's Life from the Shadows

Perhaps the most sophisticated form of misdirection is controlling the stage and scene of your opposition's life from the shadows. This tactic involves manipulating the environment around a target without directly involving yourself. By using others to create chaos, confusion, or conflict, you can destabilize your target without ever revealing your hand.

For example, one might spread anonymous rumors or manipulate other people into acting against the target, creating a web of discord that gradually wears down the target's mental and emotional defenses. This is especially effective when the target's reputation or social image is a priority for them. By creating a climate of uncertainty and discomfort, you can cause the target to become emotionally unstable, leading them to make poor decisions or lash out in ways that damage their reputation.

This form of misdirection relies heavily on psychological manipulation and the careful orchestration of events. The goal is to control the narrative without appearing to do so, ensuring that the target never suspects that they are being manipulated. This allows the orchestrator to remain in a position of power while their target becomes increasingly destabilized.

The art of misdirection is a powerful tool that can be used to manipulate situations, gain influence, and control others without direct confrontation. Whether through faking emotions, mimicking interests, eliminating sources of happiness, or controlling the narrative from the shadows, misdirection allows a person to achieve their goals by diverting attention away from their true intentions.

While these tactics can be highly effective, they also require careful planning and subtle execution, as being discovered can lead to severe consequences. In the hands of a skilled practitioner, however, misdirection can be a highly effective strategy for achieving dominance in both personal and professional arenas.

The Importance of Experimentation in Misdirection

The ability to master the art of misdirection is not something that can be attained overnight. Like any skill, it requires practice, patience, and a deep understanding of human nature.

One of the most effective ways to develop this skill is through small-scale experimentation with unsuspecting others. These exercises, though seemingly insignificant, allow the practitioner to refine their techniques in real-world scenarios without exposing their true intentions.

Experimentation serves as a valuable training ground, providing opportunities to test various approaches, gauge reactions, and learn from mistakes.

In the realm of misdirection, subtlety is key. By conducting minor experiments, one can gradually build the confidence and experience needed to execute more complex maneuvers with greater precision. This process is not only about learning what works but also about understanding what doesn't. Through trial and error, the practitioner gains insights into human behavior, emotional responses, and the nuances of effective manipulation. These insights are invaluable in the journey toward mastering misdirection.

Learning the Art of Poise Through Experimentation

Experimentation with misdirection is not just about external manipulation; it also plays a crucial role in developing internal discipline.

One of the most important aspects of misdirection is the ability to maintain poise under pressure. In situations where the stakes are high, even the slightest crack in one's composure can give away their intentions. Therefore, it is essential to cultivate a sense of calm and control, regardless of external circumstances.

Small exercises in misdirection help practitioners develop this poise by placing them in situations where they must remain calm and focused while executing their tactics. These experiments provide the opportunity to practice keeping emotions in check, maintaining an air of confidence, and masking one's true thoughts or feelings. Over time, this practice helps to build an unshakable composure that becomes second nature in high-pressure situations.

Furthermore, experimentation allows the practitioner to confront and overcome the emotional triggers that could otherwise disrupt their concentration. By repeatedly putting themselves in challenging scenarios, they learn to detach from the stressors or distractions that might weaken their resolve. This detachment is crucial for maintaining the clarity of thought and focus necessary for successful misdirection.

Detaching from External Influences That Weaken Focus

An essential aspect of mastering misdirection is learning to detach from external influences that have the potential to weaken focus or dilute the effectiveness of one's tactics. In a world filled with distractions, it is easy to become swayed by the opinions, actions, or emotions of others. These external forces can chip away at a person's confidence, muddle their thinking, and ultimately compromise their ability to execute a well-planned strategy.

Experimentation provides a safe environment for honing the skill of detachment. By practicing misdirection in controlled scenarios, the practitioner learns to identify and resist the external influences that might disrupt their focus. Whether it is the pressure of social norms, the emotional responses of others, or the fear of failure, these distractions can be confronted head-on in a setting where the stakes are low. Over time, the practitioner develops the mental fortitude to remain impervious to external noise, allowing them to stay fully focused on their objectives.

Detachment does not mean becoming completely indifferent to others nor does it mean allowing others thoughts and situations to become a focus point; rather, it is about maintaining control over one's own mind and emotions. By practicing detachment, the practitioner ensures that their thoughts remain sharp and clear, free from the muddling effects of outside influences. This clarity of thought is essential for executing misdirection with precision and confidence.

Strengthening the Mind Against Mediocre Influences

In the pursuit of mastery over misdirection, it is vital to strengthen the mind against mediocre influences that can impede progress and weaken performance. These influences often come in the form of societal expectations, superficial judgments, or even one's own self-doubt. They can undermine the effectiveness of a practitioner's tactics by planting seeds of insecurity or causing them to second-guess their actions.

Through experimentation, the practitioner becomes aware of these influences and learns how to counteract them. By repeatedly placing themselves in situations where their misdirection skills are tested, they build the mental resilience needed to resist mediocrity.

Each successful experiment serves as a reinforcement of their abilities, gradually replacing doubt with confidence and clarity.

Experimentation also allows the practitioner to refine their thought processes. By engaging in small exercises, they learn to streamline their thinking, eliminating unnecessary distractions and focusing only on what is essential to the task at hand. This process of mental refinement is crucial for achieving the level of precision and effectiveness required for advanced misdirection techniques.

The journey to mastering the art of misdirection is one that requires both internal and external development. Experimentation with unaware others provides the necessary real-world experience to refine one's techniques, while also serving as a training ground for developing poise, detachment, and mental strength. By engaging in small-scale exercises, the practitioner learns to maintain focus under pressure, resist external distractions, and overcome mediocre influences that could otherwise hinder their performance. Over time, these skills coalesce into a powerful toolkit that allows the practitioner to execute misdirection with confidence, precision, and subtlety.

Examples:

1. Western Powers and Muammar Gaddafi

In the early 2000s, Muammar Gaddafi was lulled into a false sense of security by the Western powers. After years of tension, Gaddafi began making diplomatic overtures to the West, including renouncing weapons of mass destruction and cooperating in counterterrorism efforts. He believed he had gained their favor, receiving praise from leaders such as Tony Blair and even rebuilding relationships with the U.S. However, behind the scenes, the CIA and MI6 had been supporting and training Khalifa Haftar and his units, . Haftar, who had lived in the U.S. for years and was trained in Virginia, would go on to lead rebel forces against Gaddafi during the Libyan Civil War.

Gaddafi's misjudgment of Western intentions contributed to his downfall in 2011, as NATO backed the rebels Haftar helped to lead. Gaddafi underestimated the responses that the European Nations would have to his developing plans for a United States of Africa that included restricting Foreign European Nations from having access to Africa's Natural resources.

This maneuver of Gaddafi would've crippled Europe and many other Nations when it came to certain minerals and resources that their technology and advancement in technology depended upon as Europe has no significant natural resources of any kind.

Gaddafi was also about to initiate a new global currency backed by the Africa's natural resources such as gold, diamonds, plutonium, cobalt and others which would've put many Nation's currency at a second tier in comparison like the American Dollar that is only paper called a promissory note which means a promise by the Federal Reserve to compensate the possessors if the Dollar if the currency were to fail because there's nothing like gold backing the Dollar.

2. Operation Fortitude (World War II)

Another brilliant example of military misdirection during World War II was Operation Fortitude. This was part of the larger deception plan to cover up the real location of the D-Day invasion (Operation Overlord). While Operation Bodyguard (mentioned earlier) focused on deceiving the Germans about the timing and location of the invasion, Operation Fortitude created a false impression that the Allies were planning to invade Norway (Fortitude North) and the Pas de Calais (Fortitude South). The Allies used fake radio traffic, inflatable tanks, fake dummy people ,and even a phantom army commanded by General George Patton to convince the Germans that these were the real invasion points. This misdirection contributed significantly to the success of the Normandy landings by keeping significant German forces stationed far from the true landing site.

3. Napoleon's Feint at the Battle of Austerlitz (1805)

One of Napoleon Bonaparte's most famous strategic deceptions occurred during the Battle of Austerlitz in 1805. Prior to the battle, Napoleon appeared to be in a weakened and defensive position, even feigning weakness by retreating and abandoning key positions. He used this misdirection to lure the Russian and Austrian forces into a vulnerable position, convincing them that they could easily overpower the French. Once the enemy was overcommitted, Napoleon executed a surprise attack on their weakened center. His feigned retreat and the misdirection of his true strength led to a decisive French victory and one of his most celebrated military triumphs.

4, Toussaint Overture's Defeat Of Napoleon's Army   In Haiti

Toussaint Louverture's defeat of Napoleon's army in Haiti was a groundbreaking moment in the history of warfare. Facing a better-equipped and larger French force who possessed major cannon weapons, Toussaint employed the West's first major acts of guerrilla warfare. His troops, mainly ex-slaves, used hit-and-run tactics, ambushes, and knowledge of the rugged terrain to outmaneuver the French. Misdirection played a key role, as the Haitians often lured their enemies into difficult positions, giving the illusion of retreat only to strike unexpectedly.

This unconventional strategy not only demoralized the French but also showcased the effectiveness of insurgent tactics against colonial forces.

Many Europeans who glorify Napoleon attempt to downgrade Toussaint Louverture's strategic beating of Napoleon's Army as a simple unintelligent slave uprising but the facts say there's no way a simple unorganized slave revolt could have overcome assaults of cannons and other major strategies and weapons of Napoleon's Army by luck as such tactics and weapons of the same Napoleon Army destroyed disorganized and poorly armed Armies in Europe easily.

CHAPTER 16

The J. Edgar Hoover Strategy

J. Edgar Hoover Tactics: A Legacy of Surveillance and Manipulation

J. Edgar Hoover, the first Director of the Federal Bureau of Investigation (FBI), redefined the meaning of power and control in 20th-century America. Over his nearly five-decade career, Hoover amassed an unparalleled ability to manipulate, influence, and coerce people whether they were private citizens, celebrities, or political figures.

Hoover's tactics were built upon an insidious but highly effective framework of spying, surveillance, and blackmail. These tactics exploited the darker aspects of human nature, particularly the weaknesses, vulnerabilities, and secrets people desperately wanted to keep hidden. As his power grew, so did his ability to bend even the most influential individuals to his will.

At the heart of Hoover's strategy was his obsession with information. For Hoover, knowledge was power, and he was relentless in his pursuit of people's secrets, legal or otherwise. His surveillance networks were vast, stretching across the nation, encompassing political opponents, civil rights leaders, intellectuals, and even U.S. presidents. By keeping meticulous records of his targets' personal failings, he built a library of scandals and secrets that he could use as leverage to blackmail them when necessary. His tactics allowed him to exert influence over decisions and actions at the highest levels of American government and society.

The Hoover strategy is still the main standard operating procedure and tactics of all law enforcement ,Criminal Justice Systems ,and Politicians. It is also highly relevant to any social class or setting.

Hoover's approach was not just about finding illegal activity; he was just as willing to manufacture scandals or magnify minor indiscretions. For him, it wasn't about what was legal or illegal ,it was about what could be perceived as damaging in the public eye. One of Hoover's most infamous targets was Dr. Martin Luther King Jr. The civil rights leader was relentlessly monitored by the FBI, and when Hoover couldn't find sufficient damaging material, he sought to create it. Hoover authorized the wiretapping of King's phones and sent him anonymous letters threatening to expose alleged infidelities. The letters went as far as encouraging King to commit suicide. The aim was not simply to destroy King's reputation, but to manipulate his actions and impede his activism through the threat of exposure.

Hoover according to his own records in the Co-Intel papers was even the one to initiate the beginnings of the split between Elijah Muhammad and Malcolm X and Elijah Muhammad's Son Warith Deen Muhammad by way of letters to both Malcolm and Elijah Muhammad's son about discrepancies with younger women of whom one was an old girlfriend of Malcolm X that Malcolm X wasn't aware of until Hoover's letters to an acquaintance of Malcolm X.

The higher a person's position in society, the more susceptible they became to Hoover's tactics.

Politicians were frequent targets of Hoover's machinations, including U.S. Presidents. While Hoover was technically subordinate to the president as FBI Director, in reality, he wielded a frightening level of autonomy. Presidents were wary of firing him because they feared what Hoover might have on them. As early as the Truman administration, presidents were aware of Hoover's powerful blackmail strategies, but Hoover's files on presidents, including their private lives, became a powerful shield, protecting his career while ensuring he retained influence over the highest office in the land.

Hoover's tactics were rooted in an understanding of human nature and the way society viewed morality. While Hoover publicly espoused the values of law and order, patriotism, and the fight against communism, his private actions were often ethically dubious and legally questionable. He operated in a moral gray area, exploiting society's expectations of moral uprightness, especially for those in power. By gathering evidence of personal or professional misconduct, even if unrelated to the law, Hoover could hold this over the heads of his targets. The higher their position in life, the more they had to lose, which made them particularly vulnerable to Hoover's influence. Thus, a paradox emerged: the more successful a person was, the more susceptible they became to being controlled.

Hoover's legacy is a chilling reminder of how power can corrupt institutions meant to protect the public. His surveillance methods blurred the lines between legitimate law enforcement and the invasion of privacy for personal gain. Rather than solely focusing on preventing crime or protecting national security, Hoover often seemed more interested in using information to consolidate his own power. By controlling people's secrets, he could effectively control them, manipulating decisions and actions through the mere threat of exposure.

As time passed, Hoover's reign was increasingly seen as a symbol of the dangers of unchecked power. When he passed away in 1972, his files were still intact, containing an immeasurable amount of blackmail material on some of the most powerful people in the country. His influence waned after his death, but the methods he used continue to serve as a warning of what happens when surveillance becomes an instrument of coercion.

Today, the tactics used by Hoover raise important questions about privacy, ethics, and the balance between national security and individual rights. The FBI, under his leadership, became a tool of personal gain rather than purely public good. His use of blackmail to manipulate and control some of the most powerful individuals in society illustrates a dangerous abuse of power. The greater the heights individuals reached, the more precarious their positions became in the face of Hoover's methods. Hoover's legacy, while rooted in the notion of preserving national security, ultimately became a story of power, control, and the dangers of manipulating the vulnerable by exploiting their darkest secrets.

In retrospect, the Hoover era highlights the profound connection between power and ethics, and how far-reaching the consequences can be when someone is willing to weaponize the personal lives of others for political and personal gain.

The strategy employed by J. Edgar Hoover to amass power and influence over others was based on a practical understanding of human behavior, particularly in the context of social and political hierarchies.

By systematically investigating and uncovering personal secrets often of a damaging or compromising nature, Hoover was able to exert control over people who were in positions of authority or influence. The effectiveness of this approach rested on several key factors: the inherent fear of exposure, the potential reputational damage, and the leverage gained through the use of confidential information. This combination allowed Hoover to manipulate decisions and actions across various levels of government and society.

At its core, Hoover's strategy was highly effective because it tapped into a universal aspect of human psychology: the fear of being exposed. Individuals, especially those in high-profile positions, typically have personal or professional secrets that, if revealed, could tarnish their reputation, undermine their authority, or jeopardize their career. In an environment where public image plays a crucial role in maintaining power, the threat of exposure becomes a potent tool for exerting influence. Whether these secrets were related to illegal activities, personal indiscretions, or ethical lapses, their mere existence made individuals vulnerable. Hoover capitalized on this vulnerability by collecting and storing such information for future use.

Moreover, the higher a person's social or political standing, the greater the potential consequences of exposure.

For politicians, corporate leaders, and public figures, reputation is often synonymous with power. Their decisions and influence depend heavily on public perception and trust. The possibility of a scandal, whether true or exaggerated, can severely diminish their standing, causing them to lose credibility, supporters, or even their position.

Hoover's ability to uncover and hold onto such information gave him unparalleled leverage over these individuals, making them more compliant to his influence. The strategic timing of a threat whether explicit or implied ,allowed him to direct their actions or decisions in ways that served his own objectives.

Another key aspect of Hoover's effectiveness was the expansive network of surveillance he created. Through wiretaps, informants, and clandestine monitoring, Hoover was able to gather information that many believed to be private or inaccessible. The scope and depth of his intelligence-gathering operations ensured that few people of significance escaped his notice. This omnipresent surveillance fostered an environment in which individuals became hyperaware of the possibility that their actions were being watched, further increasing their susceptibility to manipulation. By maintaining this constant watch, Hoover could uncover potential leverage points at any time, expanding his sphere of influence across different sectors of society.

The utility of Hoover's tactics extended beyond simply uncovering past misdeeds. He often used surveillance and investigative methods to create situations that could be construed as compromising. For instance, in cases where a target had not engaged in outright illegal activity, Hoover could focus on morally ambiguous behavior or politically sensitive actions that could be framed in a negative light. Even situations where no laws were broken could be spun into damaging scandals.

The ability to control the narrative around these behaviors is crucial in giving someone power over others. In effect, someone could manufacture leverage where none previously existed, further increasing one's control over key figures or simple ordinary everyday targets.

Hoover's success was also amplified by the self-preservation instincts of those in power. Most individuals in positions of authority understand the risks associated with scandal and public scrutiny, and they are often willing to take significant steps to protect themselves from such threats. This fear of potential downfall made many targets of Hoover's surveillance more cooperative and willing to acquiesce to his demands, whether they involved personal favors, policy decisions, or avoidance of actions that could diminish Hoover's influence.

By positioning oneself as the gatekeeper of others' reputations, one is ensured to hold significant power over their actions.

Another factor that contributed to the effectiveness of this strategy was the implicit understanding that the threat of exposure was often more powerful than actual exposure itself. Once a scandal is made public, the leverage it provides is lost. The individual becomes subject to public judgment and potential legal action, but their decision-making is no longer directly influenced by the fear of the unknown. Hoover recognized this and used it to his advantage, often keeping damaging information in reserve rather than immediately acting on it. This gave him sustained control over his targets, as they were constantly aware of the possibility of exposure but never knew when, or if the information would be released. This uncertain dynamic placed Hoover in a position of perpetual influence, able to direct or steer the actions of those he monitored without resorting to overt threats.

Hoover's strategy was highly effective in gaining power and influence over others due to its reliance on key psychological and social factors, including fear, reputation management, and the ability to control sensitive information. By exploiting personal vulnerabilities, maintaining extensive surveillance networks, and using the mere threat of exposure as a powerful tool, Hoover was able to manipulate individuals at the highest levels of government and society. His methods created a system in which those with the most to lose were often the most vulnerable to his influence, allowing him to maintain control and power for decades.

This strategy is effective in any social setting for example, If one is engaged in some particular illegal activity and it's only matter of time before the Police Detectives come, there always those in dire positions such as drug addicts who will say or do anything for drugs like having their children to lie on Police Detectives which could be used as a future discredit of the main Police Detectives in a Police Department as long as they're baited to come to a certain home at a certain time which will justify a false complaint being filed at the police Department. This will work also against any other enemy with modifications and variations being made.

This strategy requires the learning of available resources which is vulnerable people and the things they desire or need and have a price that will influence them to do it. Such people also require dirt or something critical being manufactured against them that will force their impenetrable silence about it.

Hoover's history ultimately gives the unique understanding that an individual or group of organized people will only be as effective as their intelligence network positions them to be.

CHAPTER 17
12 Laws Of Strategic Ghost Tactics

In the complex world of strategy, subterfuge, and manipulation, the concept of "ghost counterattacks" emerges as a highly sophisticated approach to dealing with adversaries.

Ghost counter-attacks involve using others to execute offensive maneuvers from multiple directions, at different times, and through various fronts. These tactics are designed to confuse, distract, and undermine any attempt to analyze or predict the orchestrator's true intentions. By enlisting unwitting participants who, over time, prove themselves to be useful yet expendable, the practitioner of ghost counterattacks can achieve their objectives while maintaining plausible deniability. There are twelve core principles of ghost counterattacks and counteractions, which are essential for effectively executing such strategies.

Principle 1: Multiple Fronts of Attack

The first principle of ghost counterattacks is the use of multiple fronts to advance a single or interconnected agenda. By dispersing efforts across different areas, the orchestrator ensures that no single attack draws too much attention or scrutiny. The key is to create the illusion that the attacks are disconnected and random when, in reality, they are all part of a carefully orchestrated plan. These fronts can take the form of social, psychological, or even professional attacks, ensuring that the target becomes overwhelmed by the constant barrage of problems from different directions.

The tactic of "multiple fronts of attack" is designed to overwhelm and scatter the perception of the target, making it nearly impossible for them to pinpoint the source or intent of the assaults. By striking from various angles—through rumors, planted evidence, or subtle manipulations—the target becomes consumed with addressing the chaos caused by these disruptions. This tactic is particularly effective because it attacks multiple aspects of the target's life: their relationships, career, and personal identity.

As the target struggles to comprehend the breadth of the attack, doubt seeps into their mind, particularly concerning their morals, ethics, or actions. Friends, family, and colleagues begin to question the target's integrity based on the orchestrated evidence, further isolating them. This sense of isolation magnifies the emotional toll, often leading the target to behave erratically in an attempt to reclaim control.

The psychological effects are profound. Constantly bombarded with doubt and suspicion, the target becomes increasingly anxious, paranoid, and vulnerable. As they attempt to address each individual disruption, they become consumed by the chaos, unable to see the broader picture. This vulnerability often leads to emotional breakdowns and behavioral dysfunctions that can jeopardize everything the target values—both personally and professionally—leaving them shattered and disoriented.

Principle 2: Timing and Patience

Ghost counterattacks are not about immediate results. Timing is crucial, and the successful execution of these tactics requires patience. Attacks are spread out over time, allowing the target to lower their guard or believe that the threat has passed. This creates an element of unpredictability, as the target is unable to anticipate when or where the next attack will come from. By staggering the attacks across different time periods, the orchestrator ensures that the target remains perpetually off-balance, unable to fully recover from one blow before the next one lands.

Principle 3: Using Others as Pawns

In ghost counterattacks, the orchestrator never acts alone. Instead, they use others who are often unwittingly maneuvered to carry out plans that they themselves aren't aware of the nature and results of. These "pawns" are carefully selected based on their behavior, thoughts, or actions that render them susceptible to manipulation by an enemy.

Over time, individuals often qualify themselves to be used as pawns through their lack of loyalty, untrustworthy behavior, or self-serving tendencies. The orchestrator leverages these weaknesses to manipulate them into serving their agenda, often without the pawn realizing they are being used.

Principle 4: Disguising Intentions

A fundamental aspect of ghost counterattacks is ensuring that the true intentions behind the actions remain hidden. By disguising the real motive behind a series of seemingly unrelated events, the orchestrator can keep their target from recognizing the broader strategy at play. This creates confusion and prevents the target from formulating an effective counterstrategy. The orchestrator must ensure that each attack appears innocuous or disconnected from the others, preventing the target from realizing they are part of a larger plan.

Principle 5: Creating Chaos and Confusion

One of the primary goals of ghost counterattacks is to create chaos and confusion in the life of the target. By launching attacks from multiple fronts, at varying times, and through different channels, the orchestrator ensures that the target is unable to focus on a single problem. Instead, the target becomes overwhelmed by the sheer number of issues they must address, each one pulling their attention in a different direction. This confusion serves to weaken the target's defenses, making them more vulnerable to further manipulation.

Creating chaos and confusion in others' lives through manipulation is an intensified tactic often rooted in deception. This strategy involves planting false ideas within relationships by leveraging secondary connections, such as friends or acquaintances of the target. By subtly introducing misleading information through these intermediaries, the target becomes isolated and distrustful, destabilizing their personal relationships. This approach can also extend to professional environments, where associates or friends of colleagues are used to introduce misinformation. In corporate or career-based settings, the stakes are higher, and the consequences more severe, as such tactics can undermine trust, productivity, and reputations.

Paid participants may also be incorporated into the scheme, performing slight yet calculated acts that appear suspicious, further implicating the target. This additional layer of manipulation increases tension, making it harder for the target to distinguish between real threats and orchestrated deception. These tactics thrive in environments where trust and reputation are paramount, especially among high-positioned figures, whose influence makes them prime targets for manipulation. However, while such actions may yield short-term disruption, the long-term consequences such as damaged relationships, ruined reputations, and possible legal repercussions for the target make these schemes ultimately highly destructive.

Principle 6: Emotional Manipulation

Ghost counterattacks often involve the manipulation of emotions, particularly negative ones such as fear, doubt, and insecurity. The orchestrator may use gossip, rumors, or subtle psychological attacks to plant seeds of distrust and anxiety in the target's mind. These emotions gradually erode the target's sense of stability and security, making them more susceptible to further manipulation. By keeping the target emotionally unbalanced, the orchestrator ensures that they remain unable to mount an effective defense against the ongoing attacks.

Principle 7: Creating Self-Doubt in the Target

Another key principle of ghost counterattacks is the creation of self-doubt in the target. By subtly undermining the target's confidence, the orchestrator can weaken their resolve and make them more prone to mistakes. This may be achieved by planting doubts about the target's relationships, professional abilities, or personal integrity. Once the target begins to question themselves, they become easier to manipulate and control, allowing the orchestrator to further their agenda without direct confrontation.

Principle 8: Testing and Qualifying Individuals whose own actions dictate their position.

Ghost counterattacks require the careful selection and testing of potential pawns. Not everyone is suitable for use in these strategies, and it is essential to identify individuals who have already disqualified themselves through acts of untrustworthiness or disloyalty. The orchestrator may conduct small tests to gauge the willingness of these individuals to act against the target, either consciously or unconsciously. Once a person has proven their susceptibility to the influence or manipulation of any oppositional force, they are qualified to be used as a pawn in the broader strategy. The first primary law of loyalty is that there are no second chances although it is a necessary tool to deceive others into believing otherwise.

Principle 9: Sacrificing Pawns Strategically

In ghost counterattacks, pawns are expendable. The orchestrator must be willing to sacrifice them when necessary to achieve the ultimate goals of the whole where no individual is greater than the sum of the unified whole . This may involve allowing the pawn to take the fall for a particular action or using them to divert attention away from the orchestrator's true involvement. The key is to ensure that the pawn's sacrifice serves the broader strategy, whether by misleading the target or allowing the orchestrator to maintain their cover. A sacrificed pawn is deserving of loyalty during any fall because it builds trust about hard situations that most people aren't willing to do for even their children, mothers, or siblings.

All pawns aren't necessarily a negative or in a bad position because organization at some point necessitates that one or some be willing to sacrifice themselves for the advancement or preservation of an organization and any eho doesn't support the sacrificed pawn are in reality an enemy to to well being of any organized body and its agendas.

Principle 10: Remaining Unseen

A core principle of ghost counterattacks is the importance of remaining unseen. The orchestrator must operate from the shadows, ensuring that their involvement in the attacks remains undetected. This may involve using intermediaries, spreading anonymous rumors, or planting subtle suggestions that lead the target to draw their own conclusions. By remaining unseen, the orchestrator ensures that they can continue to manipulate the situation without being directly tied to the attacks.

Principle 11: Exploiting Distrust and Suspicion

One of the most effective ways to weaken a target is to exploit existing distrust and suspicion within their social or professional circles. Ghost counterattacks often involve sowing seeds of discord, leading the target to question the loyalty or intentions of those around them. By exploiting these pre-existing tensions, the orchestrator can cause the target to become isolated and paranoid, making them more vulnerable to further manipulation. The key is to amplify the target's suspicions without directly implicating the orchestrator in the process.

Principle 12: Long-Term Strategy

Ghost counterattacks are not designed for quick victories. Instead, they are part of a long-term strategy aimed at gradually wearing down the target over time. The orchestrator must be patient, allowing the various attacks to build upon one another, slowly eroding the target's confidence, relationships, and defenses. This long-term approach ensures that the target becomes more vulnerable with each passing day, eventually leading to their complete defeat.

The twelve principles of ghost counterattacks and counteractions offer a highly effective framework for manipulating adversaries from the shadows. By using others as unwitting pawns, attacking from multiple fronts, and maintaining secrecy, the orchestrator can advance their agenda without ever being directly implicated. These tactics rely on patience, subtlety, and a deep understanding of human psychology, allowing the orchestrator to slowly erode the target's defenses over time. While these strategies can be incredibly effective, they also require careful planning and precise execution, as any misstep could lead to exposure and failure. Nonetheless, for those who master the art of ghost counterattacks, the rewards can be substantial.

SECTION 5

The Ultimate Tools Of Seduction & Deception Of The Heart

CHAPTER 18

Changing & Redefining
The Game Of Love

Know & Understand Targets Who Live For It (Love), & Project An Image Of Wanting it & Needing It

Attack & Destroy All Assumptions To Reveal Targets To Themselves As Knowing Nothing About Love To Heighten Their Thirst For It ,Thirst For You ,& Need Of You

Love, as an abstract concept, is one of the most fertile grounds for deception. It is one of the most deeply desired things by humans, yet its true definition has never been presented and still remains elusive across time and culture.

Despite its omnipresence in art, literature, and daily life, love has never been universally defined. This ambiguity creates a vacuum, allowing individuals or institutions to exploit the idea of love for their own purposes. Because people inherently seek love and validation, they are susceptible to manipulation by those who claim to understand or embody its essence.

The main unrealized fact is that even those who constantly use the word or claim to know it, both crumble into fake artificial pieces when presented with real questions and that is the greatest opportunity for you to not only take the spotlight from any and all but also presents an indomitable level of manipulation that will allow you to influence many to close the doors on many whom your new position will can and will prove them as being fake, incapable of true love, and practicing deception.

By the fact of Love being universally undefined, it becomes a blank canvas, onto which you will redefine and redirect people's desires, beliefs , and lives for your own advantage.

Leaders, religious figures, or even personal partners who claim to hold the key to "true love" often wield great power of influence and control.

In a world where no clear understanding of love exists, he who provides a definition becomes a central figure and a savior for many . Others rally around this person or ideology, often without realizing they are being guided by someone else's assumptions of love, rather than an objective truth. This is where the potential for deception lies.

People are easily misled when they are yearning for something intangible, something they have never fully grasped.

Love, in its abstract form, can be used to manipulate emotions, control actions, and dictate relationships.

The power of deception within the realm of love's many avenues will ultimately allow you to possess the power to cause break ups in others' lives when you learn the necessary tactic to subtly press the right questions to cause someone to begin to doubt the ones they're romantically involved with.

Without a universal or concrete definition, those in power have been able to twist love into whatever suited their goals because no one has ever risen with the capability to effectively challenge and destroy that position.

As long as the world remains uncertain about the true nature of love, the opportunity for deception will always thrive.

The individual or group that convinces others they hold the answer to this mystery becomes the architect of human connection and, ultimately, control.

Why does it seem like most people aren't good at solving problems and difficulties in an efficient and sufficient manner? It seems like and is an event where numerous people arise to give socalled advice that has never worked at doing anything but pacifying the problems until they manifest themselves again in different situations with different people but of the exact same nature.

Why is that? Because you can put a new face, a new time period, and new title on a method that didn't work in the past on any significant large scale and the same results of failing to alleviate the problems at their root will continuously reappear again and again with the problems getting worse and worser with each generation that tries to implement such as a remedy.

The most significant question is, could there be a clearer readily accessible solution to the reoccurring situations of always being stuck with limited ineffective options whenever you're faced with problems and difficulties?

Yes, there is and you're about to become that answer from the shadows of a superior deception in the name of love.

There's a fundamental law of power that you must remain consciously aware of at all times within any deception of the heart and love, it has been a major component of the human psyche in modern times to accept almost any and everything as long it has a good title or name placed upon it. This is a designed position of powerlessness.

If your position is to start and remain a position of power, you must know, understand, maintain the next principle of never accepting anything from those you deceive or intend to deceive because each everything they have either thought or felt before you was undefined and Always at risk of being changed or discarded..

**"TO ACCEPT ANYTHING ON FACE VALUE WITHOUT AN IN DEPTH KNOWLEDGE AND UNDERSTANDING OF THE NATURE OF THE SUBSTANCE BEHIND & WITHIN WHAT IS GIVEN IS TO OPEN ONESELF TO THE UNEXPECTED & UNDESIRED, AND , SHOULD SUGGEST TO ANY BALANCED THINKING PROCESS THAT SOMETHING ISN'T REALLY WHAT IT IS PROJECTED AS BEING WHEN ITS EFFECTS CONTRADICTS THE PROJECTED INTENT OR PURPOSE OF IT BEING
GIVEN."**

The Beginning Of The Deceptive Teachings

No matter how one phrases it, the word love is a symbol that is supposed to represent some particular substance.

There is a simple formula of **symbols and substance** that dictates that in order for a symbol to represent reality, the truth, or that which is right, then the symbol must possess a substance behind it that is congruent with what the symbol represents and proves the symbol as a correct representation of an actual substance.

For example, words are written and sounded symbols that are meant to represent the existence of physical substances like "sand" which represents the existence of a material substance that we know to be on the ground.

Ok what if the word "sand" became altered and was made to represent the substance that we know as "clouds in the sky" ?, then that symbol "sand" would cease to be backed by its correct substance and would become a false representation. Another example is a concept such as a stop sign.

The Stop sign is a physical representation of a rule or law that means to cease motion in a vehicle but what if someone said that the stop sign personally meant for them to speed up? Would that not be a misinterpretation and misrepresentation of the substance behind the stop sign which is the rule of the road or driving?

What would be the effect of it , would there not be increased crashes if the misrepresentation was followed by everyone?

Would that not be a factual incongruent state between the stop sign and the substance that the person replaced the original rule with? "Stop sign means to speed up"

Those examples relate to the voids we create in reference to love and many of life's most important things by the uninformed thoughts and perceptions we formulate and the uninformed decisions and actions we make that seek to redefine the natural order and function of things according to uninformed and incorrect personal assumptions which create the heart of all dysfunctions in our lives.

The representation of something without its correct inner substance which is a clear and direct parallel to the reality of love in the lives of people of the world.
How so? Simply by people using the word love and putting whatever they choose behind the word as if it is a true representation of love.

We as people will only grow into a better knowledge and understanding of love only after we learn one of the most hardest lessons in life, anything we as individuals didn't create such as love , can never be just exclusively defined and confined for own personal individual wants or desires.

That is so because love by its very nature doesn't and won't conform to any one's desires , it influences conformity to it so that many can be connected in one accord that it alone defines.

Love's ultimate purpose is bigger than any one person's desires , thoughts, and expectations, so much so until it produces , incorporates , and influences the existence of stages in how it must be facilitated in order to reach its highest manifestations.

The number one example is where the right Male/Female relationships naturally produce the right family structure and the right family structure.

What the complexities of relationships often reveal are dysfunctional qualities that can challenge even the strongest of bonds.

These issues ranging from breakdowns in communication to unresolved conflicts can hinder the growth and health of all human relations.

However, there's a new and more effective strategies for addressing these problems that have persisted for centuries in ever occurring cycles.

All of the negative cycles have occurred for one central reason. This world has not truly known or understood love.

These writings emerge to provide hope and new innovative practical solutions for modern relations like friendships , relationships , family , and marriages in a unique way and method that emphasizes the importance of going beyond the ineffective assumptions and theories of the past.

Theories that didn't provide an actual knowledge and understanding of love but rather added to the problems with artificial ideas and academic theories that still remain comparable to this scenario:

"A dog trying to provide a tree with emotional intelligence , empathy, and active listening skills as foundational tools to help

the tree help humans to overcome the dysfunction factor in human relations."

This sets the foundation for us to understand the nature of the complexities involving the dysfunctions of human relations in the world but will as well help us to begin to know and understand some very significant things about one's self and what we thought we knew and understood about love.

Ultimately, gaining a deeper understanding of love itself is crucial.

Love is not a feeling or an emotion but actually exists as something much more profound and consequential not only to ourselves but in the way we connect with others.

There are many impediments that either prevent us from receiving love or prevent us from being able to facilitate love in its TRUEST expressions with a solid base of consistency.

In-depth knowledge of love also involves acknowledging and respecting the boundaries that love naturally produces in one to prevent negative , hurtful , and destructive things from being done towards the object of one's love.

One of the main questions that the world of psychology has failed to answer is a fundamental question that most average people have never been able to answer themselves also ,whether they're willing to admit it or not. "Do you know what love actually is?" Not what it does or how it performs like caring , kind , and etc.

The most profound form of ignorance in the world is a form of ignorance that thr majority of the people in the world guard more than anything they've ever had in mind and that is their ignorance of love.

Everyone enjoys using the word love and those who enjoy using also dread a moment where they're put in the spotlight and questioned about love.

Everyone gas an extreme compulsion to use the word love but no one is ever willing to engage in a real conversation about love and what they actually know about love. This is the point where they are most vulnerable and can be stripped of one of their most prized possessions and destroyed. The impact of the questioning is even more destructive when others are near or present to witness the questioning that exposes them as a fraud and knowing nothing about love. Why? Because if one claims to capable of love or searching for love yet have no idea or significant knowledge of what love is, then their position becomes exposed as a senseless position of searching for something that one doesn't even have a clue about what they're searching for.

Ultimately, the target of the questioning will naturally take a defensive position but there is no defense for ignorance and a selfimposed mentality of stupidity that proposes to be able to give done something or find something that doesn't even know.

Such questions as :

What is love and where does it originate from? , If love is an emotion or feeling, then why is it that love doesn't have the same nature as a feeling or an emotion? Emotions are internal reaction to external things which means they're very nature is dictated by external things. If love is such then it can have no internal basis ,right?

How do you know you're experiencing love and not ust what you want yourself to feel? Or how do you acquaint yourself with love?

Is love up for personal interpretation? Or is there universal principles to it? If it is a personal interpretation, how can it ever be the same for everyone? How can there ever be a way to connect something that is meant to be personalized, thereby different from other's personalized versions of it and no commonalities?

Is love an action? If so, then by reason of the conscious actions of supposed caring and other such things, since actions originate from conscious thought, then you should be able to define love and how it influences the act of caring in your own mind, right?

CHAPTER 19
Setting The Trap With A Sweet Treat

The one thing to keep in mind that the most attractive position to take is the high one that stands on the high ground of pointing out the flawed and wrong perceptions and understandings that most others have about love and offer the explanation as saving reason that explains why others have not truly seen the and understood the target or why others have mistreated and misused the target.

There is a prominent false premise which assumes that when it comes to love, people can simply disregard anything that they don't consider relevant to what they're doing or trying to accomplish.

It is by this very approach that people become willing to use love as a personal tool to acquire what they want

One might wonder, how is that possible? Its more than possible.

To immediately present inescapable boundaries for the one ones you have begun to express thongs about love to, its important to state theses restraining reasons that begins with

"Because-"

1.)   We don't and can't control love.

2.)   **Love brings its own definition, method, and function of how to do things**

3.)   **Love is formatted so that it has to begin with and within an individual first which means that you have to learn to love self (entirely).**

The thought, feeling, and actions of loving yourself for who you are isn't easy or as simple as just doing it, to be able to love yourself adds some prerequisites to the whole ordeal where you first have to know who you are as your gender and your race and how that defines you in your individuality.

In most of our minds ,the only thing that matters is the opposite sex that we're chasing or interested in. To most of us that's the only love that we care about and the only one we're truly interested in.

Within this thinking is the underlying idea and assumption that this is where love truly begins.

Its like out of nowhere with no clear justification, people just simply believe they can just simply approach love from any direction that they choose without there being any requirements of truth as a guide.

In order to give you a simplified analogy of what is being expressed, consider the fact of a seed ,the seed needs things beyond itself in order to grow and until these things like the appropriate environment (dirt or soil) is added , the seed in and of itself cannot and will not grow.

Why? because there are other prerequisites that must be present before the seed can even begin its process of growth and development like water after it has been placed into the dirt.

The lack of water or soil in either case is a void. Unknowingly to most people, love works along similar principles where certain things must be present before it can become awakened.

Then at another stage in its growth as a sprouting seed that has pushed upward above ground, it still needs the soil and water but at this next stage it must have sunlight or it will begin to wither away.

Even in this analogy, according to the knowledge that the average person has about the dirt or soil in the growth process of a seed, it is a highly unknown fact that the soil itself contains certain minerals and elements that must be present within the soil in order for it to even help grow a seed. It is the same with love.

This is seen in certain situations where certain seeds are placed in a soil that has a certain pale color to it with nothing growing from it and the seed is placed in this particular soil and it doesn't even grow at all.

Another analogy is one dealing with a particular building with an advertisement sign over the front of the building that says it's a clothing store and then there is another smaller sign posted on the entrance door that says "Now open for business " but there isn't one single clothing item, shoe, or any other retail item inside of the building.

The point is that the building is not an actual clothing store yet and will not truly be open for business or become what it is meant to be until the actual clothing items are placed in the building.

Both of these analogies apply to love in ways that most people have not even considered.

People can think what they want to think about love all day and continue to only experience the failure of what they assumed was love.

As a direct result, the fact shall remain that there will always seem to be something that is missing from those assumed love experiences because there actually is and those things are the contexts through which love must be facilitated in order for it to actually become a true reality in the mind, heart and life of anyone.

Why and how is that a fact? Because when you take something that is incomplete and try to complete someone with it, what you end up producing is a void or vacuum that holds no true substance by which that person can become the totality of that which they are meant to be.

In other words you only produce and foster a partial identity platform with no means to actuate and activate the fullest potential and capability that a complete identity naturally empowers one with.

On the other hand, if what you seek to define your life by, is false and unreal, then all you'll be doing in the end is once again producing a void or vacuum but from this false platform, the void or vacuum will handicap people from being able to correctly perceive themselves , function, and react within the fabric and context of reality and truth.

That context is the state and condition of the very nature of the society , countries, and world that we live in.

The present order of the world along with all of its faculties of learning and the systems that derived from it is the result of conquerors and all conquerors had one main thing in common, to either destroy, hide or distort anything with a unifying nature to it because all conquerors came to divide people and the most effective method was eliminating or distorting the knowledge of who those people were so that they could be maintained in a fractualized existence by the only unified force, that of the conqueror.

This is the main reason that any theology or religion that originated from a conqueror has not produced uniity or love amongst the nations who currently adhere to those teachings

In the world of psychology, academic theories , and religion people are prone to think , believe , and express the idea that something is wrong with the way in which people either think and act or don't think and act.

This is always said as though that is getting at the very heart of the dysfunctions in human relations or as if that is telling the whole truth about the way people think and how they came to think a certain way.

In fact it is something totally different, much deeper, and more crucial to the facilitating of Love by humans than anything else and that particular thing is the state, quality, and condition of the actual human beings mindstate and the uninformed norms that has influenced it to be that way.

The world of psychology , Academic Theory , and religion proposes to fix everything dealing with humans while in and of themselves not possessing an actual knowledge and understanding of the human being itself , thereby making it impossible for the world of psychology ,Academic Theory ,and religion to fix something that they do not have an actual and factual knowledge and understanding about.

What does that actually mean?

Principles of truth and right are foundational contexts through which love manifests and expresses itself. This is something that may make some people feel uncomfortable or angry because it's a norm for many to think and feel they can lie and deceive and yet remain a perfect facilitator of love.

In the world of reality, there's no such thing as a little white lie or a partial liar and deceiver.

If you aren't disciplined enough to not lie and tell even an occasional lie, you're a liar. There's no in-between line that allows you to be both at the same time. "An honest person" is a definite and conclusive title that signifies the nonexistence of a lie or deceit. It signifies **ABSOLUTE CONSISTENCY** in being honest.

That is something that most people will have a problem with because of a need to make excuses and make such a thing as being impossible and unrealistic for someone to do.

In other words a disguised justification for not being consistently honest nor desiring to be such.

The question that hangs in the balance is " Is it truly possible? " and the simple answer is "yes" but you'll discover more later on along with how it's more than possible with love.

The moment the words or act of deception happens, the person is no longer "an honest person."

Contrary to what most people think and believe, there's no such thing as an honest person being honest in one area but not others.

That person is only one capable of truth while possessing an inclination to lie. Thus a liar and not totally honest.

The Principle Of Position & Space

5..)"NO TWO OBJECTS CAN OCCUPY THE SAME SPACEAT THE SAME TIME. LIKEWISE, A LIE & TRUTH CAN NOT CO-EXIST TOGETHER. THEY ARE TWO OPPOSING NATURES THAT CAN'T AND WON'T THE SAME PLACE OR CONDITION OF MIND AT THE SAME TIME."

Love can't and won't exist within a lie.

The inclination to lie doesn't and won't just affect the certain area in which the lie was told, the lie's nature causes a fluctuation or void in one's ability to facilitate love because love by its very nature influences and solidifies rightful and honest **CONSISTENCY.**

If you have a world that has been built upon the distortion of truth , the hiding of truth and deception about truth, why wouldn't the same world seek to distort the truth, hide the truth , and be deceptive about the one principal foundational element that exclusively defines, produces, and directs the course of human nature and human potential? The so-called female?

Through such deception, there's no way that any female would have knowledge of who she actually is and what that actually entails as far as the nature of a female and the unequaled natural power, abilities and purposes that go with it.

Being female is a context through which love manifests and expresses itself and so is male and Race a context through which love manifests and expresses itself.

The lack of knowledge and understanding of these contexts and numerous others are prerequisite conditions that have made love impossible on any significant large scale throughout the world.

This is one of the major misunderstandings about love.

In a unnatural world, people naturally have the unnatural notion that love only applies to that which immediately affects them or immediately serves their particular individual self-interests.

This is a predominant misperception that most people have as though individuals have the unquestionable right and power to define and confine love within the set perimeter of who they are and what they want, to the exclusion of others that are not immediately connected to them.

Contrary to popular thought or feeling, love never confines itself to any particular limitations or specific areas.

Love in all of its magnificent and indomitable power by nature seeks to encompass each and every avenue of human thought and behavior, nature around us, and the universe as the exclusive means by which it as the ultimate definer and director of all, assigns degrees of positive and powerful results to all things according to how much a thing is in accordance with the nature in which it was created.

Simply meaning, the degree to which a thing is in accordance or direct alignment with its nature determines a thing's degree of access to its natural abilities and a prescribed degree of power with a natural balance that gives a high degree of efficiency and sufficiency in all that it conceives, intends, and performs.

Why? How? Because that is the apex definition that determines whether a thing is right or wrong.

According to that same principle of nature, the degree to which a thing is out of accordance or alignment with its nature determines the degree to which it lacks access to its natural abilities and produces an imbalance (dysfunction) that prescribes either a low or non-existent efficient and proficiency level within all that it conceives, intends, or performs towards positivity.

Most people who are out of alignment with their nature have a high tendency towards producing negative thoughts and situations that effect others in a counterproductive way although the thoughts and situations may serve their own interests quite well but only at the cost of disregarding the needs and feelings of others.

Why? or How? Because that is the apex of being wrong.

HooLike the Male redefining the so-called female's position, role, and power according to an unnatural egotistical masculine desire to be superior and to deny the so-called female her equality and superiority in areas that her nature was specifically designed for.

Areas that aren't about physical strength but rests as the very essence of man's physical strength.

Do you men know what the nature and power of a so-called female's nature is? Do you so-called females even know or understand it?

Yeah, it's been said until it's worn out that her nature is to comfort but that's on the extreme outer edges of it.

If one as a so-called female doesn't know or understand what it is, then how can she ever fulfill her natural position or destinies? How can anyone truly understand why there's an imbalance in the family structure and the entire social construct? And how can one even claim to be able to fix these dysfunctions without having a sufficient knowledge and understanding of the natures of the individuals involved?

The answers are readily observed in the effects of the socalled psychological and religious remedies that all have the imbalanced masculine ego as its origin and have only pacified and enlarged the negative effects of the dysfunctions.

How so? the divorce rates continue to climb even while setting new records in the divorce rate, violence and kidnappings against the so-called females continue to rise at record numbers, child abuse and child neglect continues to rise, the masculine based culture of so-called female disrespect (Hoes, Bixxhes, etc.) continues, abortions continue to rise (The #1 killer of all people of color),Black relationship spans continue to shorten.

That is quite a list of things but not even the tip of the iceberg as the saying goes.

CHAPTER 20

Placing The Sweet Enticement Within The Trap

"THE VERY BASIS OF ANY SELF- DELUSIONMENT AND THE DAMAGE IT CAUSES IS WHEN AN INDIVIDUAL OR GROUP OF PEOPLE SEEK TO DEFINE THEMSELVES AND THEIR LIVES BY THAT WHICH THEY KNOW THEY DON'T TRULY KNOW OR UNDERSTAND BUT GO TO THE EXTREME TO PROJECT OTHERWISE "

THE POWER TO ATTRACT , INFLUENCE, AND MANEUVER THOSE WHO VALUE AND SEEK TO BASE THEIR LIVES UPON LOVE WILL BE ACQUIRED ONLY WHEN ONE CAN ATTACK , DESTROY, AND REPLACE THEIR IGNORANT ASSUMPTIONS AND BELIEFS WITH (CRUMBS) OF THAT WHICH THEY DON'T KNOW , CAN'T DEFEAT , OR CAN'T ARGUE AGAINST

How is it that someone can claim to love someone else but cause them so much pain, disappointment, and sadness in their lives?

How is it that the majority of the world's people can claim to know and understand love or claim to be loving others in friendships, relationships, family and marriages but only end up causing that which is negative, hurtful, trifling, and destructive?

How is it that the prevalence of those negative elements are so widely spread throughout EVERY city of EVERY nation until love seems non-existent except in a few isolated examples?

A few isolated examples themselves that have proven to seem one way on the surface but turned out to be something totally different underneath the surface.

A very significant example is numerous 80 + year old couples having been married 50 + years but didn't have a clue about love but considered love to be caring, companionship, and compromise etc.

The most alarming fact about it was , none of them could in the least amount define or explain what it was that they were calling love. Thereby revealing a central fear of loneliness and a acute fear of being without companionship as the main reason that bonded them together for so long thus not love.

The answers to these seemingly vast problems and dysfunctions have confounded many of the academic world for centuries mainly because they tried to understand and define a natural thing and a natural process by artificial standards and the outer appearance rather than the internal where the essence of all things exists.

This explains clearly the part that the world of academics has played in adding to the dysfunctions.

Not surprisingly, the origins of the modern academic understanding of the human being and human nature was limited or distorted by theologies with no basis in fact.

The basis of what the world has assumed was love originates from the Eurocentric Greek Fathers of Greek philosophy and other Greek Philosophy.

The same Greek Father's of Philosophy and the same Greek philosophy that proved to be nothing more than hypothetical and theorized teachings full of ideas about the existence of things that they nor the level of Greek Civilization's technical science could prove the existence of or provide a confirmable model for.

The Greeks had 6 to 8 words for love and neither one of them and the defini8or Philosophy attached to them ever revealed what love exactly was in and of itself.

1. **Agape** – Love for family, spouse, children, etc. (Modern Christians try to interpret this " Agape " as meaning

"Unconditional Love" but there is no factual basis for that misinterpretation because there was no Greek word signifying (Unconditionally) ever attached to it and how the Greeks during the time of the great philosophers interpreted "Agape".

2. **Eros** – Romantic Love

3. **Philia** – Affectionate Love

4. **Storge** – Familiar Love

5. **Mania** – Obsessive Love

6. **Ludus** – Playful Love

7. **Pragma** – Enduring Love

8. **Philautia** – Self Love

Just as there are physical laws of nature such as gravity that dictate the realm of human potential and possibility, likewise there exists laws of thinking and behavior that dictate the realm of human potential, possibility, and impossibility. What one will experience or won't experience.

All of which is directly relative to love, the dysfunctions that prevent the facilitation of love, the remedying of those dysfunctions, and the actual nature of love itself. A nature that exists outside of the boundaries of what a foolish world has tried to define it as.

It may come as a surprise to learn that we as humans are subject to laws of existence that are beyond our control and are the most influential and determining factors of who we are, what we think ,and what we do no matter how much we may deceive or fool ourselves to think, feel, and believe otherwise.

It is that exact self- delusionment that also lies at the very heart of all dysfunctions in human relations.

The prime example of these (Laws of existence) is one that exists as an unavoidable prerequisite to all that we could ever think or do. So much so until it actually determines whether one will be either at the mercy of others or the master and sole controller of ones own destiny.

7..)"THE NATURE BY WHICH WE APPROACH A THING, DIRECTLY DICTATES THE NATURE OF THE RESULTS RECEIVED."

That being expressed is proven by our approach to love in all of its numerous forms and degrees of intensity and power. An approach that in of itself actually creates the dysfunctions in human relations (friendships, family, relationships, and marriages).

The nature of those approaches are best formulated and measured by the following scale.

- **Improper Fraction Of Perception :
Seeing Is knowing & Understanding Love.**

- **Individualized Love**

- **The Need To Be In Control: Its bitter & Poisonous Fruits Of Preferences and
Conditional Intent**

- **The Standard Communication Process:
A Symbol Without Substance**

- **Infatuation's Delusional Stance As Love**

Improper Fraction Of Perception: Seeing Is Knowing & Understanding Love

When it comes to our initial approach to things in life, it is our faculty of sight that primarily acquaints us with something, and the matter of love is no different in that regard.

Our first impressions of love , even from a very   young age , is based upon our observation of the various interactions between male and females, with certain actions, holding hands, hugging, spending time together, or even kissing.

That particular stage is very significant because it is an initial stage of growth that carries on into our older age groups of young adult and adulthood with a primary perception and understanding of love based upon what we have observed.

Unknowingly, this places us in a situation that is comparable to the situation of an adolescent boy or girl seeing older children riding bicycles.

The child just by the mere fact of seeing the act of riding a bicycle, immediately believe they can do it.

Feelings then come in and deepen the premature thinking that it's easy and simple enough as just merely getting on the bicycle and copying what was seen but then the critical moment arrives when the adolescent boy or girl gets on the bicycle only to experience fall after fall.

Experience then brings the child into a fuller reality about bicycle riding that their level of observation didn't and couldn't reveal to them or prepare them for.

That necessary element of the acquisition of balance and coordination upon a bicycle that could only be developed through practice and experience.

What was the result ? It was a hard and painful lesson learned that taught the adolescent child that observing and trying to copy other's actions and just simply getting on a bicycle wasn't a complete thing in and of itself but was actually just stages in a process that involved other necessary elements before riding the bicycle could even be possible.

What is the point of that bicycle analogy?

It is basically symbolic but highly relevant to the human approach to love that has barred the human & our human experiences from actually consisting of love and being able to bring love into an actual reality within our lives and the world.

Why? How? Because love isn't some external object or external event that one can observe, measure, nor understand and perform from the basis of a seen interaction between material objects in material circumstances outside of the human.

Why or how is that so? because love exists an internal force of positive power and influence whose exact state or condition (basically it's form) is undetectable by the human eye and ultimately is only available and approachable through a process of introspection that love itself generates and compels within the one in whom love has become awakened.

This is a position that is naturally going to make some people very uncomfortable because it takes away one of the main senses that we humans use to analyze and measure things in our external environment. This position in reality is not a bad position at all, it's a position that will force us to become more acquainted with the principle internal vision of the heart and mind.

Love and one of the primary significant elements of its nature's function is to emanate from within one person's mind and heart in an outward direction towards another or others so that it can connect with another part of itself in others and become a greater degree of itself in expression, power, and influence beyond the limited but highly necessary singular existence within just one person for the purpose of establishing self love in that person.

A love for self that exists in moderation, never to the extreme because only in moderation can that love have the ability and power to truly interact with others and connect with them from one of love's main defining directives that love compels one to naturally think and act from.

"…..love the next person as one loves self "

Why ? or How ? because love doesn't discriminate, it recognizes itself in ALL persons whether it has become awakened in them or not and facilitates the truth, purity ,goodness, and fairness of its nature towards all according to another defining element of its nature's function, (Unconditionally) so that it may in time influence its existence in others to become awakened.

Seeing with the physical eyes and initially basing everything upon that is a stage of learning and perception that is natural when it comes to our learning experiences.

It is through our learning experiences that we come into the realization of a proper and improper process of learning about how to truly learn to know and understand things.

8..)"THE NATURE OF THE THOUGHT INVOLVED DIRECTLY DETERMINES THE NATURE OF THE ACTIONS TO BE PRODUCED WHETHER WE ARE CONSCIOUS OF THE EXACT NATURE OR NOT. THUS EXPLAINS HOW PEOPLE CONSTANTLY THINK ONE THING BUT CONSTANTLY ACT OUT OR RECEIVE THE EXACT OPPOSITE OF WHAT THEY ASSUMED THEY WERE THINKING. INCORRECT THOUGHTS PRODUCES INCORRECT ACTIONS "

Initially, our very first experiences should teach us at an early age that what we see and observe is never the complete picture or complete knowledge and understanding of a thing's nature and true existence.

That is a lesson that very few of us have learned and as a serious consequence, this is where the initial beginning of the dysfunctions in human relations began and continues to originate from.

It is through the mentality of "Seeing is knowing and understanding" that has caused us to improperly perceive the role that our eyes play in actual knowledge and understanding of love.

Instead of properly perceiving sight and observation in its proper context of only being a very minute element, we've made it the most significant element that determines what love is.

The decision to place sight, actions, and external events and their external circumstances in the primary position has as a consequence produced the means by which we would be missing love altogether.

Why? Or How? because this fixation on what our eyes can see and observe has in an unnatural way made perceivable actions the primary defining factor of what love is to us and has also made the outer materialistic part of things the total and complete manifestation of what love is us as well.

In truth and fact, the physically observed actions are only a small secondary link in the expression and functions of love.

Contrary to what people have heard or been deceived and influenced to think, love isn't an action but manifests a portion of its intent through actions.

Actions represent physical indicators that love may be present but not necessarily present.

How so? Because of (2) main reasons :

1) Actions are not the exclusive domain of love & do express other things besides love

2) Because there are emotions and desires that can influence the exact same actions as caring, companionship, and tenderness but have nothing to do with love.

How so ? because the actions that originate from love bear a totally different nature, lifespan, and purpose that is always unconditional, consistent ,and supremely enduring of all situations, circumstances, and time periods, thereby being contrary to all that we as humans have constructed and defined as love, that has always been momentarily, limited, inconsistent, and highly conditioned upon other things of a trifling, insignificant, and selfish nature.

The imbalanced and immature mind is always grounded upon the superficial aspects of external things of a physical nature.

A person can say or believe that love is an action all day if they choose but the one explosive fact will remain, Actions aren't a cause within themselves.

Actions are an effect of thinking which means that if you're conscious of a deliberate action then that person should be able to define and express somethings :

3.) Exactly what the nature of the thoughts and feelings are behind the actions.

4.) How they originate from a particular inner substance called love

5.) which also happens to include defining what that substance consists of (Not what it does-Actions), where it resides, and its nature of emanating from within and outward into the external factors of life beyond individual self.

Which none in modern times have done , maybe coming close but in no significant way.

Sadly, most people refuse to even consider love without trying to focus on the action as the point of the defining and that is where people then miss the internal things of the heart, and love's internal and eternal place of existence that the eyes can't observe.

In light of that, it shouldn't come as a surprise to learn that that is the exclusive reason why the world's views and assumptions about love naturally positions all things and all relations that are based upon it into the unavoidable position of always being predetermined to fail.

Why is that position naturally inclined towards failure ? Because as the external things and situations it is based upon are always changing , this as a consequence disrupts the original form and position of what was liked and repositions such things into being undesirable so that they no longer hold any attractiveness, and just simply outlived their purpose. Although a trifling purpose.

Don't get the wrong understanding here. This isn't just about what you call romantic love.

This also applies equally to the love that we as humans call ourselves demonstrating with and towards ourselves, in our family structures, and friendships.

Our past observations and experiences with family love were based primarily upon our observations and experiences with various situations that we were either apart of or observed others engaged in which formed a reference point of what to do or not to do and how to think or how not to think in regards to certain situations and events that occurred in the family.

This very reference frame for thought and actions within the family structure is the number one reason and origin for child abuse, child neglect, gangs, teenage runaways, and foster children.

How so? because that so-called family love was expressed continuously but always manifested itself as being something totally different.

Prime example:

"I love you" but actions showed that :

"My fear of something or someone is greater than my love for you"

You might wonder how this could ever be a realistic situation involving that principle of thought.

Imagine a parent or parents , grandparents, or aunts and uncles who have called the police on a child or teenager under their guardianship and reported them to the police as having either committed a crime or about to commit a crime.

What kind of family would do such a thing? Its one thing not to condone bad behavior or illegal activities but its something totally different when a so-called family member will be the cause of another family member going to jail or prison because they disagreed with the family member's activities and valued or feared man's laws more than they loved their own flesh and blood.

Laws by a particular kind of man (Caucasian) who have NEVER applied any of their laws equally to Blacks or other people of color.

"I love you" but actions showed : " **My want of a girlfriend or boyfriend is greater than my love for you"**

"I love you" but actions showed that : "My hatred for what you do or how you think is greater than my love for you ... .so get out of my house".

There are certain situations where a parent or guardian must remove a family member from their home because of a security risk they may pose to the home like it being targeted for a shooting.

Surprisingly,   there are innumerable incidents where teenagers or young adults are being forced out the home just simply because they refuse to think and behave like the authority figures in the home.

"I love you" but actions showed : **"You're in trouble with the law so deal with it on your own... no letters from me, visits, or**

support but once you're out of jail or prison, I will love you again"

What kind of real and true family member does this?

What kind of real and true friends do this?

Obviously, this is the basis of what is now called being the natural way that family and friends treat people they claim to have love for.

As the course of time moves on, there has been a rapid deterioration of the values and standards of what a family and friend are composed of and it's only going to worsen.

 or even

"I love you" but actions showed : **" You're only as valuable as what i can get from you"**

" I love you " but actions showed: **" If you can't and won't be like me and do as I say, then I don't want to deal with you"**

Or within friendships…

" I love you" but actions showed : **"We can't be friends unless you agree with me or like what I like"**

This kind of artificial love exists because of what people saw and observed being done towards others as children in a family structure or being done by society or even saw and observed being done towards them as children by the family structure or society which naturally transferred into adulthood as a reference frame of how to think and act within a family or friendship, or relationship structure thus continuing the cycle of dysfunction in the name of love.

The proliferation of the world's dysfunctional human relations lies heavily at the feet of the academic world that is not only educational universities with psychology but are also facilities of learning that seeks to define or influence human thought and beliefs thus religious institutions as well that have been influenced primarily by man under the disguises of The Creator's names.

Psychology and the majority of man's religious teachings have historically taught and still currently teach that love is an emotion or feeling.

All of the things that are classified as emotions and feelings such as anger, disappointment, fear, happiness, and loneliness are essentially defined as reactions to things (Situations,

Circumstances, people, physical objects etc.) external to one's self.

Love isn't a reaction to anything so if love is just an emotion or feeling as the so-called experts say and teach, then why and how is it that love is capable of overpowering ALL other emotions, setting boundaries and restrictions for ALL emotions and feelings that they can not overcome? Why and how is that love can even cause all emotions and feelings that are not conducive to its purpose to become voided?

That indisputably infers and solidifies the fact that love's ultimate nature is significantly different from the emotions and feelings that it has been classified with.

The answer is not only very refreshing and enlivening but is indomitable as well.

Love is not an emotion or feeling although it facilitates both in the process of making itself known to the one or ones in whom it has become awakened.

INDIVIDUALIZED LOVE

When it comes to people in the world being asked about love the response that one usually gets is that they have their own particular idea and opinion about what love is.

The thought never occurs whether anyone else can relate to it or not or whether how it can cause negative and detrimental effects towards others.

Most people do not see anything wrong with this particular perception because they feel like love is something that they should be able to define based upon their own individual experiences.

No one perceives this particular position as being wrong in any way.

Why? because people want to believe that love is under their control and that they have a right to direct their love towards whom and whatever they choose like "love interests" to the exclusion of anything else or a family to the exclusion of everything else.

This is a very significant perception that most people in the world have about love that stems from ignorance and selfishness. This belief that we as individuals can define and direct our love in any way that best suits us as individuals and places everything beyond our individuality as a nonessential to love is actually the catalyst through which numerous dysfunctions are produced.

The idea of one even thinking of this individualized love as being a dysfunction and as well creating dysfunction is something that is bound to make someone very uncomfortable and highly disagreeable out of the feeling of someone attempting to wrestle something from them that they have an exclusive right to conceive and implement in any manner that they so choose.

It has been said that there are nine wonders of the world that cause awe and wonderment but one of the most highly underrated wonders of the world that should be added into that category is :

"How is it that individuals can think, feel and believe that they can conceive of things with their own definitions and ideas about a particular thing that has no basis in reality or nature and then wonder why it is so hard and impossible for others to connect with it and receive anything positive and nurturing from i?"

This particular perception of individualized love in reality is not designed to be about others ,it's not designed to include the feelings ,wants, desires or needs of others. It possesses no true or genuine position in regards to others at all , it is all about an individual.

There is a widely spread assumption that one can have their very own perception and understanding about love, although true in one minor way, that is totally false and wrong in all of the most significant and most defining ways about love.

How so? love brings its own standards ,definitions ,and reasons to the table of Human Experience where although it manifests itself to and within different individuals, every manifestation has the same basic Foundation ,nature, intent ,aim ,purpose and Direction within the different contexts of different people's lives so that all of the different people can be unified or connected on the same page of love with the same positive nurturing principles involved.

There are approximately close to 5 billion people in the world and the problem comes about with the idea, belief and perception of one being able to have a personal individualized love that is exclusively defined by them.

When you have close to five billion people with five billion different ideas, opinions, and feelings about love ,what you naturally end up with is the current state of the world ,massive dysfunctions in human relations where almost five billion different ideas and opinions about love that conflict with each other, have no common aims, purposes, directions or meaning. So much so until these almost five billion different ideas and opinions about love cause nothing but conflict, confusion, chaos, pain ,hurt ,and misunderstanding in the Name of Love.

Some people to hide their lack knowledge and understanding about love will argue to the extreme about their individuality and their right to perceive things as they choose.

They argue as if their individuality is subject to the laws of human nature as everyone else is. One went so far as to say that gravity was only a theory and when asked if she could jump off of 30 floor skyscraper and not fall as everyone else? She avoided the answer. The woman continued the conversation along the same line of thought about her exclusive individuality and exclusive right of defining things as she felt But when asked " Oh so everyone else's brainwaves all flow according to the same patterns ,the same principles the make perceiving possible and the same directions but your brain has a exclusively different shape of its own and your thoughts originate and flow in a different way than others, like your thoughts

What are the origins of the idea of there being such a thing as an individualized love?

No one who thinks and feels such away about love has ever asked themselves the question of what makes them better qualified to define love better than love itself?

In our immature mentality and expressions of human nature we act as though love came into this world the moment we as an individual came to exist.

There are numerous reasons as to why a person would want an individualized version of love but two of the main reasons are that no one likes to be in a position of having to admit they just don't know something about a very significant thing due to an exaggerated fear of being positioned as powerless, stupid, or unworthy and incapable of having something or someone desired.

No matter the actual amount of the reasons available to explain this individualized love , all of them have a common nature that derives from selfishness and ignorance taken to its extreme point.

As with any dysfunction, the basic definition of dysfunction is the inability of a person ,place ,thing, or idea to function in the way it was designed or intended.

With all of that being said, what is presented to us is a unique position that is bound to make us initially uncomfortable but within that position lies the central remedy to any dysfunction.

That position is in fact a question that we must ask ourselves and depending upon how honest we are willing to be with ourselves ,we will either open the door to finally being able to fix our dysfunctions or we will continue to lie to ourselves and continue to produce the exact impediments that are causing the dysfunctions in human relations in the name of love.

That very question is, did you yourself create or originate love? If you realize that you didn't ,then your answer at the same time must be allowed to reposition your thinking into realizing and understanding that there exists a predetermined model and standard of what love is, that must be conformed to rather than us in our warped and immature thinking believing that we as individuals must always distort or force everything around us to conform to us as an individual and our individual limitations and defects.

In reality this whole idea, opinion, and theory about individualized love is to a greater extent about the kind of individual and the individual desires that individuals like to disguise under nice and shiny names like love so that ulterior motives and intentions can attract other people to them so that they can receive some form of benefit at the expense of others kindness, sincerity, and dignity. That can be money, financial security, sex, social status, or even just plain old influence and control over another.

Okay I understand that presents another major problem of (you) not knowing where to find that predetermined model or standard of love because this world hasn't produced it, although they would like us to think, believe, and feel otherwise. But you'll find it here.

The Need To Be In Control :Its Bitter & Poisonous Fruits Of Preferences & Conditional Intent

This is a critical point in the Seduction because it lays the foundation for one to take away some of the defenses in a way that subtly takes away the target's feeling of needing to be in control of their dealings with love.

This desire or compulsion of needing to be in control in part stems from a mentality saturated with impatience, frustration and an overwhelming feeling of wanting what one wants in an instant. It's comparable to instant microwave popcorn or dinners with the thought "Oh I'll just put this prepackaged love in the microwave and I'll have it instantly with a minimum wait and no risk factor."

The control Factor says "It's My Life ,my wants ,so I'll determine the time it needs and when it's ready regardless of any instructions involved"

Sadly, this very thought process isn't about popcorn, this is the main idea that the world has in reference to being able to ultimately control love.

Everywhere you go in this world ,one of the main first things you'll hear people say when it comes to them seeking a relationship or Love is "I'm looking for that which is drama free" not realizing that in a world built upon being Loveless, the moment you find true love the world is going to bring you drama up close and personal in constant streams to test it and to tear it apart. Tests that more than often involve a problem that makes one or both involved very uncomfortable, frustrated, or depressed.

This is the critical moment when those who feel the need to be in control react with the usual response to such. "This isn't what I was looking for"

That is the strange and sometimes funny thing about life in this world when it comes to people and the things that they believe that they want. When it comes to most things that people believe they want ,usually they're only looking at maybe one or two particular things while excluding the existence of other things that naturally exist with the particular thing they believe they want.

Naturally when they reach a point in dealing with that thing that they say they wanted, they discover that there are other elements there that present a totally different set of contrary circumstances, requirements and experiences that they either didn't consider, didn't want or wasn't ready for.

With most people this is that defining moment where they then change their minds and say "oh this isn't really what I wanted"

Most times this type of situation will always be blamed on others as something bad or negative that others did to them when in fact, the blame always rests upon the one who assumed that a particular thing is naturally only one sided or one dimensional in the way they wanted it to be. It's a hard truth to face but it's their own limited immature thoughts and desires that blinded them to the complete reality of what they thought they were wanting.

The need to be in control, a widespread aspect of human behavior, leads to significant imbalances in personal and professional relationships.

The desire for control derives from an acute fear of uncertainty and an exaggerated desire for predictability.

In personal relationships, such as those between partners, friends, or family members, the drive to control can manifest itself in the form of attempted dominance, manipulation, or coercion which results in an imbalance within all relations that such a mentality becomes involved in.

Whenever there exists one individual or groups of alike individuals who consistently seeks to enforce their will, it undermines and destroys any potential for respect, empathy, fairness, trust and equality to exist which are necessary essentials for healthy interactions.

The inevitable result of this dynamic is the production of resentment, the erosion of trust and genuine communication, and the loss of any moral compass which to most individuals who seek to be in control, doesn't even matter because when all is said and done, it's all about what they want, how they want it, where they want it, how much and how long they want it without regard for who gets hurt, used, or deprived unfairly as a result of it.

When it comes to the subject of love, this approach of needing to be in control manifests itself in numerous forms.

It derives from a delusional mentality that an individual in of themselves can dictate meaning, purpose, and function to all things in life dealing with it or surrounding it.

That particular method and mentality usually produces good consistent results when dealing with material things and material based situations such as jobs, careers, hobbies, and sports because they are all the product of human thought and planning but have not , do not, and will not produce the good or right results when it comes to love.

The need to be in control, while often felt to be a strength, can lead to significant personal negative and counterproductive ramifications.

Control is perceived as the only means by which a sense of order and predictability can be established in their lives, enabling individuals to control or restrict life's uncertainties with confidence.

At its core, the desire for control stems from a basic human need for security and stability. When individuals feel in control, they believe they can prevent undesirable outcomes and dictate control over their lives.

When it comes to love the need to be in control manifest itself in the form of such thoughts as :

"I don't want to be heartbroken or deceived so I'll confine my idea of love to certain areas and only deal with certain types of people who are more susceptible to what I want and how I want it without regard for themselves "

"I am willing to consider a person a possible love interest only if they can fit within the confinements of my lifestyle "

" Love is defined by me as something that won't challenge or disrupt what i think is best for myself and the way I want my life to reflect only what I consider to be valuable and comforting. "

"Love isn't a reaction to anything external "

9..)"LOVE ISN'T & NEVER WILL BE A REACTION TO ANYTHING EXTERNAL (PERSON, PLACE, OR THING).

LOVE IS OF AN INTERNAL FORCE OF POWER , INFLUENCE , & EXISTENCE THAT PERCEIVES & CAUSES ALL ETERNAL THINGS TO REACT TO IT & BEAR THE DEFINITIONS OF ITS DIRECTIVES."

This can lead to a crucial paradox where the pursuit of control becomes a source of stress and tension not only to the individual seeking control but to those who have to deal with the controlling individual because there persists a constant striving to control every aspect of one's environment which also in a major way involves the relentless attempt to control other people and the interactions. It is the unpredictability of life that inevitably disrupts these efforts.

Furthermore, the need to be in control negatively impacts all relations with others.

People who exhibit controlling behaviors often seek to impose their will, desires ,expectations and standards on others which always leads to conflicts and resentment. This can result in a cycle of misunderstandings and emotional distance.

In addition to interpersonal issues, the need to be in control hinders personal growth.

Embracing the uncertainty factor of life is a crucial component of learning and development. When individuals seek to control their experiences within a small perimeter of their own making , they limit their exposure to new ideas and new opportunities.

With the individuals who feel a need to be in control, there's always the delusional idea that this position is in the best interests of themselves and others.

Preferences

We as people are by Nature beings who initially perceive and interpret everything about ourselves and around us according to the senses (sight, taste, touch, smell, hearing, and sound).

As we grow mentally through our experiences with the physical surroundings a Form of Intelligence should have been developed in the mind that suggests and compels us to know and understand that living things are defined more precisely and correctly by the inner substance of their minds which will reveal their very nature and the realm of potential and definite situations that can or will occur in an experience with those things.

Contrary to that, 99.9% of people have developed an ignorant approach to the relations that are meant to provide us with love and as a consequence, it has become a highly common result to end up with that which is other than love.

That ignorant approach is the development of some sort of preference for particular facial and body features or financial situations or other similar external circumstances that a person has to possess in order to be considered possibly the right one for us, beautiful, hot ,handsome, desirable ,or suitable for ourselves in dating, relationships, and marriage.

The preferences themselves aren't ignorant, it's when these preferences are positioned as a prerequisite to love that defines this approach as ignorant and foolish.

How so? First and foremost this preference approach presupposes to dictate to love a set of Standards by which it would be willing to be open or susceptible to love but if these standards aren't present in a person, then they are concluded as being unacceptable and not even up for consideration.

The ignorant and selfish basis for these particular preferences lies more often than anything up on the principle of a sexual attraction that arouses excitement within us upon seeing these particular individuals.

This sexual attraction is then taken out of context and turned into a warpcd standard of measurement that precedes to define not only the potential or lack of potential for an individual to possess the distorted version of love (that we have in mind) and is sought after by us but as well proceeds to define the ultimate worth of an individual by his or her material outer characteristics.

This is the particular distorted ,incorrect, and delusional ideas that people have formed in their minds and hearts about love in order to cheapen what Love Actually is, so that it presents no particular responsibility, meaning, or dictates to them in pursuing such shallow-minded things that they have designed and titled under the Name of Love.

These particular preferences are in and of themselves a unique status of insanity that are based upon an external perception and definition that seeks to disqualify any other particular significant element as a defining factor in what a particular thing is so that the nature, event and circumstances surrounding it all will become simplified and based upon an animalistic urge that incites the senses.

Such a one who is possessing these particular preferences acquires that which isn't lasting, stable, or consistent as love is, then they naturally assume that the problem is with other people rather than with themselves who initiated something that wasn't love and naturally received results that didn't have anything to do with love.

The insanity then deepens to the point of formulating the idea that if they change the locations, age groups, or social status of where they look for love, then the results will be different.

All along setting themselves up for the same results no matter what they change or restructure because they haven't changed the essence of their perceptions and approach which is those shallow minded preferences that believe the substance of love is to be found behind outer symbols as a set category of particular outer appearances.

Once again you cannot define an inner eternal process of a spiritual nature by the restraints and confinements of that which is physical and readily seen.

Whether you believe in spiritual or spirituality or not, the mind and the process involved with thinking is and shall forever be that which is composed of unseen positive energy that derives from a more powerful source than thought itself and that is a particular standard and rule of judgment that is based upon the definitions and principles of the ancient civilizations of the world.

Ancients who were more in sync with that which is called spiritual than modern people have ever been.

All of those ancient civilization's (non Greek, Crete, Roman) mystery schools of higher teachings equated spirit with mind and thinking, the particular feelings that derived from such thinking, an inner source of energy that rested as the source of the mind, that not only connected human beings at the very essence of who we are but also connected the essence of human beings to all things in the universe along with the effects that thinking was able to produce upon the external environment.

The most profound thing about this need to be in control is that it also invades and seeks to define a significant aspect within that which some people call their religious beliefs.

In the Biblical scriptures, it is said that "God is Love" but when it comes to love, most of those in the church or those who claim to believe in God and that biblical verse will tell you anything from their mouths about God being in control or how one must give

God control but when you see them in action and listen to them outside of the church, what you discover is a total different reality.

A reality where even they are bound by having the same preferences and a overwhelming need to be in control of who they chose to love and how they chose to love which in reality says

" God is love but this is my life, my heart, and my right to choose something according to my own standards so I'll just put God over there in the corner with God's love because I can't sleep with God, kiss God, or be held by God".

What does that ultimately mean? The Creator is love? It means that humanity's approach to love is a direct reflection of humanity's approach to The Creator.

10..)"IN ESSENCE, PEOPLE'S DESIRE & INTENT TO CONTROL & DEFINE LOVE ACCORDING TO THE IMMATURE, PETTY, & SUPERFICIAL PRINCIPLES OF HUMANITY'S WARPED THINKING IS A DIRECT REFLECTION OF HUMANITY'S BELIEF & THOUGHT THAT IT CAN CONTROL & DEFINE GOD AFTER THE IMAGE OF MAN'S THOUGHTS & PERCEPTIONS

Conditional Intent

"Conditional intent" is the most defining nature of the world's overall view, understanding, and application of what it falsely calls love.

This is probably the hardest fact that one has to face when it comes to what they call love or have been indirectly taught about how love works in the world.

When it comes to people loving others in this world, what you find is the majority of the people in the world who are always at some point in their life where they tell someone that they love them or are in love with them and on the surface this would seem to imply that this is a commitment of loyalty, respect ,and honor forever.

Time and time again it is realized that these are only mere words to people that people use to gain particular things that they desire or value for temporary moments in time.

What usually happens is that those words translate into contradictory words and actions that actually mean

"I love you as long as you think and act the way I want you to think and act"

" I want to be around you as long as you do those things that make me happy",

"I love you as long as you're willing to give me what I want or need"

, also two of the all time favorites,

"I love you as long as you have what I want"

and " I love you as long as you're near me"

which means that if a problem or difficulty arises that takes you away temporarily, then it's **"out of sight ,out of mind".**

This explains why the average friendship, marriage, and relationship never last because those who have entered into these particular relations have known deep in their heart and their minds that they have only entered into these particular relations with certain conditions attached to it , although they may lead others to believe otherwise.

This conditional intent as well applies to the dysfunctions in the family structure because the love that is supposed to be there naturally isn't there, what is found in its place is something that's masquerading as love and most of the times usually ends up being very hurtful, disrespectful, disloyal, dishonest, and uncommitted to the ones they are saying that they love within these particular family structures.

Sadly, it always boils down to something else being more valuable than the one that is said to be loved and this particular love is always applied with conditions.

It's like "as long as you do what we want you to do we will love you", "as long as you behave within the confinements that we have set for you we will love you" or as long as you pattern your life after our lives, standards, and expectations then we will love you but when you fail to do so and choose to be different ,we can no longer love you".

These are some of the most hurtful and destructive characteristics displayed in many families all across the world in the Namc of Love.

Surprisingly, the conclusion is that most people who believe in love this way and demonstrate love this way actually find something wrong with the person that they demonstrated this particular perverted caricature of Love towards rather than finding something wrong with their application of what they considered to be love.

There is an ultimate truth when it comes to misunderstanding love and the dysfunctions that are produced from these misunderstandings and that ultimate truth actually involves another major element of the nature of real love.

Love acts unconditionally in a continuous flow towards the object of Love's Focus.

Loving someone and the facilitation of that love towards someone must always remain continuously and unconditionally regardless of what the object of our love does or thinks that is contrary to our particular expectations and standards.

Love is not blind , love is not ignorant ,love is not foolish but love exists and overcomes all of these particular things in its realest form.

Love doesn't mean that you have to accept anything from a family member that you disagree with.

What it does mean though when it comes to love and truly loving, if it is real, it will always outweigh that which is disliked about a particular family member and will come to exist even more stronger with the best of wishes and hopes for that particular family member as we love them enough to allow them to have to experience some things in life on their own that will teach them the lessons that mouths and words can't.

It may come as a surprise to many but even on their own, the love positions true family members to always make it known, "If you need us, we are always here with open arms".

Love doesn't prejudge no one because love knows that people must get their own experiences in life which means making their own mistakes but no human is ever beyond change or redemption and as long as a person lives, change is forever possible.

The Standard Communication Process: A Symbol Without Substance

---

It's a well voiced idea that communication is the key
to   solving   misunderstanding,   problems,   and
        many   other dysfunctions that plague Humanity's relations with each other.

That is true to a major limited extent and that is expressed as being so because when it comes to the human relations such as friendships, relationships, family, and marriage, what is more significant than just the communication process itself is the nature of the communication.

The substance of the communication, and the origins and nature of that substance to be instilled within the communication is the most determining element of it all.

When it comes to relationships and the presence of a dysfunction within it ,the first cliché that gets stated and repeated is "there's a breakdown in the communication process" but the hard hitting truth in that matter is that the reasons most relationships ,marriages friendships, and family structures fail is because there never was truly a real communication process established there from the beginning.

Therefore in reality, the thought or act of attempting to eliminate or heal the elements that are causing a breakdown in the communication process within the particular relation is more like trying to fix something that's never been there in the first place.

How can that be said and proven as a fact and truth? Quite easily.

Okay, from the very beginning of your relationship or relationship that evolved into marriage, what were the exact substances conveyed in the conversation between you and your socalled love interest? Was it not just simply favorite colors ,favorite foods, favorite movies, the revealing of each other's birthdays, each other's likes and dislikes, jokes, family background, each other's job status and job nature, what each wanted in life, fashion, Club, Church, each other's belief or disbelief in God and religion, the desire are not for children, what each other was looking for in a relationship, descriptions of each other's characters such as openminded, Reserved, spontaneous, and any other thing that the world considers major building blocks towards relationships and friendships ?

Next, after the relationship was established or made official and remained so for a few months or a year, what was the substance of the communication? Was it not just the usage of words and phrases that you'd heard(love, in love, etc.) but at no time did either you or your love interest define in your conversations what love actually was? Was it not the disclosure of what each other was feeling about certain situations or events in life that affected one in a good or negative way?

Lastly, at some point the relationship marriage or friendship reached a plateau beyond which it could not grow and began to feel stale.

There are a few exceptions of counseling being used as an attempt to fix the problems but it only seemed to work temporarily and then everything returned to the same stale Plateau of no growth. Sadly ,through all of this there has and will always be some few who keep experiencing the ever-present feeling that there is much more to a connection between two lovers than what one has been experiencing, there is much more to a friendship than what one has been experiencing, or much more to a family than what one has been experiencing.

The question that many have failed to ask is why didn't any of this work even with the communication process being active?

Some think and believe that the communication process wasn't functional because the other in the relationship or friendship wasn't very expressive of their thoughts or feelings beyond insignificant things.

Those kind of thoughts are conceived as if it explains the core reason for the failure of the relationship marriage or friendship as though the fault must be placed solely upon the other with no blame on oneself.   Once again it's stated:

" The Nature in which we approach a thing dictates the nature of the results received"

I know, truth sometimes hurts but when it does, it's always necessary to disengage you from something that you've invested a lot of sentimental and emotional value into that's not only not good to you but isnt good for you as well.

99.9% of the time the initial spark of interest in another for what one considers a love interest has nothing to do with love. Yes, that physical attraction again.

99.9% of the time we as human beings feel that we are loved only when we are paid attention to, held in someone's arms, giving valuable time, or bought things.

Sadly, this is best termed "The lapdog syndrome " where an individual's idea of love or of being loved is the exact actions that a lapdog craves and receives from its owner. Tender Caresses, treats (gifts), being held, quality time, being provided for (clothing, food, shelter), pedicures, paid hair treatment ,etc.

First of all contrary to what the world has taught you or influenced you to believe, the foundation for any communication process that you could ever attempt to establish between you and others actually begins within you between you and love .Yes that's right ! shocking is it not?

Actually, what people fail to realize even more about love is the fact that love can't exist within you without it suggesting and influencing some thoughts within you whose very purpose is to be released to others in conversation and communication.

What does that ultimately mean? It ultimately means there is no real or right communication without love being involved when it comes to our search for love in another.

Why? How? Because love as well brings its own language to the table of human experience that utilizes communication as a facilitator of what it has to teach and Implement in a continuous never ending flow within the minds of the ones under its influence.

A continuous process of communication that ignites thoughts, perceptions, and feelings within one that becomes naturally transmitted to the other, who in return receives those thoughts and allows them to interact with and connect with all that has become embedded within one's memory through experience ,where those deep thoughts originating from love engages and transforms old understandings from old experiences into new, better ,and rightful understandings.

Those rightful understandings about unlimited things are then in return released back (in the form of words) into the thinking of the original one who initiated the expressed thoughts.

Inevitably causing the originator of the expressed thoughts to receive a more elevated version of the thoughts that originated from them but were returned to produce growth.

This is just a general outline of love's communication process that causes a mutual catalyst of continuous growth, rejuvenation, and unification within the minds and hearts of those truly connected by love.

Within this communication process of love, the growth primarily involves the growth of the couple or groups of people connected by love but that unified growth is predicated upon the growth of the individual that it is receives through one's consciousness of love and the redefined experiences it affords the individual so that the benefits of it can be transferred and contributed by each individual into the whole of the connection or relationship with another or others.

When true love is involved between people, the magnitude of love's influence and power within the connection doesn't allow any thoughts or feelings that one is getting tired of the other's presence, the connection is getting old, or that one needs a break from the other.

Why? Or how is that possible? Because love never tires of the object of its focus. Every moment in the presence of the object of its focus is relished as a moment to directly connect with itself within the other person so much so until the other person could just be describing an experience with a fly on the wall and in the ears of the other, it will seem as the greatest expression ever formulated in the world.

Once again, it may be questioned as to why or how that is possible? Simply because of the fact that love redefines and transforms the process of communication into its highest and most significant purpose that produces the highest and most significant and meaningful results.

Love's Redefining and transformation of the communication process establishes communication as the most powerful conduit that facilitates the mutual exchange of pieces of one another's essence with the other or others involved until what is expressed actually becomes a part of the other and begins a continuous mental and soulful process of assimilation within each until each begins to mirror the other at the very core of who they are. Two minds and hearts in sync as one.

The communication process is by no means easy from the very beginning, it as everything else in life must evolve through stages of imperfections, mistakes, and difficulties.

It is love that pulls two or more hearts through those imperfections with love's primary Influenced thought and understanding that each imperfection and mistake made is to be overcome and accepted as necessary steps to equip the one's involved with the greatest tools of life, unbending faith and assurance that as long as the communication is what is, no problem in life will ever be able to approach and survive love's communication process that exists between them.

Infatuation's Delusional Position As Love

The origin of the word infatuation comes from a Latin word (Infatus) which means foolish desire or perception.

Frequently confused with love, infatuation is typified by a strong, fleeting desire that has its roots in idealization and fantasy rather than reality. This deluded mindset causes people to exaggerate and distort the actual existence of the thing or person it is focused upon which undermines relationships.

Infatuation is defined as a foolish desire because the motivating idea behind it is trifling in nature and has no real significance or purpose to it.

The only purpose behind infatuation always amounts to the desire to use ,possess or experience a person, place, or thing for the fulfillment of momentary happiness, sexual pleasure, recreational pursuits, or egotistical endeavors of control over a perceived inferior. Thus many prey upon people of the opposite sex with low self-esteem under the disguise of love.

Disillusionment ,dissatisfaction, and frustration arise when the infatuation fades and the gap widens drastically between the fantasy perception of the person and what the actual reality is concerning this person. When this becomes apparent and undeniable.

Conflicts, misunderstandings, and emotional distress are frequently the outcome of these irrational expectations. Therefore, sincere connection and mutual understanding—two prerequisites for a strong, long-lasting relationship—are compromised by the deluded condition of infatuation.

When you watch soap operas and romance movies or read romance novels and this becomes the blueprint from which you construct your understanding of love, then you are delusional and just infatuated with the idea of love or of being in love and not love itself.

Some are so caught if in their emotions of needing to be noticed by someone or needing to be wanted by someone until they're easily susceptible to the actions of infatuation from another because infatuation can and most times does mimic or project actions associated with caring, being kind, and considerate while in pursuit of its goals.

That is something that may be hard to accept but it needs to be accepted if you truly desire to begin the process of learning to know and understand what love truly is.

We as people need to also learn the difference between liking something and loving something.

The two seem so similar to most people until they're used interchangeably to express the idea of just simply enjoying something because of the happy feeling things bring us, but liking and loving present two totally different sets of feelings for two totally different reasons and purposes.

One is shallow, the other is at the very essence of things. One is a reaction to something external, the other is the basic foundation of all that is mentally and consciously internal.

CHAPTER 21

Locking The Trap : Exposing All Others As Fake

This stage is very important because this is where you begin to make any other in your target's eyes look fake where they begin to doubt the validity of past or present relationships to give them what they need by the fact of them not knowing or understanding what love is.

Do you truly know what love is? Is a very hard question for some to answer but then again it's easy for two kinds of people.

1.Those who actually know and understand the reality of love and

2. Those who foolishly rush to repeat clichés and other instant microwave statements they've either read or heard.

How does one tell the difference? Easily by the actions that reveal the decisions they've made in mind and heart that have no resemblance to right or fairness, some of love's main principles.

The fact of what is truly known or not known is also revealed by the longevity of the things they're parroting but have no experience of.

How so ? because at a short period after the repeating runs out, thus the true substance of (not knowing) will stand revealed where they can't think or relay anything of fact or reality outside of the boundaries of those parroted clichés and statements.

The actions that reveal the fact that one doesn't know is shown in their decisions to continuously look for love according standards and methods that have nothing to do with love or actually producing love.

Revealing actions that demonstrate one considering and choosing others who are no more suitable for love than a bucket of gas is for putting out a raging house fire.

Contrary to the experts and those disguised as knowing love, no amount of loving from one can ever impart a value or need for love into another nor impart a knowledge of love into another.

Why? because love is initially a personal realization that one has to become conscious of themselves through a narrow path of personal experience that teaches and redevelops that one according to the internalized lessons of right attitude, right thinking, right intentions, and right actions becoming solidified into the very heart of who they are until those principles of right are so well grounded in them until the demonstration of them are easily manifested consistently without a minor feeling of a want or need to deter, thereby love is finally awakened.

There are many who will disagree but disagree without one solid base to stand upon. Just a personal feelings and assumptions born out of a want to have love and anything else of true significant value and importance to come easy and in submission to petty human desires to have things instant, without a process, without a requirement of patience & humility, without rules of order that they can't circumvent or manipulate, and the petty human desire & exaggerated egotistical motive to recognize nothing or no one as the ultimate director and controller of that which they want, not even God, The Creator, or Supreme being.

Lastly, the main thing that reveals one as not knowing what love is, is when one is questioned about love and they proceed to define love as existing in one singular (one size fits all things) theoretical way, when in fact, the only way to even begin to answer the question, is actually with another question that in and of itself is the only thing that can give clarity and a point of direction in which to answer appropriately, that question is ...." What degree of love's expressive nature, function, and context are you asking about?

How so? because love isn't just love. There are multiple dimensions of expression (points of meaning, acting & revealing) that love operates from and each has a specific context in which it applies and emanates from.

The context is where many run into problems because they try to apply one context of love to situations that deal with another context like the way people call themselves loving pets or vehicles.

It's no joke because the majority of the world's people only feel loved or feel like they're loving others when there exists the acts of taking care of them, spending time with them, feeding them, taking them places, considering their wants, and buying them things to make them look better, or when the acts of caressing and holding are present.

The idea of verbal expressions of the love within someone in communication has to take the backseat to the actions even though the consistent and constant verbal expressions of the deeper feelings and perceptions of love that exist in one for them is a rare phenomenon in the world that they've never had or experienced.

There is an even more decisive element that reveals who knows and who doesn't know what love is.

When one truly knows and understands what love is, in a loveless world full of loveless people and loveless situations stemming from those people, those that truly know and understand, either find themselves alone and without a love interest or find themselves moving outward and away from the ones that are only pretending to be capable of loving.

How is that possible? because when love is awakened or already active within self for self, love equips one not only with the necessary inner definition and inner depth of thinking that allows one to approach or be approached, engage, and then analyze any particular person at the very core of who they are with the right questions that are so penetrative until it allows them to be able to rightly determine the extent to which love is either already awakened or still dormant and inactive within a person.

This is how the active presence of love provides one with a precise method of thinking and reacting that helps avoid the unnecessary negative and hurtful situations that another person may pose in regards to a relationship or friendship.

In human relationships, the authentic nature of our interactions can significantly impact the quality and depth of our connections. Yet, people often find themselves pretending to know or understand the central essence of their relationships, often influenced by societal expectations, cultural norms, or personal insecurities.

Pretending in Romantic Relationships

Romantic relationships often originate with a set of assumptions about love, roles, and behaviors, most of which are influenced heavily or predominately by academic assumptions, internet portrayals, television portrayals, cultural traditions, and norms of society.

People may pretend to understand the dynamics of love, thus leading to miscommunication , misunderstandings, and unfulfilled expectations.

1. Assumptions about Love & Its Origins.

Most people in the world base their knowledge and understanding of love on observed portrayals in movies, books, and social media. These sources often promote an exaggerated view of love, thus leading individuals to form unrealistic expectations and unrealistic methods to acquire those unrealistic expectations.

2. Consequences Of Pretending in Romantic Relationships

Pretending to understand the dynamics of love can create a superficial connection, where partners are not fully honest about their true intentions and feelings. This most times leads to frustration, resentment, confusion and the inevitable natural demise of a superficial and unrealistic connection.

3. Examples

Consider a couple where one partner believes that extravagant romantic actions are necessary for expressing love, while the other values everyday acts of just spending time together. If both pretend to adhere to the other's expectations without communicating their true stance , the relationship dwindles and ends.

Pretending to Know & Understand Love In Family Structure Dynamics

---

Family structures are often governed by unspoken rules and expectations based upon assumptions about love and how to apply what is assumed.

Family members may pretend to understand or pretend to be genuinely committed to their roles and responsibilities while situations occur that reveal otherwise ,leading to strained relationships, uncaring words and actions, and sometimes disrespectful words and actions.

1. Family Expectations :The Pressure to Conform to Something One Doesn't Truly Value

In many families, there is an expectation to adhere to certain roles, such as the dutiful parent , the supportive sibling, or the authoritative parent. These roles can be based on cultural norms, family traditions, or personal expectations.

2. Examples of Pretending to know and Understand Love in the Family Structure

For instance, a parent might pretend to be interested in the children's activities to meet their children's expectations but the parent's actions show a bare minimum of interest because of secretly harboring other aspirations. This pretense can lead to frustration and a lack of fulfillment in a family structure.

Example:

When family members pretend to know and understand what love is, it can lead to misunderstandings and a lack of true connection.

This can exaggerate family bonds and create a sense of fakeness that forces the genuine at heart family members to separate themselves from those family members who generate the fakeness or this can foster a family environment where no word is perceived as dependable and nobody is perceived as dependable or caring in the situations where a family member needs another family member the most.

That is another element within the origins of gangs in society that society refuses to acknowledge as their fault.

Most dysfunctional families are dysfunctional for various reasons that originate from simple misplaced attitudes :

1. Grown ups who think and feel that a parents love doesn't mean having to listen to the children or that the children are their robots or some human A.I android figure to be programmed and regarded as possessing no thoughts or feelings that matter.

2. Children (especially teenagers) who always think they're grown before their time and are always in disagreement and at odds with rules of the house and punishment.

The parents or guardians of such children are most times only at fault when they misperceive their love as requiring them to force children into submission by any means.

This type of response is a result of a misplaced attitude that they know what's best for them better than they do which is always true but necessitating a different method.

Love in this family context isn't always about enforcement , its more so about loving this type of child or children enough to realize and remember what it was like to be that age and just because the grownup's parent or parents methods worked with them , it doesn't mean that method is appropriate for a new generational child or children.

Sometimes even though the grown up feels they love this type of conflicting child or children , love in its most simplistic and realest terms dictates that you have to allow the child or children to experience the harsh and cruel consequences of their own disobedience that the world will inevitably bring upon them.

That's not saying to abandon them or restrict them from your care and concern but in dire situations as that, the best way to implement that care and concern is with unconditional positive advice and encouragement.

A major lesson has to be learned that the grown up can't learn for the disobedient children.

That lesson is, The main and most significant difference between grown ups and children is experience and the knowledge and understanding of things that can only come by experience.

1. What basically will work and what won't work

2. What thoughts and actions are more prone to lead to positive results and which one's more prone to lead to trouble, harm, or dissatisfaction

3. The full and complete extent of the dangers and dangerous people that await outside of the child's or children's bedroom, school environment, and neighborhood.

4. The main reason why some children excel in life more easily and less complicated than others even though they have the same or similar intelligence.

    That determining factor being that the easily excelled listen to and incorporate the benefits of their parent's guidance and its knowledge, understanding, and experience into their thoughts and decisions so that they're prepared to confidently and efficiently approach and overcome life's difficulties and problems with ease based upon what their parent or parents taught them and their trust in their parents guidance as the best course of thought and action in order to achieve success more so than their own limited, inexperienced, and incomplete ideas and perceptions about life.

To watch a child of yours make mistakes that are thoughtless and sometimes dangerous will never be easy or comfortable and do so is never unloving or heartless, it's a decision born out wisdom that knows that no amount of talk, fussing, or punishment will detour a conflicting and disobedient child from running their head into a wall that they're determined to challenge with a stubborn head.

A lot of parents and family members just give up on other family members who at some point are rebellious, criminal minded, promiscuous, or stubborn and many there are who have changed for the better and became successful from even the most lowest of positions in life like jail or prison.

That is a lesson in itself, Love never prejudges anyone because all have the potential to change in time and the length of how long it takes isn't up to another, the only choice that reak love naturally influences them make is to be an unconditionally loving support with an undying faith in that family member's ability to change.

Not many family are capable of learning that lesson because they didn't possess any real love to give in the first place.

Such unloving family relations should never be a hindrance or discouragement , it should be rather a motivation to stand on one's on two feet ,to succeed in spite of the unloving family relation , and to become greater by being all that they were not to another who was or is in that same position or another who just simply needs someone to be there as that dependable element they've never had but always desperately needed.

Pretending To Know & Understand Love In Friendships

Friendships are often said by the experts to be built on shared interests and mutual ideals without a single mention of love.

However, it is the superficial expectations of love and assumptions about love that lead to false pretenses eroding the condition of these friendships that were doomed to fail from their very beginning because they lacked any real substance of love but were rather based upon temporary principles of thought and action.

Society often influences the idea or standard of how friendships should   look and operate while society (government, religious congregations ,social groups etc.) itself shows in everyday dealings that they only consider friendships to be situations of benefit or compliance which leads the normal average individuals to assume they know what a friendship is composed of based upon that standard of the world.

This usually includes being constantly available, open to persuasion and manipulation, or engaging in certain activities under false pretenses.

These type of friendships are always superficial and based upon things of no real significance or importance such as a mutual enjoyment for gossip, drinking or using intoxicants, going to clubs, etc.

The Effects Of Pretending That One Knows & Understands Love In Friendships

---

When friends pretend to know and understand things that are important to others , it can erode trust.

Being authentic is crucial for building loyalty, a deep, meaningful, and lasting connection that only love can provide.

Psychological & Emotional Effects Of Pretending To Know & Understand Things We don't

---

Pretending to understand or know certain things that one does not can and will create stress upon an individual's mental health and emotional well-being.

The constant effort to maintain a lie can lead to stress, anxiety, and a feeling of inadequacy. An individual may struggle with their self-worth and experience a wide range of emotional fatigue.

The Emotional Ramifications Of Pretending To Know & Understand Something

---

Pretending to know and understand something can create an emotional burden. Individuals may feel isolated, vulnerable, misunderstood, and unable to be their true selves.

The Role Of Society Norms In Facilitating False Assumptions

1. Social norms often attempt to dictate how people think, feel, and act as well as define how relations should be, thus leading or pressuring individuals to conform to these standards even if they do not coincide with their true selves.

This perpetuates a cycle of false pretenses and blocks any possibility of any genuine human relations.

The assuming and false pretense dilemma about love as well rests at the heart of the dysfunction called racism.

There is a very significant perception that most people in the world have about love that stems from ignorance and selfishness.

The belief that we as individuals can define and direct our love in any way that best suits us as individuals and places everything beyond our individuality as a nonessential to love.

One of the most significant things that a lot of people have failed to pay attention to is the fact that even when you look at all of the major religions of the world and even the smaller offshoot branches of religion, none of their religious scriptures ever actually define love in any definitive terms or details, its either in superficial ways that describe what love produces or just the mention of love but never the exact definition of what love is in and of itself.

There is one particular verse " God is Love" that many focus upon as if thinking " oh yeah, that's the definition of love" while truly missing the universality of the statement that applies to all things.

Unknowingly, according to the specific principle contexts of all things' creation and the nature of their design, there are and always will be natural dictates that certain prerequisites be present before one can even approach and begin to possess a minute understanding of love, God, and the specific predetermined aims , directions , purposes and functions therein that each naturally influences within things when the things are existing in their natural context rather than the contexts shaped, fashioned, and directed by modern man.

This may be becoming a little complicated to some, more complicated than what some have imagined or expected but in reality that complicated feeling or perception isn't really about the content that is being expressed or about to be expressed, the feeling or perception that something is being made complicated actually derives from a simplistic mindstate that most of the world have been influenced to have and act from thereby creating a mental, emotional, spiritual and behavioral box of confinement.

A confinement that keeps one in a perpetual self-inflicted shallow consciousness that not only believes that all things are simple without a deeper meaning, significance, or understanding but as well a consciousness that only seeks that which seems simplistic.

Why? in order to avoid having to do the one thing that actually determines positions and conditions of living. Simply thinking, analyzing, and measuring things for one's self beyond the immediate appearance.

Sadly, it is the surface thinkers where most assumptions are easily accepted and transmitted into their dealings with others, thus the exact reason why dysfunctions are so widely spread in the world. Most of the time people don't even think about the fact of whether or not there could be some serious consequences attached to the decisions we make.

We as people naturally think it's okay to approach and deal with things with very little or no knowledge and understanding at all about what we're preparing to engage.

Why? Because of the belief that as long as we're sincere, everything will turn out fine. In truth there's nothing as worse and dangerous than sincere ignorance because even though damage or hurt may be produced within what we're dealing with, there's an underlying idea that things can be fixed or changed in time if we only have faith or as long as we continue doing our best.

Contexts of Existence

This next phase will deal with those different contexts that factually go against the grain of everything that has been ever taught for the last 3000 plus years

When it comes to anything in existence even deception there exists an underlying principle called (context) that must be considered in order to fully analyze and understand anything. The more you understand it, the more effective an analysis and method will be.

Whether you believe in a God, Supreme Being, Creator etc. or not. Each particular creation has its own particular nature as when it comes to that which we know as male and female.

According to the principles of the perception about individualized love, the particular individuals always perceive love as originating from one's own individual self and basically applying predominantly and exclusively to one's own individual self. The defining point in that matter is, if you do not know and understand the exact totality of what individual self is composed of and you only have a fraction of it ,then you're only going to be able to understand and demonstrate who you are in a limited partial capacity.

The direct consequential effect of a partial function is the drastic altering and rearranging of a natural process such as Malefemale relationships and family structures into that which is unnatural, defective, and counterproductive.

When it comes to a context being applied to anything or something existing within a context, it simply means the analysis of a thing with numerous surrounding factors involved like environment, habits, and natural inclinations to arrive at a more precise and more complete understanding of a thing.

Simple analogies are :

1. **If someone wanted to know or understand something about a specific high speed automobile then, the request would be for information on an automobile within the context of a Ferrari.**

2. **If someone wanted to truly know, understand, and experience the true nature and natural function of a lion, they wouldn't go to a zoo, why because a lion in a zoo is positioned in an unnatural environment of a caged confinement which is a context.**

To see a lion's natural function and nature in action, it would have to be in the context of its natural unconfined habitat or environment in Africa.

CHAPTER 22

Know Her Better Than She Knows Herself

In any case, the female should never be underrated or underestimated for 2 good and quality reasons.

The Apex Female

There's not only such a thing as an Apex male who naturally possesses the superior characteristics to stand out and perform mentally and physically above the average male but as well stands capable of matching or excelling the above average Male in the mental realm. Although other males develop by experience into the same Apex category but there is well an apex caliber of female who naturally excels above and beyond the average female with a true sense of self realization and awareness of the power she holds to persuade influence and dominate males not by sexual appeal but by the primary dynamics of her mind and natural propensities toward the foundation of thinking and analyzation.

The Apex female doesn't just influence and maneuver the average male by her mental faculties because there exists a dual aspect of the Apex female spectrum where another type persuades influences and maneuvers the average and above average male through her power of provocative sexual appeal that can ,will ,and does take advantage of the males natural propensity towards the physical and material side of human nature of which sexuality reigns supreme as the ultimate fulfillment of physical desires. Then there is such a thing as the top tier of Apex females that possesses both mental and sexual dominating qualities. The female thus by no means is weak or to be underestimated. In her case underestimation works in her favor and to her advantage in dealing with the male.

Seduction, in its most calculated and strategic form, relies on a deep understanding of human psychology. When it comes to seducing a woman, deception is to be understood here not as blatant dishonesty but as the art of presenting oneself in a certain way that can be a powerful tool. To truly seduce a woman, one must understand the essence of what a woman's heart revolves around: love. Not just the surface notion of love, but a nuanced understanding of the emotions and ideals that underpin it. This knowledge, when harnessed correctly, can create a profound connection that is difficult to resist. However, in this process, there is a key to success, to knowing her better than she knows herself.

The principle of seduction lies not merely in appearance or charm, but in creating the illusion of difference. For many women, the concept of love is both a mystery and a yearning. It's the very force that governs much of their emotional world. To succeed in the art of seduction, one must not only know how to talk about love but must also present it in a way that is distinctly different from how other men have presented it. This difference becomes the bait, a well-crafted lure that draws her in. But more than just words, seduction involves the ability to tap into the depths of her emotional experience and bring to the surface desires and curiosities she may not have even realized she had.

The cornerstone of this approach is to make her feel understood. This involves not only grasping the abstract idea of love but understanding the specific way she experiences love. Every woman, influenced by her past relationships and life experiences, has a unique emotional map. A man who can decode this map and also who can intuitively sense the highs and lows, the wants and fears is a man that can position himself as different. He becomes not just another suitor, but someone who "gets it," who knows love on a deeper, more profound level. This ability to decode her emotional landscape gives him the upper hand in presenting himself as someone who knows her better than she knows herself.

To lay this groundwork, certain questions can act as powerful tools. Asking a woman, "Has any man ever sat you down and talked to you about love?" or "Has any man ever allowed you to hear and experience love from his heart?" is to place her in a reflective state, one that causes her to reevaluate her past relationships. These questions create a sense of contrast. They plant a seed of doubt about any other man in her life, both past and present. The moment she begins comparing, wondering whether she has truly experienced a love like the one you are offering, she becomes intrigued. This curiosity is the first sign that the bait has been taken.

In many instances, these kinds of deep, probing questions are absent in her previous romantic experiences. Most men fail to ask such personal, introspective questions, preferring instead to focus on surface-level charm or physical attraction. This is where the key principle of deception enters. The goal is to present oneself as someone who is different ,not just in appearance or demeanor, but in how one understands and expresses love. Through your words, you must paint a picture of love that is foreign yet enticing, something she has never quite experienced before. This love should not be framed in generic terms, but in personal, intimate language that suggests a depth of emotion that goes beyond what she has heard from any other man.

Furthermore, the seducer must exhibit patience. Love, or the perception of love, is not something that can be rushed. Once the bait has been taken, once she begins to wonder whether you are different from other men, you must allow these thoughts to sink in. Patience is key because the woman must internalize this contrast for it to become effective. Rushing her would only result in resistance, as she would perceive the seduction as manipulative rather than genuine. By allowing her the time to reflect, the seducer ensures that the seed of doubt grows. The more she questions the depth and authenticity of her current relationship or her past experiences with men, the more she becomes drawn to the new possibility you represent.

In this process, the seducer is not only working to appeal to her rational mind but her emotional core. By presenting love in a new way, he stirs up feelings of excitement, curiosity, and even vulnerability. These emotions create a powerful cocktail that can lead to an almost irresistible attraction. She is not simply responding to the man's words, but to the emotions they evoke. By crafting an explanation of love that feels personal and unique, the man creates the illusion that he alone possesses the key to her emotional fulfillment.

But this seduction technique also relies heavily on projecting one's self as genuine or at least the appearance of it. The man must not only communicate a unique view of love, but he must also embody it. His actions, tone, and demeanor must align with the words he speaks. If there is the slightest disconnect between his message and his behavior, the deception falls apart, and the illusion is shattered. Genuineness in seduction does not necessarily mean sincerity; it means consistency. The words and actions must create a cohesive image, one that she finds compelling and trustworthy.

The principle of laying the bait and allowing it to sink deeper is perhaps the most critical aspect of this process. The seducer's role is to create doubt—doubt about the other men in her life, doubt about her understanding of love, and even doubt about whether she has ever truly experienced love. Once this doubt takes hold, it paves the way for the seducer to offer himself as the answer. He becomes the man who can provide the love she has been missing, who can fill the emotional voids left by previous relationships.

In the end, to seduce a woman successfully, one must engage with her at the deepest emotional level. It's not about flattery or shallow compliments, but about understanding the very essence of what her heart desires: love. By positioning oneself as different from other men and presenting a unique, thoughtful perspective on love, the seducer can create an attraction based not just on physical appearance but on emotional resonance. Through patience and a calculated approach, he can deepen this attraction, allowing the woman to feel that he knows her better than she knows herself. And in doing so, he becomes irresistible.

The emotional intensity of a female is a core characteristic of her nature, one that often surpasses the emotional spectrum of the male. Women, by virtue of their biological nature and societal roles, tend to experience emotions more deeply and express them more openly. This emotional intensity manifests particularly in the realm of love, where a "real" woman often goes to great lengths to demonstrate her affection and commitment. Her emotions fuel her actions, driving her to nurture, protect, and sacrifice for the people she cares about. Her love is not merely a fleeting feeling but an allencompassing force that pushes her beyond herself.

Take for example these bold and unflinching actions of females that you have rarely heard being done by a male for the one he loves :

A young woman who said she was chartering a helicopter to go sightseeing drew a gun on the pilot and forced him to land in the yard of a state prison near here today. Three inmates scrambled aboard and were flown to freedom.
As they boarded the helicopter, a prison guard tried to pull them off and was shot in the lower jaw. State and Federal lawenforcement officers began scouring the South Carolina and nearby Georgia countryside. One of the convicts is a convicted murderer.

After leaving the prison yard, the pilot was ordered to land in a hayfield about five miles north. Jerry Green, the helicopter pilot, was released unharmed. The convicts and the woman fled in a blue car. Guard Undergoes Surgery Hal Leslie, a spokesman for the State Department of Corrections, said guards at the prison, the Perry Correctional Institute, fired pistols and a shotgun at the ascending helicopter but apparently did not hit it. The prison, one of the state's four high-security prisons, is in rural Greenville County, about 10 miles south of Greenville. The $11.8 million prison, opened in 1981, has a population of about 1,150, twice its capacity of 576 inmates.

Faith Readus, 39, of Nashville, Tennessee was sentenced on September 13,2013, to serve 60 months in prison followed by three years' supervised release, for her part in a plan to obtain and use a helicopter to break a federal prisoner out of Nashville's Criminal Justice Center, announced David Rivera, Acting U.S. Attorney for the Middle District of Tennessee.

Michel Vaujour was a man who had things to do. Not *nice* things, maybe, but certainly things which were impeded by the fact that in 1985, he was convicted of bank robbery and attempted murder and sentenced to 18 years in prison. He wasn't overly concerned with that, though....before he was even convicted, he'd already been planning his escape.

THE COUNTERPART

Every good prison break needs an outside associate, and Vaujour had one ready and waiting: his wife, Nadine. Nadine, for her part, wasn't afraid to roll up her sleeves and get in on the action. As soon as Vaujour was arrested, she began taking classes to obtain her license as a helicopter pilot. With that in hand, in the months leading up to the event she became a regular customer of a helicopter rental company in southern Paris. The owner of the company noted that she showed up twice a month like clockwork, sometimes with a friend and sometimes alone. Renting a helicopter at the time cost roughly 2,200 francs ($315) per hour, and Nadine exclusively paid in cash....in retrospect, a glaring red flag which the owner managed to steadfastly ignore for more than five months.

THE ESCAPE

At approximately 10:30 a.m. on May 26, 1986, a helicopter flew low over central Paris. Nadine Vaujour ignored a hail of radio warnings and brought the machine to a hovering stop over the roof of one of the prison buildings. The warnings over the guards' radios of a helicopter on the roof were eclipsed by a far more intense situation developing inside the walls, and eventually Vaujour and

Hernandez emerged from an access door and jogged unchallenged across the roof.

In contrast, there exists a certain type of woman for whom love does not hold the same significance. These women are often characterized by emotional detachment, a lack of loyalty, and a selfabsorbed nature. Their inability or unwillingness to connect with the emotional essence of femininity can make them appear coldblooded or indifferent. Unlike emotionally intense women who seek deep emotional bonds, these individuals may prioritize personal gain, status, or surface-level gratification over meaningful relationships. They lack the emotional depth that drives a "real" woman to demonstrate her love in profound ways.

Ultimately, this emotional detachment can be a vulnerability. One way to subtly expose the cold-blooded woman's lack of femininity is through subtle attacks on her emotional disconnection. By emphasizing the emotional richness of true womanhood, one can spotlight the gap between the emotionally detached woman and those who embody genuine femininity. The cold-blooded woman, being disconnected from this essential aspect of female nature, may not recognize her own deficiency until it is subtly pointed out. These women can be deceived by appealing to their insecurity about their lack of emotional depth, subtly making them aware of the emptiness in their detachment from their feminine emotions.

Thus, while some women may seem detached or indifferent, this emotional detachment can serve as a point of weakness. A true, emotionally rich woman demonstrates her love with intensity, loyalty, and care, while those lacking this depth remain trapped in self-absorption, vulnerable to the realization of their emotional inadequacies.

This emotional detachment is viewed by these types of women as a shield or wall but in reality it's welcome mat for deception to turn it all into her own disadvantage.

The principle of femininity, often associated with qualities such as nurturing, creation, and balance, can be observed and validated consistently throughout nature and the universe.

This principle of femininity is not limited to the human or animal species but transcends into an illimitable array of natural processes, biological systems, and even phenomena of the universe's very fabric of existence.

By analyzing these aspects, we can gain a deeper understanding of how femininity permeates the fabric of existence itself everywhere.

In nature, femininity is prominently displayed and showcased in the reproductive processes of most living organisms.

Female organisms are often an unequivocal component essential to the process of creation, the of nurturing new life , and the natural systems that facilitate them all.

Example :

In many species, the female's role in childbirth is critical. This process is not only a significant biological function but also a principal nurturing act, where mothers provide care, protection, and sustenance to their babies.

This maternal principle of instinct ensures the survival and continuation of species, emphasizing the importance and high necessity of feminine principles in the natural world.

Beyond the scope of individual organisms, ecosystems also exhibit feminine qualities through their innate balance and interdependence. Ecosystems thrive on cooperation and the delicate equilibrium between various species and their environments.

That balance is a direct image of and intricate sister of the nurturing and harmonious aspects of femininity.

Example :

The delicate but highly efficient symbiotic relationships between pollinators and plant life such as bees, demonstrate a mutual nurturing that structuralizes , supports , and ensures the health and vitality of entire ecosystems.

Those highly organized interactions are essential to the reproduction of plants and the survival of pollinating species. That is a demonstration of the pervasive power and influence of feminine principles in nature's interconnected spectrum of life.

In the sphere of plants, femininity can be observed in the reproductive structures and processes that sustain life across numerous spheres of life for plants and humans alike.

Although plants possess both male and female reproductive organs, it is often the female part, the ovary, that develops into fruit thus providing new seeds for the next generation of its kind.

This cycle of growth, reproduction, and nurturing new life not only mirrors the human so-called female but is actually directly connected and aligned with her through that feminine principle of energy so that none has ever equalled the so-called female in not only growing plant life but also understanding every use of plant life for medicines and vitamins until so- called female was most equipped to be the original doctors of the ancient world.

That amongst other understandings of the ancients is why the question of the so-called female's equality was never in doubt or up for a vote and why the penalty was unquestionably death for disrespecting the so-called female.

The principle of femininity extends vastly beyond even all of that into geological and scales of the universe. The Earth itself is often personified as a nurturing mother, providing resources, sustenance, and shelter to all forms of life.

That view is validated in various cultural mythologies and scientific understandings of the Earth as a self-regulating system, often referred to as the Gaia hypothesis. This concept suggests that the Earth functions as a single organism, with its various components working in harmony to maintain the conditions necessary for life, exactly like a mother tending to her offspring.

On a larger and more powerful scale, the universe exhibits feminine principles throughout the processes of creation and destruction that drive its development. Stars, often referred to as the "nurseries" of the universe, play a crucial role in the creation of elements and the formation of planets and galaxies.

The very birth of stars themselves from clouds of gas and dust, their life cycles, and eventual demise in supernovas contribute to the ongoing creation and transformation of the universe.

That continuous cycle of creation, nurturing, and renewal is a reflection of the feminine principles at the deepest and most powerful level of any scale of measurement.

Furthermore, the existence of dark matter and dark energy in the universe can be directly linked to feminine principles.

Those mysterious but real and largely unseen forces are thought to constitute the majority of the universe's mass and energy, governing the structure and expansion of the universe.

The nurturing and guiding roles designated specifically to dark matter and dark energy resonate with the unseen but pervasive influence primarily equated with femininity.

In conclusion, the principle of femininity is so intricately embedded into the fabric of nature and the universe.

From the reproductive processes of individual organisms to the balance and interdependence of ecosystems, and from the nurturing Earth to the cycles of the universe and the process of creation, femininity plays a crucial and Unequalled part in the perpetuation and harmony of life.

The most hidden truth in her regard is the fullness of the socalled female's identity and power that connects the so-called female to the Unequalled feminine energy throughout the universe and directly from The Creator of whom she is a direct part of.

Understanding these principles of Unequalled power and influence should not only escalate and solidify our appreciation of femininity's profound universal impact and significance beyond cultural and human contexts but it should as well cause a redefining of how we perceive and approach the so-called female.

Throughout all that has been expressed and validated by the natural and principal workings of femininity in nature and the universe, a pattern developed that showed us Numerous (but not all) principles of femininity that are in of themselves prerequisites to any family, community ,society, government, and civilization that is to be just, nurturing, and positive.

Undeniably, what was also shown and validated was one central theme if the feminine nature's natural and unequivocal propensity to produce, sustain, and advance the core of all primary systems.

So it should no longer be a mystery why or how the feminine nature excels at mathematics and the principle dynamics of science more so than the masculine essence.

How could anyone ever degrade , disrespect, and devalue one such as her unless they're truly sociopathic and barbaric by nature and from cultural proclivities that reflect the same nature?

Until relationships are realized, known, and understood in their proper context and nature as a natural system based upon the feminine and masculine essences being in their proper positions and contexts in relations to their individual selves and each other, the dysfunctions will continue.

Most females and males perceive relationships as genies in a bottle that just pop up naturally as expected or desired and perform according to a natural pattern by its own accord . As if no right knowledge of the process is required on order to produce and main the results.

To the average female in current times and even in the past times being female mint and basically means today simply having children, relationships with men ,laying on your back having sex ,flirting ,being sexy ,and that is about the extent of it.

There is the predominant thought that being female is all about the moment, all about the era in which one lives, all about the activities that one experiences as an individual female while the individual female lives.

Never realizing that the feminine aspect is more about that which is transmitted into the later generations of the female.

Just because you no longer are able to have children does not nullify the continuance or activation of you being female on another level.

It just means that you can no longer demonstrate the principles of your femininity on one level and that is meant to be so by nature but that doesn't nullify the existence of other levels and other responsibilities that one's femininity dictates.

In the ancient times of news numerous civilizations of old there was the existence of teachings and schools by females that was passed down from female to female so much so until in some civilizations such as Egypt and Sumerian there was particular schools that was specifically for the female so that the principles of femininity could easily could be taught, implemented ,and passed to later female generations.

This was a particular established systematic continuation of the proper demonstration and expression of the proper feminine principles of power from one feminine generation to the next.

Within that system, the females even had their own language called : **Eme - Sal** dialect.

What does that mean ? It means that grandmotherhood has duties and obligations of femininity to their Children that birthed their grandchildren and to the female grandchildren to help reinforce and advance the feminine principles according to their frightful nature.

This idea makes the average female cringe with dislike and disagreement because grandmotherhood is their retirement plan. Why ? How could any female feel that way ? Because of a lack of true love and appreciation for their Feminine nature.

Within the context of Male/Female relationships, each gender is analyzed according to the ancient origins of each and the original positions , functions, and natures that was originally applied to each as well as demonstrated by each.

This is an area that has historically been intentionally mislabeled as myths by a world that wanted to supplant these histories with its own distorted and deceptive stories and histories about the origin of things.

So-called histories like Adam and Eve that was borrowed from their very own histories and has all the elements that are said to define something as a myth but can't and won't consider it as a baseless myth even though it exists with no historical or archeological ties to any ancient times it claims to describe.

Is that false or a lie? Is that the sign of a uncover Bible hater ?

No, it's the sign and most powerful indication of an extreme history lover and researcher who studies ALL histories from ALL races of people without one natural bias or prejudgment.

The fact remains that the book of Genesis or Bara' sit in Hebrew, has records about itself and the time in which it was first documented, catalogued, and made to be scripture and its not only not ancient at all but also there's no original ancient manuscript scrolls or pieces of a ancient scroll for it from the time period that

Genesis describes. There is only pieces of scrolls specifically dated from the time in which Yeshua (Jesus) supposedly lived.

The Dead Sea Scrolls aren't even ancient scrolls. They're also from the time period in which Yeshua (Jesus) supposedly lived.

Why is this significant? To defend the only real histories that are ancient enough to give someone the original natures, functions , and relationships of Male and female so that the original dynamics can realized and used as measuring principle to understand the root origins and causes of the dysfunctions.

Context significantly impacts our understanding of gender,.

It is the lack of such that has ensured a continuance and reinforcing of intentional misleading misinterpretations.

It is the current cultural, social, and educational factors who derive their base and standards of measurement and definition from Eurocentric influences that continue to transmit misperceptions and deceit about Male/ Female natures, roles and their proper relationships.

Without considering these contexts, one might misunderstand the nature, function, and purpose of gender, reinforcing stereotypes and biases that distort the complexities of male-female interaction.

Those particular relations were meant to incorporate each of the female and male essences within their natural respective positions and roles of thought, feeling, and identity as equal contributors to the relations in which humans would interact but according to the nature of each.

When it comes to the very basis of life itself, human life, or even other things in the universe. There is always a natural context attached to it that facilitates the way such things will behave and function in continuous cycles, a natural environment it will exist within, specific acts it will perform , and certain actions it produces to naturally align it with other things it is meant to be connected to in order to produce other elements within a system of nature or the universe. The human being is no different or exempt from such principles of existence.

Most people have a limited knowledge therefore limited understanding of the historical precedents of love and how it was originally defincd, demonstrated, facilitated and maintained.

Unknowingly to the mass majority of the world, when it came to ancient civilizations and the particular knowledge that they possessed in reference to the human being.

Within the very languages that connected them, there was always a feminine and masculine element attached to the very words and physical objects that they utilized and interacted with. Such words as earth, wind , spirit, energy, sound, and even the life force and the mind itself are all feminine since it was considered spirit and energy.

(Source: Ancient Hebrew language Encyclopedia)

How are these things relevant to love? Because it gives one a more precise knowledge and understanding of not only what love is but also gives one the precise knowledge and understanding of how love was facilitated and the understanding of the differences in human relations when these contexts are acknowledged and implemented.

It is a well-worn out cliché that says "one must love self first before being able to love others". But if you do not know or understand what the individual self actually is composed of, then it can be said that you do not even know how to begin to love oneself.

Any person's given name is not that particular person's actual identity.

Each human it's going to be either female or male first. Each female or male is not the original first female or male so this dictates that no modern Male or female can define themselves and their very nature according to their own definitions and be right.

If one looks and studies into the ancient civilizations like the Sumerian, Egyptian ,and the Indus Valley Civilizations, one would readily see an acute difference in the cultural norms from those of modern times.

Cultural differences involving what is termed male and female and these particular differences were the defining points that actually allowed these civilizations to have better quality and better positioned relations without all of the dysfunctions that are now experienced in the modern world for the last past three to four thousand years.

Ultimately the questions are what did these particular civilizations and people know and understand that modern people don't know and understand? How does that show and prove a significant difference?

What those particular civilizations in history show even in the before mentioned languages and perceptions is a true, positive, effective, and efficient relation between the so-called female and male.

Within these civilizations is the exact nature of the particular male and female and how these particular elements were not just existing as what we know as male and female but were distributed all throughout nature on various levels that were highly significant in the overall functioning of all living and material things.

When it comes to those particular elements or essences that are considered male and female, these are modern terms that has been placed upon these particular essences by men in history with the ulterior motive of hiding and also redefining the knowledge of the female's true identity so that an exclusive male dominance paradigm could come into existence.

A new Masculine paradigm where the being mislabeled as female ,would become repositioned from a state of equality into a position of inferiority and under control, thus the creation of an imbalance and dysfunction within the Male-female relationships and the family structure.

How so? Because in all of the major ancient languages that which is known as female was considered to be an feminine energy and power that was different but never inferior to that which is considered to be the masculine energy or male existence.

If you look at words in the Hebrew language such as the act and power of creation, it is a feminine energy and power. Also if you look at the word "love" in Hebrew and Sumerian and other ancient languages the word love is always feminine. This is the reason why in many of the ancient languages and cultures, like Egyptian, Summer, Indus valley, or even the latter civilizations as Greek, Hebrew, and Roman, love is personified in the form of a female figure.

Hathor - Egyptian

Ishta - Sumerian

Radha - India (Indus Valley)

Xochiquetzal - Aztec

Ma-Tsu - Asia (modern China)
Benten - Asia (modern Japan)

Ixchel - Mayan

Inanna - Sumerian

Astarte - Sumerian

Freya - Norseman (the origin of the week day Friday)

Aine - Celtic

Asherah - Original Hebrew

Many people have been given a misconception and misinterpretation of these ancient histories and teachings in order to facilitate a lie that these cultures worshiped statues in order to deter minds from looking back there and finding the truth.

Why was this personification of love in the form of a female very significant even now? Because it gives one a knowledge, understanding and perception of love in its most powerful forms that determines a lot in the realm of humans.

How so? Because the first love that any human being ever comes into contact with is from that of his or her mother while in the womb of this mother.

Not only was the love of a woman in ancient times considered to be second to only that of the Creator but it was also considered to be the most powerful and the only unconditional love in the human realm that did not have to go through a particular process in order to exist ,it was natural for a mother to love the child just simply because it was a part of her and began to exist within her.

So there is evidence that love is not just simply love and that it does have a context through which it operates ,functions , and is to be facilitated and that is according to the nature of the individual in which love has become awakened.

Therefore, the love that is facilitated through that which is known as a feminine essence is expressed and implemented within all human relations according to that which the feminine nature has to specifically impart and so forth also with the male or masculine essence.

When it comes to that which we know as female and woman, these are titles that originated from a masculine pparadigm ulture and psychological mind frame that was bent on redefining the gender known as woman to a position of inferiority within a new paradigm of Male dominance that was of Eurocentric origins.

From Roman General/ Conqueror Scipio Africanus, King Minos of Crete , Roman General/ Emperor Julius Caesar, Roman General/ Emperor Hadrian, Alexander The Great, Emperor Constantine, and The Maykop Caucasian Civilization (The oldest of Caucasian settlements).

All of these Caucasian Conquerors and Civilizations had one thing in common

1) A hatred for women and social/Political norms to deprive women of any rights, designate women as property belonging to their husbands, a theology that women were on the intellectual level with children and much more.

So what is the point of all of this? The main point is that the titles such as female and woman were designed to not only Implement a state of mind but also a teaching and condition that would exemplify the idea that that which is known as the feminine person (female) would be defined only by that which is determined by male or man , this in itself inferred that the woman didn't have any separate existence or foundation in nature that was not defined or determined by man.

Fe - male = feminine version of man

Wo - man = vagina version of man (as "wo" signifies womb (a vagina)
 History all depends on what end of the history you identify with ,that of the conquerors or the conquered. In any case history has a way of redefining things and validating things that never existed sich as the " Canaanites "

There isn't and never was an ancient people named Canaanites.

As a matter of fact, there's no ancient recordings or archeological evidence of there ever being a Canaanite race of people or a Canaanite political, religious, or social group calling themselves Canaanites or being called that by anyone in any of the histories of the ancient nations that occupied the so-called Mesopotamia or middle East.

A Civilization was discovered in the middle East in 1928 and was named (Ugarit) but sometimes called (Ras Shamra) and the first thing the converted Judaic Nation of Israel and its Rabbis and Christian flunkies did was start proclaiming that The Ugarit Civilization and the Ugarit Texts that were found was the long lost Canaanites.

Factually, NOTHING that was found in what became named Ugarit ever mentioned a Canaanite people or called themselves such. As liars and deceivers normally do, they just threw a name at it and said **" Oh, we found it validating that name and the existence of the Canaanite People we've been**

looking for."

(Reference Book: **The triumph of Elohim, From**

Yahwehisms To Judaisms, By : Diana V. Edelman).

This reference book contains numerous top Biblical Historians and scholars who present indisputable evidential facts both archeological and ancient texts that contradict everything about the modern mainstream propaganda about what the Hebrew Religion historically consisted of.

It also proves that "Asherah" was more prevalent as a belief than the temple version of Judaism which was for the educated, not the average Hebrews.

Thus also in those same biblical scriptures it is said that they both (male & female) were called "Adam."

The ultimate question is where is this particular expression found to be a fact in nature and the natural functioning of a living organism? and what would change if such was proven to be a fact?

That answer is also very simple. In ancient times there was a specific mind shattering reason as to why the act or process of creation was of a feminine essence and that particular feminine expression of love was considered to be second to only that of the creator but yet divine in nature.

The reason is, because if you look at the very process that enables the continuation of the human species ,you will see at the very heart of it a particular element of creation in childbirth that mimics the power of the Creator to create.

A process of originating within her a unique human. A divine process that actually determines the very nature and foundation of all human thought processes and all foundations of thought to be found in the human being ,right there within her who is called the female.

What you see in childbirth on the outside is nothing compared to what is actually taking place on the inside of the female. What you don't see is that the development of the child is directly connected to the thinking of the female, so much so until the very thoughts of the mother are what influences the brain cells in the unborn child.

What does this ultimately mean? It means exactly what the ancient teachings of the ancient civilizations knew, which is that cultures and civilizations are not defined by the man but by the woman because it is the woman through which all humans must come and must be initially influenced by.

As the woman is the first teacher of all humans and the determiner of the potentials that each and every child will possess or not possess based upon the nature of her thinking while the child is being developed during pregnancy.

The ancient people and their ancient civilizations all knew one fact that would destroy the egotistical and exaggerated false psychological mind frame of modern man.

That explosive fact was and still is :

" The world of people pray for change and Saviors and the answers to those particular prayers have always come through the woman who gives birth to that special person destined to produce that change in the affairs of men and that person isn't and NEVER will be always be a man."

When it comes to the way in which love manifests itself, there are not only contexts through which it expresses itself and makes itself known, there is as well stages of development within these contexts that are to be followed and implemented within a process of growth that one can not and will not escape.

1. Only the knowledge of Self can lead and qualify one to love self & then others.

2. Truly loving others naturally establishes loving relationships with others.

3. Loving others is influenced by love to produce relationships that produce family of the same race and friends.

4. **Families through love naturally connect and combine to construct communities of the same race.**

5. **Communities of a race are Influenced by love to connect at the very essence and to think, act, decide, and judge in accordance with the collective consciousness that is produced for the self - preservation, self- determination, and self-advancement of the race.**

These are the natural basic structural contexts of love that love naturally influences, everything else is built upon and around these.

Everything except the contexts of Gender and race, truth and right, respect and empathy, and justice and accountability, duty and responsibility, and loyalty and commitment which are defining context cornerstones in the structural context.

These contexts are essential not only to how love functions but also how love is intricately embedded within the very nature of who we are.

Most people are unaware of these quintessential elements but will feel forever in your debt when you explain them to people.

The main thing that must be realized is that the more one studies this information and incorporates into their mentality, the more effective it all becomes.

If you approach it with mediocre effort, mediocre results shouldn't come as a surprise.

No matter how much deception a man intends toward a woman, there are always women in their lives whom they strongly dislike the idea of them being deceived like daughters, sisters, or even Aunts.

For those who would like to shield their women from deception of the heart, the following (2) books are a must. There are none on the market that even comes close to an in-depth knowledge and understanding of love, the questions to ask to discover deceit or whether someone truly knows or understands what is.

Although it helps many ,the content your reading, neutralizes those books and allows one to go undetected.

Most people are fascinated with the idea of love, being in love ,and even being loved but very few are actually able to commit themselves to the struggles and Imperfections that must be endured in order to reach what is termed love.

Once again , the event of the microwave age in which we live is brought to your mind because when it comes to love as stated multiple times before ,the average person today thinks that love is something instant as if they can wake up one morning and say **"oh I am in love, i know what love is ,or I Feel Love."**

For someone to come along and express the idea that people cannot have love the instant they decide to possess love like some Hocus Pocus magic is involved.

That very thing is sure to cause some severe agitation and aggravation within a lot of people to the point where they want to scream :

" Why can't i have love like that ? or why can't love work that way ,if I want it to ?"

The answer is quite simple and in accordance with human nature which dictates that :

"No human being can or will truly know or understand a particular thing themselves without experience being involved
"

"Someone can tell you anything and it may be the truth to them but until you actually experience it for yourself ,what you were told, is only a statement with the possibility of being true."

Automatically, what comes to mind next is another question which is why would one need to have some type of experience before being able to know or understand love?

This may be a little hard to accept or understand but once again in accordance with human nature "No human being can fully appreciate something without having first experienced certain conditions and circumstances over and over again through a protracted period of time with the exact opposite of what is desired."

In this case, the exact opposite of what love is.

Why is that so ? Because only by experiencing the exact opposite of love can one not only grow into a unconditional appreciation for love but also grow into an unconventional application of love which is where things like preferences, the need to control, and conditional intent dies.

In the realm of human behavior and activities, nothing solidifies a thing within us as an unchangeable principle more so than the tragic and excruciating experiences that we find ourselves creating for ourselves by having the wrong ideas and making the wrong decisions that naturally result from those wrong ideas.

With experience this is not always the case because experience acts as a two tipped flame that can burn you so that all of the unnatural impurities can be released and eliminated or experience can burn you and leave an internal wound to the heart so deep and vast until the hurtful effects of the experience become infected and worsened.

How so ? Infected and worsened by way of particular emotional reactions that are produced such as resentment, hate, and the need to primarily blame the other person for the experience.

That is the most common reaction, rather than looking at the experience for what it is, a lesson taught and a lesson learned that has only resulted in a deeper outcome that was to make one a better, deeper, and wiser, person because it and it's gift has cemented within one the inability to ever have the same ideas and make the same mistakes again.

Experience also has a way of internally changing a person from a previous position of character ,mind State, and behavior that naturally repositions them to be a totally different person and thereby a perfect match for someone whom love has truly awakened whom they weren't previously compatible with in their previous state.

Compatible at the essence where it truly matters.

Experience and the intricate workings of love within has a way of having to allow us to go through some painful experiences over and over again until we are forced to let go of things that we have become sentimentally attached to that unknowingly to us are a hindrance to our development in the right direction.

What right direction? That very positive right direction that more times than anything else isn't about what where we want to grow but about how and where we need to grow in order to qualify for the balance in life that only love can initiate, nurture, and produce.

What balance in life? That balance of thinking and doing that which is not only good to us but good for us. That balance of finally acquiring that which is not only good to us but good for us as well.

It is experience and the many mistakes we make in life that are there to teach us and guide us into improving in the areas in which mistakes were made.

This is a hard lesson for most people to become aware of or to even begin to learn and by their own stubborn persistence in ego tripping, selfishness, and ignorance, end up missing the very things they claim to want or need.

Those most meaningful things such as a true experience with true love. An experience that very few actually realize starts within themselves through a correction of themselves that only experiences can influence.

Love doesn't come easy because there is always a price that one has to pay in order to truly have love awakened in us so that we can see through the eyes of love rather than through the lenses of our own short sightedness and imperfections.

That cost is the sacrifice of every single element of an emotional and psychological immaturity gained from our prior tunnel visioned perceptions and conclusions about the nature of our past experiences.

There's a point while in the midst of our seemingly heartbreaking and soul ripping experiences where we have numerous moments of thinking about giving up on the idea of love or being truly loved.

It is from somewhere deep inside of us there always seems to be a small urging that keeps pushing us to try again.

Sometimes we go through a period of trying to ignore it or bury it by focusing on work or things to occupy our mind and time but time and again that small urging keep pushing us to not give up on love.

Unknowingly to us, that is the small spark of love within us pushing us to continue the experience so that it can finally be realized and fully awakened in us through the conscious mind learning the hardest but most significant lessons in life that rests as the sole key to love's awakening.

"Regardless of what the external world and its unloving people do to me, I love myself enough to never again give the world the power to determine my worth, my potential, or whether i will or won't be loved. "

" The love in me lets me know that it is enough until its other half is through being developed and positioned by time and experience especially for me."

"The power of love in me for me and the power of faith and patience it gives me is stronger than the power of any hurt, disappointment, disrespect, or misuse the world could ever cause me."

While in the midst of our numerous experiences in the course of our lifetime, it becomes easy sometimes to focus more on the pain and the seemingly damage that it does to us more so than the positive things that are always there accompanying the negative things in the different human relations.

So much so until sometimes it's easy to believe that we're destined to be hurt and disappointed over and over again without an end in sight.

Surprisingly, what we fail to realize is that even though each time that we are hurt by someone it seems to go deeper and deeper for a reason.

While in the mist of excruciating pain disappointment and confusion of being hurt, it is not easy at all to realize that the negative has a counterpart that is actually equally positive and outweighs any significance that the negative could ever pose towards us.

How? Because with every experience that involves our hearts, the intensity of what is felt grows stronger and stronger and within every one of those experiences we are exposed to different higher degrees of certain elements both positive and negative that gives us glimpses of the one that life, experience, and love is preparing for us.

The positive being the higher degree of the right and healthy things that will be experienced and the negative being a higher tool of influence that helps shape, mold, and fashion the highest standard of positive measurement within us toward others. " Treat others as we want to be treated".

The negative side of any relationship or any other human relation gives one the ultimate reason for not doing such to others, because we know and understand how it feels and therefore can't and won't do it to others.

Sadly, it seems that there is a reverse effect with many of the world where the negativity incurred within relationships or other human relations influences quite a number of people to turn up the heat and Flames in their experiences by choosing to allow the negativity within their experiences to influence them to feel that they must inflict as much pain ,disappointment, and suffering upon others as it has been inflicted upon them which only increases the power and intensity of the negative situations that such ones will attract for themselves.

This is a very pivotal point in any of our lives where numerous lessons are materializing in our lives through experiences that naturally include other people or things we do in of ourselves that hurt us , disappoint, and frustrate us with the effect of always confusing us or either angering us.

During the trials, tests, and sometimes crushing predicaments that life's experiences takes us through, we never realize and do the one main thing that all contrary and contradicting experiences are trying to force us to do for our own good and benefit,

Simply just stop, take time, and reflect upon the one main element that has the power to change the nature of the experience and eliminate it altogether, the changing of our minds ,the nature of our approach to life and the changing of our perceptions of things, situations, places, people and our methods involved towards all of those things.

Why? Because to change your thoughts and mind is to redefine who you are and the nature of your position & power.

(Emotional Clarity)

Experience is a multifaceted thing that serves as a teacher through our life experiences, revealing invaluable lessons to us about the consequences of our wrongful decisions. At the very center of our experiences, is the workings to expose our vulnerabilities and insecurities, producing a space where we are more likely to encounter people, things, and situations that challenge our judgment.

These experiences, although often painful and very disappointing, are essential to reshaping our thoughts, beliefs, and understanding into a necessary growth.

When we make decisions in the context of feeling, we are driven by emotions that are prone to cloud our rational thinking. This leads to crucial mistakes, such as trusting the wrong kind of people, making sacrifices that are not reciprocated, or staying in unhealthy relationships out of fear or misplaced attachment.

At no time during any situation are you powerless to change or modify the conditions and events in which you participate or live. Within the diameter of all relationships, friendships and other relations such as family. It takes the difficulties and problems within these particular relations to actually help us to understand not only our connection to others but the connection that others have with us and what that connection means to them from their individual perspective.

Most times it takes connected people having to go through difficulties and problems along with the sometimes heart wrenching emotional stages of fragility and inner turmoil in order for us to gain a better and deeper grasp of who we are as individuals and our prescribed contribution to the ones we are connected to.

Sometimes it is the excruciating experience within our connections with others that influences us to think that we must isolate ourselves from the one or ones whom we are connected with and in doing so there is always the high probability that our isolation from the particular ones that we are connected with, will deepen the gap between us if love isn't allowed to do what it does best.

Love influences and establishes boundaries in our hearts and minds that always inevitably restricts our thoughts and actions from causing hurt and damage to the ones we are connected to so that any feeling of a need to isolate ourselves from the ones we love is only brief and never prolonged.

It takes these difficulties to arrive at a better understanding of our connections with others and our primary duty and obligation of love to the others to contribute love in its purest form to aid, assist, and support them in maintaining the connection or reestablishing their position within the connection even their failings, doubts, or confusion may involve our very own selves.

It takes the heat and pain of misunderstandings and miscommunications to teach us the true value of the others involved and ourselves.

There's nothing like the power of love and the faith it inspires to stand strong and relentless in our pursuits to allow our love to encourage and heal others whom we are connected to even when the world has given up on them.

Through the fire of experience verily one finds the true power of Love that is relentless and all persevering in regards to the one our love is focused on and connected to.

The teachings of love that are offered through experience give us a deeper insight into the intricate workings of Love within our hearts and Minds that otherwise would not be discovered and incorporated into who we are for the expressed benefit of helping and supporting others to empower themselves.

We learn through the severe tests and trials of experience that we can never force by might or petty bickerings a necessary change that our loved ones may desperately need because we can never make the changes for them, love's role and purpose is to exist as the ultimate unconditional encourager and supporter until love and its realization awakens in others that we are connected to.

Sometimes the fire of experiences forces us to realize that the one or ones we are connected to need other things other than us to become better and the connection isn't for us.

Surprisingly, of the rarest nature, love sometimes through another accomplishes that miraculous event of encouraging and influencing the needed betterment in the one or ones that are loved.

It is the nature of love and its position in our overall connection to others that determines whether the connection is right or wrong for us.

We as humans according to our proclivity to make mistakes as an element of learning and understanding, can never force our feelings to be love when they are not nor force our mere feelings into the power of love when such feelings don't and can't even come close to doing so.

That delusional frame of perception and feeling is and shall always be a highly favored means by the uninformed that only makes things worse for themselves and others.

If nothing else, experience will inevitably force one to know whether they truly know what love is by the measure of them either continuing in the dysfunctions or the measure of them resolving the dysfunctionalities of their lives and relations with others by them finally having love awakened within them.

No matter what our opinions are, experience has a way of showing us our the errors of our misguided thoughts and feelings, it is very few who actually pay attention, most have to create and go through an emotionally and mentally torturous cycle of their own making before they learn.

Contrary to our usual perceptions while in the midst of wrongful and

hurtful experiences, the wrongful decisions we made to arrive at that point are not just errors; they represent opportunities for us where we are compelled to initiate some pivotal introspection of ourselves.

The pain and regret that always seem to follow our mistakes forces us to reflect on our actions and their impacts on ourselves and others.

Through this reflection, we find better understanding and insights into our priorities, boundaries, and needs.

Experience, therefore, aims to teach us resilience and the importance of self-respect and self-awareness. Each experience of heartbreak or disappointment is a lesson in determining what is truly important and not important in relationships , what basic decisions naturally lead to the mistakes, and how to better direct our emotions and choices in the future.

Furthermore, in this way, experience not only highlights our wrongful decisions but also guides us towards growth, helping us to make wiser and more informed choices in our relationships.

Through experience, it is meant for us to learn the greater lessons of integrity, self-worth, the enduring strength of faith and the true value and importance of what it means to be well informed.

Experience serves as the most powerful instructor in emotional responsibility whereas it guides us into making choices that are more in alignment with truth and right when we engage in relationships.

Experience exposes us to a wide range of emotions and scenarios that challenge our current faulty and counterproductive decision-making process and influences us to replace them with those decision-making skills that limit or eliminate the power and influences of negative people in our lives and the negative situations that come with them.

Our experiences, both painful and enjoyable, are very instrumental in teaching us the consequences of our actions and the importance of making choices that uphold principles more suitable towards producing positive outcomes for ourselves and those whom we encounter.

At the heart of those experiences is the intent to equip us with a new standard of judgment that truly allows one to see themselves for the very first time and the total cause and effect of wrongful decisions—whether it be through dishonesty, neglect, or selfishness—we not only harm others but also ourselves.

Such choices tend to create emotional turmoil and guilt, revealing the negative impact of our actions on our well-being and the integrity of who we are.

These painful outcomes serve as crucial lessons that highlight the importance of emotional responsibility.

CHAPTER 23

The Nature Of Love In The Web Of Deception

Anyone who tries to commit themselves to the concept of love opens the door to being deceived because the concept actually influences at some point or another a blind faith .

Blind faith is a fantasy world where anything can be made possible based solely upon the idea that if you believe something, then it is already either possible or already a fact.

This is what makes love the perfect area of deception because people fool themselves into believing that they want or need love while having no clear and precise knowledge or understanding of what love is. It is always a thing that someone is waiting for another to help them understand love whether they voice the position or not.

This is the moment that's been highly anticipated. So without hesitation, lets enter this slowly.

In all pursuits these particular principles should be internalized into the mind because they are very significant to any method you devise.

" Love is not a feeling or emotion although it facilitates both in the process of making itself known to the one or ones in whom love has become awakened "

" Love is a spiritual thing that isn't physical or material based but exists as the essence in and behind all that is physical and connected or unified. "

"Love isn't defined by nor confined by time, distance, circumstances, place , the presence of a person's body or the lack of a person's body.
Love escapes and defies the boundaries of all things to exist as the most powerful force by which all things are connected, grown, healed, and changed into the best results possible even when the odds of it seem too overwhelming to happen or become true. "

" The degree to which one learns to believe and trust in love unconditionally directly determines the degree of love's power to accomplish what it is meant to accomplish in the lives of human beings "

Love is an inner spiritual force of consciousness that has the power and ability to assimilate and supersede any and all dimensions of the mind's thought processes and redefine its underlying foundation until all thoughts ,feelings , perceptions .and attitudes are filtered through love's directives and made to bear the imprint of its influence.

An influence so powerful to the point of being able to give more vibrant radiance and in depth definition and purpose to things and people in the surrounding environment that previously seemed to hold no real aim, purpose, or meaning until seen again by the one or ones now able to see through the eyes of Love.

It is as well an inner force of divine magnetic properties consisting of a inner intelligent energy that emanates from the soulful essence of one's being, then on through the very mental fabric of thought as a means to implementing it's expressive and informative nature through channels of influence so that it may transcend from its internal (heart) position of existence within one person into the internal (heart) position of another person to seek expression and connection there so that it may or can seek to Aid in the awakening of another dimension of itself within the other person.

Where ,when or if combined, then truly grows, develops, and becomes nurtured into a greater and more Fuller degree of power and expression of itself within the connection with the other.

There is an alarming and very disturbing characteristic of thinking, perception, and feeling not only within modern times but in much of the past eras of time as well that has prevented love from truly being in the world on any significant or widespread level.

The alarming and disturbing characteristics of thinking, perceiving, and feeling that has done this is a continuum of dislike and disregard for the positive nature and positive aim, direction , and purpose of things like love that bring its own rules , principles, and requirements that must be complied with in order to be allowed to approach it , truly realize it, and experience it along with the fullest benefits and possibilities incorporated within the results that are produced only by the event of total compliance with the dictates of its nature.

People have been fond of quoting , giving an unlimited amount of speeches and writing enough volumes to fill 4 or 5 N.F.L. Football Stadiums about love in the Bible and what it means.

None of them has yet to give the true meaning of love as it is used in those (2) New Testament verses because of :

- The true nature and roots of that which surrounds the word love in the scriptures ,
- The nature of the hearts of the people today behind the interpretations and leadership with the Bible.

Historically, the true meaning wasn't conceivable because when they were written (2 Centuries after the time that Jesus or the Disciples supposedly lived) , the comprehension of them escaped their grasp because of the nature of their hearts and the intent for the Bible (Conquerings & forced conversions / Emperor Constantine + Council of Nicaea to formulate New Testament Scripture).

Romans Ch. 13 vs. 8 - " The one who has loved another has fulfilled the law "

Romans Ch. 13 vs. 10 - "Love is the fulfillment of law "

Why use those verses used ? How are they relevant? Just simply to prove a point about something .

The basis of one of love's most influential and most defining principles is something that people who like thinking wrong and doing wrong have a intense disregard for. (What is right). How does that relate to love ? The basis of law is to influence and enforce what is right with penalties of punishment for the breaking of those laws. The fear of the punishment is meant to influence compliance to the law.

To fulfil the intent of the law means that one has grown to love the doing of right so much until they think and perform what is right not out of a desire for a reward or due to the fear of a punishment, they just simply do it unconditionally out of a love for right.

Everything else is to be considered and based upon an ulterior motive other than the right one.

So the point is that the basis of love is (RIGHT). The totality of what is right is The right thoughts, the right intentions, the right attitude, the right perceptions,   and the right actions which consistently produces the right results as the nature of love intends and ensures.

The fruit of thinking and doing what is right to others is : fairness , justice, equality and healthy relationships. Something that the governments, Educational halls of learning, and the major religions of the world can't and won't do because they're all from the basis of a world order that was built upon wrong, thus a natural impediment and to love in the world.

CHAPTER 24

The Feminine & Masculine Nature

The Nature, Basis, & Dynamics Of Male-Female Relations

This is where you learn to put all of the pieces of love together in a perfect little basket for tour targets so that they can realize that you know the nature of the male and female relationships

So what does all of this really mean? It means that the feminine and masculine essences each has a particular role and function to fulfill that is neither lesser or greater in regards to each other but rather individual pieces of a whole with their own natures designed to complement and complete each other in areas that one may have qualities better suited for things that the other doesn't possess to the extent or degree that the other does.

One of those particular areas is physical strength which the ancients knew to be balanced by the fact that the feminine contributed to the essence of that which determines physical strength

Ultimately through the influences of her feminine nature is the main defining factor that brought moderation to the usages of man's physical strength and helped to keep man's physical strength within boundaries of moderation.

The Foundational key & Lock To Human Progress Or Stagnation

The first comfort that any man knows is that of a mother because the woman by nature is the ultimate comforter, balancer, moderator, developer, and the ultimate conceiver , thinker, and maintainer of essential things (especially an eye for details) and many more qualities of importance.

All of those principles of nature when properly perceived and connected to by man ,naturally translates into positive balanced causes and effects in every avenue of civilization.

The so-called female and her feminine essence is fulfilled, grown, and sustained continuously by mainly acknowledging, respecting, and connecting with the masculine essence in man in a complimentary role that helps produce harmony, balance ,peace, and growth between the two essences of feminine and masculine.

The man by nature is better suited for physical tasks of the enforcement and maintaining of the security of the household, society, and civilization as well as the implementation of his nature's propensities towards shaping, building, facilitating, directing , maintaining, and securing along with numerous other elements which also translates into relationships, household, society ,culture, and governing but in a way that acknowledges, respects, and connects with the feminine essence in a complimentary role that helps produce and sustain harmony, peace growth , and balance between the two essences of feminine and masculine in all areas of Civilization. Which means that no area of civilization could ever be truly healthy , balanced, or complete without the representation of equal participation and imparting from both Essences.

The dysfunction in the relationships , household, family structure, and society originates not only out of a lack knowledge and understanding of love but also from both men and women lacking a knowledge and understanding of their own individual essences and the roles dictated by them.

Today, many women out of necessity have had to take on roles of the male in the family and household structure due to the lack of a fatherly presence in the household and the children's lives because of incarcerated ,dead, or trifling fathers not fulfilling their responsibilities or roles and it's been that way so long until it's become a cultural norm for women to fulfill the functions of the male which becomes hard for women to switch back from even when some male appears in their lives because their efforts have been the only dependable force in their lives or their children's lives which has a dire consequence of influencing female children to think and believe that their mother's or grandmother's example is the only real choice and example to emulate.

The before mentioned examples and information were intended to cause both sides of the coin both feminine and masculine to rethink and reposition themselves into accordance with their nature so that the source of the dysfunctions can finally be addressed and begin to be taken through a healthy process of elimination within every human relation.
Strangely this is the representation of a process that many are not going to be willing to acknowledge, consider ,or even implement because of certain negative roles and expectations that both feminine and masculine beings have become entrenched within.

Most men feel that they not only want to believe but have to believe that the being we call woman is lesser than them in order for them to feel Superior and that the woman is best suited to be a plaything ,servant or subservient being to all that is male in the name of entertainment, fun ,and sex.

Equally, the majority of the incorrectly named feminine beings known as woman feels a want or need to remain in a negative passive role of being and doing that which gives credence to the male's disrespectful, condescending, and devaluing egotistical views of females and their perceived purposes for females of the same nature.

It is the lack of knowledge of self and one's true feminine nature that influences these ignorant choices of a self- inflicted confinement that prevents the majority of so-called females from even knowing and understanding how and why to have love for self.

Until this particular dysfunction and all of its elements are alleviated there will never be a universal demonstration and implementation of Love within male and female relationships to no great or significant extent.

This is about one having love within the context of their very nature and demonstrating it from that particular context because to do otherwise is to attempt to initiate and facilitate a false perceived notion of Love out of context and perpetuate the damage , disorder, and unnatural effects produced from this ignorance.

This is only a sample of what it means to go beyond the surface.

There are some regardless of what is said and how it is proven ,they will continue in the same course of thought ,belief , and action. This is the kind of person who should still be shown unconditional kindness , respect, and care because experience is the best teacher and it isn't up to us to determine when and how that person changes the course of their thinking , it one's duty to only plant the seeds of suggestive thought and direction then allow time and experience to produce the proper elements necessary for growth.

The realm of truth and love are unconditional but it is people's reactions that are conditional and based upon a desire to resist change because change has a way of leaving us naked , exposed , and in need of being redressed according to the dictates of a new idea and truth whose time has come.

There are four questions, one for the so-called females and the others for the male and all four are the most explosive and most indomitable questions to ever be implemented within the discussion of the dysfunctional Male- Female Relationships.

Questions within themselves that are so intense and forceful until no choice is left in one's mind except to rethink and begin to reevaluate the spectrum of ALL history dealing with the so-called female.

This question is for the so-called female :

"If modern man(of the past 5,000 + years) didn't historically treat you so-called females right, how can it ever be rational that he historically taught you right about yourself and taught the right knowledge of the socalled female?

None of this intended as an attack on the Black Male or belittling of the Black Male, it is only a means by which the Black Male must be forced to reexamine himself and the foreign unnatural standards of Manhood that have never served empower us but rather to entrap us into a design that benefits the Caucasian Male's progress in maintaining his dominance

By deception and the continued systematic strategy to alienate the Black Male from our true essence of self and its indomitable power that the world couldn't erase all signs of.

These questions are for the Male :

" If modern man (of the past 5,000 + years) didn't historically treat the so-called female right , how could it ever be rational that he would teach the right things about her ,if his intent was to conquer others and even seek to redefine man according to new limitations of artificial value and positions that would only aid in enhancing and reinforcing a domination by a select few over all men through deception ? "

Is it not a conquerors' nature to either destroy or disrupt the family dynamics of the Nation that has been conquered?

" What better way than to redefine both gender definition, potential ,and positions in a way that not only disrupts the

cohesion of those nations but as well kills those conquered Nation's collective consciousness? "

The modern male ego is a very fragile thing that has been set up for complete failure and collapse when faced with facts that exist in a way that contradicts also everything man has ever thought and believed about himself.

To have to face something that seems to crumble one's whole psychological foundation under him is comparable to the withdrawal symptoms that drug addicts experiences when they are deprived of a drug that they're addicted to.

In the mind of the drug addict, it may be perceived as a unjust deprivation that hinders them from feeling good and alive but reality says the deprivation is good and healthy because its taking away some poison that's harming the drug addict.

Its the same with the Male whose addicted to a poisonous lie about Male superiority that's based upon the idea of a superiority to so-called females that's meant to be and justified by a standard of man's physical strength.

That false and exaggerated position of the modern Male ego is a poison that's implanted within the Black Male that has to be thrown away before the Black Male can even begin to see himself and properly align himself with the Black so-called female.

The So-called female manifests the essence of living things (the future people of a nation-) that the male with his strength and mastery of the physical material world guides and shapes in the world. The future generations.

As opposed to the definitional constructs of Western

Civilization for the Male and female, they are in truth not and NEVER have been opposites or opposing elements of two different spectrums to be measured against each other in a unnatural standard of measurement to determine lesser and greater so that an unnatural conclusion of overall supremacy can be determined. The (2) Essences (Male & Female)

> The (2) essences are actually two components of the same unit that compliment each other and fit together by nature like a puzzle.

According to the dictates of Western Civilization and its Eurocentric cultural norms and standards. The (2) are genders that are to be defined and regulated according to the precepts of what was established in their collective ancestral history of Europe.

This particular Eurocentric model for interactions between what they call "Genders" has and will forever instigate and enforce inequalities and injustices between the two that will always favor the Male as the superior and the female as the inferior no matter what the Caucasian Male establishment does to influence the idea of them giving females equality and better treatment. It is always deception by another and another nice sounding name or policy.

How is that so? Because of one main principle that also applies to Black People (Including The Brown branch of The tree.) **No entity, establishment , or person can make or position another to be equal with it.**

Equality is a state of mind with every necessary ability and capability to make itself equal by its own selfdetermination, self-preservation actions therein that are produced and sustained continuously by that one aspiring to equal another from a self- generating process of those things that make them equal to another.

To be told you're being treated equal or that you've been made equal is only a deceptive illusion when the source of that which is said to be making one equal originates from and is sustained by the other giving you equality or equal treatment.

Do the Caucasian have to continuously vote on whether they will remain the dominant race in all of their Caucasian ruled countries? No because that's not up for discussion. Does the

Caucasian Male have to vote whether they'll give total control or access to the Caucasian female ir any other female? No because that's not up for consideration no matter how any individual females they (allow) to have certain high ranking positions.

Why? Because when you're truly equal, you don't have to petition anyone or conduct a vote for some permission to have something. You naturally have it already and don't need anyone's permission to do or use what is desired.

This is a process that applies to all human relations but in this context, it is applied specifically to so-called Female/Male Relationships.

At multiple stages in family relations ,friendships ,and relationships there's naturally going to be disagreements.
Especially in the beginning.

Why?   because at the beginning, what you have is the meeting of different thoughts ,ideas ,opinions ,and perceptions about things between sometimes similar but different minds and personalities.

The more these seemingly different minds and personalities communicate and experience one another ,the more the differences lesson as familiarity reveals connecting points up on which two or more minds and personalities can merge together on common grounds within the things that previously seemed different and contrary on the surface.

As the communication process buds a unique Bond, the developing of affections and consideration for the other begins to take shape and become stronger.

When the affection grows, there is a natural repositioning that takes place within the mind and heart of each of the ones who have grown close.

That repositioning involves valuing and appreciating the other enough to put them and what they think, believe, or perceive before their own.

When both do this in reference to one another, a natural degree of compromise is produced between them.

At that point the means by which true communication can be established and maintained has occurred.

What does that further mean ? It means that the friction base and the extremities of irrational thinking and feeling within a disagreement is no longer existent within the connection between them. This doesn't mean that disagreement will no longer happen, it simply means that the friction and the extreme irrational point of arguing and fussing has been neutralized and replaced with the real and solid principles of unification such as respect, compromise, true consideration, and understanding for the other.

This is a highly matured and balanced degree that influences each to consider the other thoughts ,feelings ,and perceptions before their own in a deeper sense that redefines the communication process and the problem resolution process.

What does that mean? That means whenever there is a disagreement, there will always be the thought of compromise at the Forefront of the two's mind that will influence them to listen to each other and then take individual time to themselves where within their own thought processes, begin to analyse and measure ways to put the other's opinions and perceptions before theirs and figure out the way to combine the two individual thoughts or ideas into one method or one course of action for them to implement together.

This is the true unification process as a result of a true communication process based upon the affections or love that exists between them. It is the direct result of keeping the proper perspective while dealing with the struggles of experience so that the outcome is positive and conducive to strengthening the connection between two people.

This is by no means an easy process. So many give up before the process even begins due to misunderstanding about what is meant to occur or a lack of knowledge about the process all together

The hardest thing with humans when their feelings get involved in something with a high intensity, its hard to keep the ego out of the way where instead of letting arguments go ,there remains a deep seated resentment and a egotistical harboring of a need to prove that the other is wrong.

This is an area that is always ripe for manipulation because in most relationships that have lasted over 2 years ,they are usually at many many points in time barely hanging on by thread and all it takes it the right set if words at the right time to break that thread and either seduce one of the couple are destroy the relationship.

Such words as "Excuse me, I know you don't really know me but I saw you and was wondering if I may ask you a question? Have you ever encountered a man (if it's a woman) that could truly hold a conversation with you about love? " "I'm just curious and ask people everywhere I go the same question. "

CHAPTER 24
The Superior Man Maneuvered Into Inferiority

The principle of masculine essence is deeply rooted in the innate physicality of men. At the core of this essence lies a natural proclivity to focus on the material aspects of human existence. The male inclination toward shaping, constructing, and influencing the physical world is a fundamental expression of this. Historically, men have been the builders, warriors, and laborers who used their natural physical strength to create and maintain the material infrastructure of civilization. This strength is both literal and symbolic in representing a man's ability to shape his environment, meet physical challenges, and exert control over the tangible world around him.

However, the emphasis on physicality often creates an imbalance in the masculine psyche. Men, because of their natural connection to the material realm, can develop a sense of detachment from emotional, intellectual, and psychological aspects of life. Their focus on solving problems through physical means often overshadows their emotional intelligence, leading to a significant gap in emotional awareness and expression. While physical strength serves its purpose in addressing external challenges, it leaves such men vulnerable in the overall settings of the external world , creating a sense of inadequacy in being able to handle their own deeper problems or those of others that require intelligence and critical thinking.

This imbalance can be exploited. The male proclivity to focus on the material can be used against him, entrapping him in a cycle of attachment and replacement. Men often form emotional attachments to material things, objects, status, or achievements because these are tangible representations of their mentality, efforts and strengths. Yet, their detachment from the deeper emotional aspects of these attachments makes them susceptible to manipulation. This is where the trap lies: when a man loses or feels he must replace these material things, he seeks new, similar objects or goals, always in pursuit of something that reflects his physical effort. This cycle of replacement becomes a never-ending chase, a distraction that prevents men from delving into the mental processes that could truly address the root of their dissatisfaction and difficulties.

Society has long capitalized on this masculine inclination toward materialism, subtly reinforcing the idea that a man's value is tied to what he can build, own, or possess. The material objects, social status, and achievements that men tirelessly strive for become tools of entrapment. Marketing industries, corporate structures, and societal pressures all push men toward accumulating more, more wealth, more power, more objects while downplaying the importance of emotional and psychological fulfillment. In essence, men are conditioned to view material success as the ultimate marker of their worth, often to the detriment of their emotional well-being.

Compounding this issue is the masculine mindset that equates physical strength or physical objects with problem-solving. Men, by nature, often approach challenges with a belief that their physical capabilities are at the heart of finding solutions. Whether it's in conflict, competition, or the pursuit of goals, men tend to rely on their physicality to overcome obstacles. While this can be effective in certain scenarios, it limits their potential to engage in deeper intellectual or emotional problem-solving. The tendency to focus on tangible, physical outcomes leaves many men ill-equipped to address more in-depth or complex challenges, such as psychological conflict, or even understanding the subtleties of human relationships.

This reliance on physical strength as the primary problemsolving tool also puts men at a disadvantage when confronted by those who operate from a more intellectual or emotional plane. A select few men, who understand the nature of thinking, can easily outmaneuver those who are stuck in the mindset that physical strength alone is enough. These thinkers use strategy, emotional intelligence, and psychological insight to navigate challenges, creating solutions that transcend the immediate, material world. In contrast, men who remain focused on their physical capabilities often miss the opportunity to engage and develop their full mental faculties, leaving them vulnerable to manipulation by those who understand how to play on their weaknesses.

The principle of masculine essence is rooted in physical strength and material focus, creating a natural imbalance in emotional and intellectual awareness and mental development. While men are biologically inclined to shape the physical world around them, this focus can be used against them, trapping them in cycles of material attachment and emotional detachment. The reliance on physical strength as the primary tool for problem-solving further limits their potential, leaving them at a disadvantage in a world where emotional and intellectual understanding is increasingly necessary.

Only by recognizing and addressing these imbalances can men fully exercise the mental and emotional capabilities that are essential for true growth and fulfillment.

Men who focus on projecting physical strength or the ability to fight often operate under the belief that "might makes right," a mindset that reinforces their reliance on aggression as a solution to problems. This tendency is an extension of the idea that dominance through physical force can substitute for mental acuity.

The Overcompensation of Physical Strength

However, this approach often traps men in a cycle of overcompensation for their intellectual or emotional shortcomings. When faced with challenges that require deeper thinking or intelligent insight, such men may default to aggressive behavior, mistakenly equating power with control or superiority.

This cycle is detrimental, as it reinforces the illusion that physical strength is the ultimate solution, preventing them from developing the mental tools needed to approach and overcome more complex issues. In social, professional, or personal settings, aggression may yield immediate results, but it fails to address the root causes of conflicts or problems. Over time, this reliance on physical dominance becomes a mask for insecurity and a barrier to growth. Men trapped in this cycle often find themselves isolated, misunderstood, or manipulated by those who can outthink them, leaving them further entrenched in the belief that only aggression can protect them from their vulnerabilities.

The overcompensation of physical strength is often a mindset fueled by emotions such as anger, frustration, rage, and spite. Men who over-rely on their physical power are frequently driven by a desire to dominate, especially over those they perceive as weaker. This creates a distorted worldview where might equals right, and violence becomes a go-to solution. Yet, this very reliance on strength becomes their greatest vulnerability, turning what they perceive as an asset into an Achilles heel.

Anger and frustration are emotions that thrive on impulsivity, clouding one's judgment and leaving little room for calculated decision-making. A man whose identity revolves around physical strength is, in essence, a puppet to these aggressive emotions. His sense of control is fragile, easily disrupted by anyone capable of igniting his temper. Once anger takes hold, his actions become predictable, driven by his emotional need to act out rather than to think strategically. This predictability can be manipulated. Those who understand this can easily construct traps or situations designed to exploit this emotional weakness.

The puppet master in such scenarios is the individual who recognizes the strings of emotion that govern these men. By triggering their anger, one can steer their actions as if pulling on those emotional strings. Their need for physical confrontation leads them into traps—whether it's a literal physical ambush or a metaphorical situation where their strength is rendered useless. The man who prides himself on his ability to overpower others is, ironically, being overpowered by his own emotions.

This overcompensation not only exposes them to external manipulation but also reveals an underlying insecurity. If their strength were truly enough, there would be no need for rage or frustration. Their aggression, then, becomes a mask for their own vulnerabilities, making them easy to predict and control.

In the end, the overcompensation of physical strength is a weakness disguised as strength. The man who allows his emotions to dictate his actions is not truly in control; he is simply reacting. And the more he reacts, the more he plays into the hands of those who know how to exploit his predictability. Like a puppet on strings, he moves according to the pulls of his emotions, unaware that this very act of aggression is his greatest liability.

Foundations Of Thought & Belief will be cracked in ways never imagined.

Many have believed themselves immune …..believed & prided themselves as being untouchable…….That's going to change

Never Be Afraid To Think outside Of The Norm.

Join us. Every thought you have is Valuable For

You and should work for You. If You Can Think, You can

Learn to Express it verbally & in writing. Looking for thinkers who want better in life. Success is Always Just A Thought Away.